British-Owned Railways in Argentina

Latin American Monographs, No. 34
Institute of Latin American Studies
The University of Texas at Austin

British-Owned Railways
in Argentina THEIR EFFECT ON
ECONOMIC NATIONALISM, 1854–1948

by Winthrop R. Wright

PUBLISHED FOR THE INSTITUTE OF LATIN AMERICAN STUDIES
BY THE UNIVERSITY OF TEXAS PRESS, AUSTIN AND LONDON

Library of Congress Cataloging in Publication Data

Wright, Winthrop R   1936-
    British-owned railways in Argentina: their effect on
the growth of economic nationalism, 1845-1948.

    (Latin American monographs, no. 34)
    1. Railroads—Argentine Republic. 2. Investments,
British—Argentine Republic. I. Texas. University at
Austin. Institute of Latin American Studies.
II. Title. III. Series: Latin American monographs
(Austin, Tex.) no. 34.
HE2907.W75   338.982   74-4447
ISBN 0-292-70710-X

For Eleanor, Geoffrey, and Christopher

CONTENTS

MAPS

ACKNOWLEDGMENTS

In a few brief paragraphs I would like to thank a number of people whose aid and encouragement cannot be repaid adequately in words. I hope that I can return their generosity at some later date.

From the beginning of this study Professor Arthur P. Whitaker has given unselfishly of his time and energy. I owe much to him. As a student in his seminar on Argentine nationalism I had an unusual opportunity to test my ideas on a group of distinguished scholars. I am forever grateful to the positive criticism of my early attempts at scholarship made by Hans Kohn. Robert J. Alexander and Joseph R. Barager also made substantial contributions to my first efforts to understand the history of the Argentine Republic.

Thanks to the Rockefeller Foundation, which funded the seminar on Argentine nationalism, I had an opportunity to work with three Argentine scholars who served as advisers to the seminar. The enthusiasm for history shown by Dr. Ricardo Caillet-Bois has impressed me to this day. He helped direct the first steps of the study that led to this book. Gino Germani and José Luis Romero also read parts of the book and made valuable suggestions. At a later date Thomas F. McGann read the manuscript and added advice for which I am thankful.

Fellow members of the seminar on Argentine nationalism also played a role in the development of this book. My thanks to Samuel L. Baily, James Levy, David Jordan, Marvin Goldwert, and Earl Glauert for their patience. On numerous occasions we sweated blood defending our pet theories and questioning each other's ideas.

Historians cannot work without the help of competent archivists, librarians, and fellow scholars who know document collections well. Since the Argentines destroyed the permanent records of the British-owned railways that had been housed in Buenos Aires until 1948, I was unable to view the Anglo-Argentine railway experience from the companies' internal point of view. Thanks to Harold Blakemore of the Institute of Latin American Studies of the University of London and Christopher Platt of Cambridge University, I was able to locate a few remnants of company records at the University of London, but only enough to whet my appetite. Officials at the Public Record Office and the British Museum were extraordinarily kind in assisting me as I used their facilities during the summer of 1968. I spent that summer in London thanks to a grant from the General Research Board of the Graduate School of the University of Maryland.

The staff of the Latin American Division of the Library of Congress, and especially Georgette Dorn, have helped me whenever I have asked them. Mr. John Hébert of the Library of Congress Map Division spent considerable time in helping me locate historical maps of the Argentine railway network. The maps in this book were prepared from maps in the Library of Congress collection by Joseph W. Wiedel of the University of Maryland who did a quick and professional job in record time. At the National Archives I found one of the most efficient and helpful staffs I have ever met. I am especially indebted to Milton Gustafson of the Department of State records for advice that has saved me countless hours of research. I also appreciate the invaluable help given me by the staffs of the Baker Library of the Harvard Business School, the Widener Library at Harvard, and the New York Public Library.

W. R. W.

British-Owned Railways in Argentina

Introduction

On the evening of March 1, 1948, thousands of cheering Argentine workers, *descamisados*, flocked into the Plaza Britania in front of the Retiro railway terminal in Buenos Aires. They came from all parts of the nation to celebrate the official transfer of the ownership of some 16,000 miles of British-owned railways to the Argentine government. Throughout the day special trains brought labor representatives to the Argentine capital from interior cities. Shops and businesses closed down early in Buenos Aires to allow employees to take part in the celebration. By six o'clock the plaza overflowed with an excited crowd in a festive mood. White-shirted workers waved placards. Banners and signs proclaimed "Now They Are Argentine," and that Argentina had gained its economic independence. Others paid tribute to *el líder*, Juan D. Perón. Latecomers found it impossible to approach the central square. They milled about, listening to speeches over the public-address system. Some athletic participants climbed lamp posts and statues to gain a better view. Others watched from rooftops and windows of surrounding buildings. The more daring perched precariously on the ledges high above the streets below.[1]

Excited Argentines had come to celebrate a national victory over foreign imperialists. Their government, under the popular leadership of General Juan D. Perón, had repatriated a major portion of the nation's railway network. Few acts have ever won such popular acclaim in Argentina, a nation given to division and fragmentation. Although some Argentines have subsequently referred to March 1, 1948, as *el dia de la estupidez argentina*, few at the time raised serious opposition to Perón's decision to purchase outright the extensive British-owned railway network. The majority of workers proclaimed Perón their economic liberator. Indeed, many went so far as to place him second only to General José de San Martín as a guarantor of an independent Argentina. Even some of Perón's bitterest opponents have considered the purchase a benchmark in the economic development of an independent Argentina.

A closer analysis of the history of the British-owned railways reveals that they had long served as a convenient reference point for diverse nationalist groups since the 1850's. As a historical phenomenon, nationalism constantly changes. The British-owned railways offer a leading example of its change in Argentina. Supported during the nineteenth century as a means of transforming Argentina into a modern, integrated state, the foreign-owned railways became despised as a chief target of rising economic nationalism during the twentieth century. They also provide a focus for the interplay between national economic policy and private business policy.

During the nineteenth century British-owned railways grew under the protection of a liberal Argentine ruling elite. The latter considered railways as harbingers of civilization and as both instruments and symbols of progress. Under their direction, Argentina

---

[1] The official ceremony of March 1, 1948, is described in considerable detail by *La Prensa*, March 2, 1948; *Buenos Aires Herald*, March 2, 1948; *New York Times*, March 2, 1948; and *El Obrero Ferroviario*, March 16, 1948.

built the largest railway network in Latin America between 1856 and 1914. The elite did not care that British capital constructed and controlled the major railways. Rather, they gave support to the foreign enterprises as Argentina became an increasingly prosperous agricultural producer and exporter during the second half of the nineteenth century. The elite attributed their prosperity directly to the major British-owned railways. As a result, the British-owned railways grew in size and power. The Britons showed little concern for the public, governed railway affairs from London, and demonstrated a calloused disregard for Argentine interests in general.

The railways they built did transform Argentina from a backward rural country into a modern food producer. The railways also helped to unite diverse parts of the country. They put an end to weak and isolated local industries and destroyed the regional markets of the interior. At the same time, they made the interior centers increasingly dependent upon east-coast port cities, especially Buenos Aires and Rosario. As in other nations, the railways tended to benefit the richest parts of the nation the most, even while developing remote regions. Buenos Aires's mercantilists easily spread their hegemony over the rest of the nation as all the major British lines terminated in Buenos Aires. An imbalance existed that Argentina has never fully overcome.

During the twentieth century an increasing number of Argentines began to view the British-owned railways as instruments of foreign domination and as tokens of retrogression and strangulation of Argentina's economic development. As in other Latin American nations by the turn of the century, nationalists began to see themselves as economically inferior to citizens of the traditional colonial powers. They resented the preponderant role of the British, especially in public utilities, such as the railways. The major companies represented on a large scale both foreign investment and foreign enterprise. At the time of the world depression of the 1930's, approximately 66 percent of Argentina's 23,862-mile railway system belonged to British companies.[2] French concerns

[2] Argentine Republic, Ministerio de Obras Públicas, Dirección General de Ferrocarriles, *Estadística de los ferrocarriles en explotación*, 1933, XLII, 48.

owned nearly 9 percent of the national total, mostly in provincial lines that did not run to Buenos Aires. The remainder of the nation's railways belonged to a state-directed railway system. Because the British controlled such a large part of the railway system, most Argentines equated foreign ownership of the railways with British ownership. As the revisionist historian Raúl Scalabrini Ortiz once noted, the terms *private capital, foreign capital,* and *British capital* are interchangeable when applied to Argentine railways.[3]

By 1948 most Argentines had convinced themselves that the well-being of their nation depended in part upon repatriating the public utility companies, especially the British-owned railways. Some may have seen the acquisition of the railways as a panacea for the nation's economic difficulties. Others saw it as one of many steps toward gaining Argentina's economic independence. But all agreed that Argentina should own its own railway system.

All studies of nationalism run the risk of becoming bogged down in semantics.[4] No matter how much they may contradict each other about some aspects of the subject, students of nationalism agree in recognizing the impossible task of defining the term. At best, nationalism poses an elusive concept which is hard to define precisely and impossible to confine. There is much truth in the words of Lester Pearson, former prime minister of Canada, who wryly quipped, "Perhaps we should merely admit that we may not be able to exactly define a nation, but we certainly know one when we see it."[5]

How have leaders employed nationalism? How have they reacted to nationalism? Nationalism is clarified when seen within a specific historical context where its usage becomes more obvious than its origins.[6] As a complex group emotion or state of mind, nationalism demands that the members of a society called a nation

[3] Raúl Scalabrini Ortiz, *Historia de los ferrocarriles argentinos*, p. 44.

[4] See items marked by asterisks in the bibliography for examples of the extensive studies of nationalism.

[5] Lester B. Pearson, "Beyond the Nation-State," *Saturday Review*, February 15, 1969, p. 26.

[6] Arthur P. Whitaker and David C. Jordan, *Nationalism in Contemporary Latin America*, p. 5.

will, by common consent, place loyalty to a state and its citizenry above all other values. Although nationalism implies consensus, it does not necessarily predicate consensus. Several competing "nationalisms" can exist in one country at a given moment. Ultimately, all nationalists accept the nation as the common denominator, the supreme power.

Unlike cultural or political nationalism, which find fuel in a nation's past accomplishments, economic nationalism looks to the future. As part of a political ideology, economic nationalism optimistically promises a better material future for a nation's citizens. It may appear negative in that it directs its attacks against an existing order. But economic nationalism sets positive goals. As a driving force, economic nationalism has two primary objectives. First, it seeks an amorphous goal of achieving as much economic self-sufficiency for a nation as possible. The second goal relates to the first and encompasses the attempts of developing states to pattern their economies after those of recognized world powers. The so-called underdeveloped nations invariably want economic equality in the world economic system. Both objectives imply that a nation can achieve and secure the well-being of the individual citizen by controlling its own economic resources. Economic nationalists believe that a nation's greatness depends upon its economic strength. They also maintain that political independence hinges upon economic power. Thus they fight for freedom from outside economic penetration.[7]

Argentine economic history manifests two prevailing nationalist traditions.[8] The first, formulated by the founding fathers, and especially Mariano Moreno and Bernardino Rivadavia, presented a cosmopolitan outlook and stressed the need to align Argentina culturally, politically, and economically with Europe. Proponents of this liberal nationalism sought to create an Argentina after the advanced nations of the Old World and, later, the United States.

[7] See Harry G. Johnson, "The Ideology of Economic Policy in the New States," in *Economic Nationalism in Old and New States*, ed. Harry G. Johnson.

[8] Arthur P. Whitaker, *Nationalism in Latin America*; also Samuel L. Baily, *Labor, Nationalism, and Politics in Argentina*, pp. 3-8. The best discussion of Rosas and his use of nationalism is found in Miron Burgin, *The Economic Aspects of Argentine Federalism, 1820-1852*.

They considered foreign ideas, immigrants, and capital as indispensable implements of change. The second tradition developed as a reaction to the first. Best typified by the dictator Juan Manuel de Rosas, who governed between 1829 and 1852, the reactionary school of nationalists practiced a nationalism directly opposed to the liberalism of Moreno and Rivadavia. Rosas based his nationalism upon xenophobia and a denunciation of foreign influences in all areas of Argentine life. By restricting his outlook to Argentine horizons, he left a memory of violent opposition to foreign influence. He had no intention of Europeanizing the country. As a leading student of the Rosas period has stated, "In the eyes of the provinces, Rosas became the most Argentine of all *porteño* governors, the only governor in fact who placed the economic interests of the nation above those of foreign merchants."[9] This type of nationalism often appealed to leaders of the interior provinces, where it has continued to enjoy popularity to the present day in the form of *criollo* nationalism. The leading characteristics of the *criollo* economic nationalism have been antiforeign reactions, combined at times with anticapitalism and hatred of Buenos Aires.

Though most observers currently link economic nationalism with antiimperialism and xenophobia, during the latter half of the nineteenth century, following the overthrow of Rosas in 1852, a liberal concept of economic nationalism prevailed. Leaders of post-1852 Argentina welcomed foreign participation in the economic life of their nation. The new ruling elite that came to power desired to modernize Argentina. More exactly, they hoped to turn it into a United States of South America. They believed that foreign capital made important contributions toward progress and ultimate self-sufficiency as they defined it. By their standards Argentina would achieve its economic independence once it became self-sufficient within a liberal international trading system. They envisioned a gradual process and relied upon foreign capital and technical skills to accomplish many of their goals. Excited by the prospect of a balanced trade relationship with Europe, the liberals moved to develop a predominately export economy based

[9] Burgin, *Economic Aspects of Argentine Federalism*, p. 242.

on cattle and agricultural production. Railways made this economic growth possible. At the same time, they opened up new regions of the country and tied together existing centers.

As the century drew to a close, radical nationalists began to challenge the liberals' free-trade and laissez faire policies. For years the elite of Argentina had excluded "out" groups from economic and political power. Now representatives of competing socioeconomic classes turned to nationalism in order to rally support against the elite. The first assault included the resuscitation of Rosas-*criollo* nationalism by cultural nationalists and by politicians, such as Hipólito Yrigoyen and Juan B. Justo. The Rosista movement manifested increasingly antiforeign characteristics. As the middle class grew in political and economic strength, a second, more reactionary nationalism grew which stressed economic factors. At the turn of the century it began to challenge the liberal traditions. Advocates of the new economic nationalism considered foreign capital a barrier to economic development and a threat to political independence. Public ownership and control of the key economic sectors became the goal of the economic nationalists. Nationalists placed more importance upon the well-being of the nation and its citizenry than on economic efficiency. As a result, they tried to break the existing economic relations with the imperial powers of the world. In the political sphere, the more radical nationalism promised two things. First, it attempted to end the domination of the nation by a *vendepatria* elite. Second, it guaranteed social justice to all Argentines, especially the forgotten urban workers. Fanned by the frustrations of the world depression during the 1930's and by the failure of organized political parties to maintain legitimate political order after 1930, this strain of economic nationalism grew rapidly. Ultimately it contributed to the rise of Perón after 1943.

1. Opening the Door

Argentina entered the railway age late. Great Britain and the United States had already developed extensive networks by 1850. Several Latin American nations had begun minor railway construction. But in Argentina bullock carts, "in appearance not unlike a *rancho* or native hut," set upon immense wheels, still plied the pampas.[1] It took months to transport goods from the interior to the east-coast population centers. Most farmers of the interior produced locally consumable goods. Few of their products reached the east coast. Indians still dominated large sections of the fertile plains. *Caudillos* remained in control of remote areas of the country, oblivious to a growing commitment on the part of many Argentines to the creation of an integrated nation. As yet the young republic failed to show any signs of the modernization process so evident in other parts of the world. Not until 1857 did a steam-driven locomotive make its first, tentative trip in the province of Buenos Aires. But within thirty years the

[1] Nathaniel H. Bishop, *The Pampas and Andes*, pp. 103-105.

Argentine railway industry entered a period of unparalleled growth. With the boom, unification of the country and political stability seemed tenable goals.[2]

A new age dawned with the application of steam locomotives, iron rails, and flanged wheels to public transportation. Beginning in Great Britain in the 1820's and the United States in the 1830's, railways made an impressive impact. Within a few decades, iron horses replaced their flesh-and-bone predecessors. Railways became the leading conveyors of produce and people. They caused political, economic, and social changes throughout the world. In England, an industrial revolution surged forward with the building of a national railway artery. In the United States, mercantilist rivalries between growing cities sparked the westward push of railways. These lines transformed the frontier and determined the course of a burgeoning industrial economy. Elsewhere the process of nation building gained momentum thanks to growing railway networks. By the late 1840's, for instance, a common rail system drew together the diverse German states. During the 1850's, India, Russia, and parts of Canada experienced similar developments.[3]

[2] The most useful studies of Argentine railways include Juan B. Alberdi, *The Life and Industrial Labors of William Wheelwright in South America*; Alejandro Bunge, *Ferrocarriles argentinos*; Juan José Castro, *Treatise on the South American Railways and the Great International Lines*; Horacio Juan Cuccorese, *Historia de los ferrocarriles en la Argentina*; Manuel María Díez, *Régimen jurídico de las comunicaciones*, vols. 1-4; J. S. Duncan, "British Railways in Argentina," *Political Science Quarterly* 52, no. 4 (December 1937): 559-582; Gregorio Etcheguía, *Los ferrocarriles argentinos vistos por ojos argentinos*; Leopoldo Grahame, *Argentine Railways*; Leland H. Jenks, "Britain and American Railway Development," *Journal of Economic History* 11, no. 4 (1951): 375-388; Colin Lewis, "Problems of Railway Development in Argentina, 1857-1890," *Inter-American Economic Affairs* 22, no. 2 (Autumn 1968): 55-75; George Pendle, "Railways in Argentina," *History Today* 8, no. 2 (February 1958): 119-125; Emilio Rebuelto, "Historia del desarrollo de los ferrocarriles argentinos," *Boletín de Obras Públicas de la República Argentina* 5, nos. 5 and 6 (November-December 1911): 113-172; William Rögind, *Historia del Ferrocarril Sud, 1861-1936*; and Argentine Republic, Dirección de Informaciones y Publicaciones Ferroviarias, *Origen y desarrollo de los ferrocarriles argentinos*.

[3] See Hamilton Ellis, *British Railway History*; Brian Fawcett, *Railways of the Andes*; Leslie T. Fournier, *Railway Nationalization in Canada*; Holland Hunter, *Soviet Transport Experience*; J. Johnson, *The Economics of Indian Rail Transport*; J. Lorne Mcdougall, *Canadian Pacific*; Estevão Pinto, *Historia de una estrada-de-ferro de nordeste*; Michael Robbins, *The Railway Age*; John F. Stover, *American Railroads*; Norman Thompson and J. H. Edgar, *Canadian Railway Development*; J. N. Westwood, *A History of Russian Railways*.

The railway age began as an exciting commercial venture. Such Englishmen as George Stephenson, his son Robert, Isambard Kingdon Brunel, Joseph Locke, and Thomas Brassey comprised an important body of railway visionaries. These men stood out because of their ability to plan railways in a total sense. They mastered the technical as well as the commercial aspects of railways in a day when most men thought that canals and turnpikes provided adequate transportation. Tireless individuals, they relentlessly tried to convince commercial men, financiers, and other capitalists that their schemes would bear rich fruits. Their work resulted in impressive rail systems.

By the end of 1850, Britain's six-thousand-mile railway network had effected a social and economic revolution. Private capitalists built a well-integrated, yet competitive system sanctioned by Parliament and watched over by the government through railway inspectors of the Board of Trade. The nation benefited as railways expanded. Receipts grew beyond the dreams of early speculators. Passenger traffic grew especially fast and represented nearly 50 percent of the total receipts in 1850. Britons of all classes could afford to travel. This led to an unprecedented movement of people and great demographic change. In a short span of years an economic upsurge took place, especially in the nation's industrial sector. Railway expansion taxed Britain's iron-and-steel industry to its fullest capacity to supply rails, locomotives, rolling stock, and other iron products. The same expansion applied to the lumber industry, which supplied crossties and bridge materials. Employment in supportive industries, construction companies, and railways gave further impetus to Britain's industrial revolution. If some shady financiers made personal fortunes as a result of the railway boom, the nation could afford the price. Britain's extensive railway network placed it far ahead of its nearest manufacturing and commercial rivals.

A similar development took place in the United States between 1830 and 1850, although along somewhat different lines. British railways primarily tied together existing cities. Railways served an urgent need for increased transportation between established commercial centers. In the United States the earliest railways united the scattered commercial centers of the east coast. By 1850 the bulk of the 9,500-mile rail network stretched from north to south in the eastern states. But soon new railways began to open up communication with a rapidly expanding frontier. Often railways preceded the western markets they hoped to serve. With the discovery of gold in California more lines branched westward to the Great Lakes and the Ohio River, then across the unpopulated great plains. Gold, the federal government's new land-grant policy, and the transpacific trade combined in the 1850's to bring about a railroad boom. The total railway mileage of the United States reached over 30,000 miles by 1860.

The experience of Britain and the United States demonstrated to other countries the benefits of railway systems. Their successes encouraged other nations to build railways to remote areas as well as between established population centers. Union generals during the Civil War in the United States and the British army during the Crimean War proved the military importance of railways. Knowledgeable Argentines did not have to guess about the potential uses of the railway. Nor did they have to invent new systems. By importing the iron horse they stood to benefit. With luck they could duplicate the success of both Britain and the United States. As in the former, railways would tie together settled areas of the nation. As in the latter, railways would develop the unsettled territories of the republic.

Although liberal Argentines wanted to emulate Britain and the United States, they had many obstacles to overcome before they could seriously entertain the construction of a vast rail system. Ignorance and economic backwardness formed imposing barriers to modernizers. Although topographically ideal for railway construction and in need of railways to tie distant cities and markets, Argentina lacked any immediate stimulus to build railways before the 1850's. In Peru and Chile railways had opened up mining regions during the 1850's. Two of the first steam railways on the continent of South America ran through the impossible Andean terrain of Peru and Chile, both feats of engineering genius.[4] Argentina,

---

[4] Fawcett, *Railways of the Andes*, pp. 15-31.

however, had no mining industry which demanded transportation to coastal ports. Nor did Argentina have export commodities, such as sugar, which needed rapid transportation from cane fields to central refineries. Cuba, Mexico, and Jamaica built small railway systems during the 1830's and 1840's to develop interior resources, usually raw materials, for export to European markets. Argentina, which still depended upon the cattle industry of the east coast for its major exports, did not build railways before the mid-1850's.

The *porteño* dictator, Juan Manuel de Rosas, further delayed railway building in Argentina. Railways served no useful purpose to Rosas, who governed between 1829 and 1852. He made his fortune from the cattle industry of the coastal province of Buenos Aires. He simply wanted to eliminate potential competition from the interior. Furthermore, he purposefully built up his political image as a xenophobe to gain popular support for his regime. He directed his xenophobia against technological innovations and improvements that would have changed Argentina. His narrow *porteño* view, his rejection of change, and his lack of vision convinced him not to build railways into the interior, or for that matter to consider any development of that vast region.[5]

In 1853, a year after the overthrow of the despotic Rosas, Argentina remained an undeveloped country by nineteenth-century economic standards. Its economic system had not changed noticeably since 1810. Some forty years of independence from Spain had seen little alteration of the conditions of the interior provinces. Primitive technology, subsistence farming, and marginal manufacturing characterized the economies of the interior and coastal regions. Livestock and agriculture prevailed throughout the central and northwestern part of the nation, but these zones did not have large surpluses. Small farmers had neither adequate manpower nor proper transportation systems. With the exception of textiles in Tucumán, raising of draft animals in Córdoba, and Santa Fe for work in the mines of Upper Peru, no export industries prospered. Even these industries suffered from low productivity

[5] Miron Burgin, *The Economic Aspects of Argentine Federalism, 1820-1852*, pp. 242-245; Henry S. Ferns, *Britain and Argentina in the Nineteenth Century*, p. 311; Ysabel F. Rennie, *The Argentine Republic*, p. 45.

and lack of adequate transportation facilities. The province of Buenos Aires still depended upon cattle for its chief source of revenue. Wild cattle provided salt beef, hides, and tallow. To date, no effort to breed purebred cattle had been made.

The introduction of the railway began to change Argentina. The first phase of Argentina's railway development took place between 1854 and 1880. During this period four of the nation's most enlightened presidents—Justo José de Urquiza, Bartolomé Mitre, Domingo Faustino Sarmiento, and Nicolás Avellaneda—worked to bring peace and stability to Argentina. They set as their primary goal the building of a new nation out of a heterogeneous group of provinces and cities. Though they often differed on important political matters, these men and their supporters laid the groundwork for Argentina's economic and political development.

Little railway construction took place during their terms of office. But these leaders did settle matters of state that necessarily preceded any large-scale railway program. They committed Argentina to a liberal concept of progress which held that economic development naturally led to political and social improvement. In this respect they represented economic nationalists who thought in terms of progress and improvement. Products of an age of unbridled optimism, they promised high economic living standards for future generations of Argentines. Like Rivadavia and other pre-Rosas liberals, they hoped to populate the land with European immigrants and to encourage foreign capitalists to invest large sums in building a new and viable economy. That foreign capital played an important role in the growth of Argentina caused little criticism at the time; it had already done so in the United States, whose example many Argentines in that period wished to emulate.

Perhaps Juan B. Alberdi, intellectual spokesman for the interior block of provinces which composed the Argentine Confederation in 1853, best expressed the sentiment of his liberal countrymen. In his *Bases y puntos de partida para la organización política de la República Argentina*, published in 1852 as a guide for framing the Constitution of 1853, he stated that "railways will bring about the unity of the Argentine Republic better than any number of Congresses. Congress will be able to declare that it is *one and indivis-*

ible: but without railways, which will draw the remote extremes close together, it will always remain divisible and divided despite all legislative decrees."[6] Alberdi realized that without railways his dictum "to govern is to populate" meant nothing. The interior would attract immigrants only if they could reach it easily. Railways could effect the kind of land settlement and development that liberals anticipated. Alberdi correctly argued that Argentina needed rivers of steel to make up for its lack of a great river system. Until goods and people moved around Argentina with relative ease and speed, the modernization of Argentina could not begin.

Alberdi's concepts found expression in Article 67 of the Constitution of 1853, according to which Congress "shall have the power to provide for all that conduces to the prosperity of the country, to the advancement and welfare of all the provinces, and to the advancement of the people by prescribing plans for general and university instruction and by promoting industrial enterprise, immigration, the construction of railways and navigable canals, the colonization of public lands, the introduction and establishment of new industries, the importation of foreign capital, by laws which protect these ends and by temporary concessions of privileges and rewards."[7]

Until 1860, Buenos Aires refused to ratify the constitution. All the other provinces accepted it and joined the Argentine Confederation. Buenos Aires, the richest province, controlled the financial resources of the divided nation. Without the revenue of the port city's customhouse, the Confederation had nothing but land to its name.[8] Foreign investors wanted assurance of minimum profits on their investments. They would not accept land in place of capital resources. Investments in the United States, Canada, Russia, and India paid from 4 to 6 percent per annum. British capitalists understandably refused to risk money on Argentine ven-

---

[6] Juan B. Alberdi, *Bases y puntos de partida para la organización política de la República Argentina*, p. 82. Unless otherwise noted, all translations will be mine.

[7] Article 67 of the Constitution of 1853, as translated by Ferns in *Britain and Argentina*, p. 295.

[8] Justo José de Urquiza's annual message of May 25, 1855, to the Congress of the Argentine Confederation, in Heraclio Mabragaña (ed.), *Los mensajes*, III, 109. Raúl Scalabrini Ortiz, *Historia de los ferrocarriles argentinos*, pp. 83-84.

tures that could not guarantee equal security. Between 1854 and 1860 the Confederation attempted to finance the construction of a rail link between the port city of Rosario and the interior city of Córdoba. Leaders of the Confederation realized that the government had to encourage railway building. They had to give incentives to foreign entrepreneurs. Other nations had used land grants, duty exemptions, and guaranteed minimum profits to encourage the construction of railways. The Confederation hoped to follow the same pattern in order to duplicate the success of the United States.

At first the Confederation limited itself to a modest and realistic goal. Specifically, railway advocates hoped to attract trade currently handled by merchants in Buenos Aires and Santiago de Chile. To accomplish this they suggested the construction of a comparatively short trunk line from the Paraná River to some central point in the interior. The Confederation lacked the population for an extensive system. But the short line would provide sufficient revenue to warrant its construction. Córdoba already enjoyed political power and considerable commerce. It had access to the interior provinces and was close to the Paraná. The government chose Rosario as the port for the railway because at the time it provided better harbor facilities than Santa Fe.[9]

In January, 1854, the Confederation's Congress authorized the government to contract an engineer from the United States to survey the best route between Córdoba and Rosario. In keeping with its limited budget, the Congress requested the government's agent not to look for a first-class engineer but for one who earned the equivalent of four thousand pesos per year in the United States.[10] As luck would have it, the agent found just such a man in Chile. In September, 1854, the Confederation engaged Allen Campbell to make the survey. Campbell had worked for the New York and Harlem Railway before the North American contractor William Wheelwright hired him in 1850 to survey a railway from

[9] William Wheelwright, *Introductory Remarks on the Provinces of the La Plata and the Cultivation of Cotton*, pp. 8-11.

[10] Argentine Republic, *Registro oficial de la República Argentina*, no. 3091 (1882), January 28, 1854, III, 98. Hereafter cited as *Registro oficial*.

Caldera to Copiapó in Chile. That railway, one of the first to run on the South American continent, served the copper and silver mining region of Copiapó, at an altitude of twelve thousand feet. It did not match the engineering masterpiece constructed by Henry Meiggs in the Andes of Peru. But at the time it represented the first leg of a projected trans-Andean railway that Wheelwright wanted to construct across the *cordillera*, eventually terminating in Rosario. Because of his Chilean experience, Campbell met the Argentines' need. He had proven himself a capable engineer in the United States and Latin America. More important, he knew the special problems involved in constructing railways in South America. Finally, his congenial nature and his ability to work hard under adverse circumstances suited him to the Argentine task.[11]

Campbell found a civil engineer's paradise in Argentina. Firm ground, few rivers, and long expanses of flat countryside contrasted markedly with the Chilean Andes he had just left. Within a year after his appointment Campbell completed his study for the Rosario-Córdoba line. He submitted his final report to Minister of Interior Santiago Derquí, on November 30, 1855. In that report he estimated that the railway would cost approximately one million pounds sterling, at a rate of four thousand pounds sterling per mile, a low figure when compared to the cost of railway building elsewhere in the world. The low cost resulted from the simplicity of constructing the railway, which needed few bridges, no zigzags or hairpin curves, and no major building up of the track bed. The expenses, besides the steel for rails, included transporting gravel for ballast and lumber for crossties from other parts of Argentina.[12]

On April 2, 1855, the government authorized José Buschenthal, a banker from Montevideo who had made heavy loans to both the Confederation and Buenos Aires, to form a company in Europe to finance the construction of the Córdoba-Rosario railway.[13] Campbell had not completed his survey at the time, but anxious officials desired to obtain financial support for the project at the

[11] Scalabrini Ortiz, *Ferrocarriles argentinos*, pp. 75-76.
[12] Wheelwright, *Introductory Remarks*, p. 36.
[13] *Registro oficial*, no. 3441 (1855), III, 207. The best biographical sketch of José

earliest possible date. Since they lacked details concerning the cost estimates, the government attempted to attract foreign investors through generous land grants and tax concessions. Buschenthal's contract guaranteed a free right of way between Córdoba and Rosario, as well as a permanent grant of a strip of land one and one-half miles wide on either side of the right of way outside the limits of the towns through which the railway passed. The government also agreed to permit the duty-free importation of all equipment and material used to construct and operate the railways. The contract limited the period of private ownership of the railway to a ninety-nine-year period. At the end of that time span, the railway and all its properties reverted to the government upon payment of its valuated price.[14] These terms differed very little from railway concessions written in Russia, India, and parts of continental Europe, except that the contract did not guarantee the payment of minimum profits to investors as did contracts in Russia and India.

Buschenthal failed to find the necessary funds. After two years of waiting, the Confederation changed the original concession. A decree issued on October 30, 1857, ordered Buschenthal to extend full partnership in the enterprise to William Wheelwright.[15] Born in Newburyport, Massachusetts, in 1798, Wheelwright had spent the better part of his adult life in Latin America. A ship he captained sank in the Río de la Plata estuary in 1823. From that date on he based his operations in Chile and Argentina. Though neither a technician nor a man of fortune, he had the vision of a good contractor. By the 1830's he began to make a reputation as a developer, especially after he established the first steamship line on the west coast of Latin America in 1835. His chief interest lay in steamships. His many accomplishments included the founding of the Pacific Steam Navigation Company of Liverpool in 1839 and

---

Buschenthal appears in José María Rosa, *La caída de Rosas*, pp. 184-186. According to Rosa, Buschenthal first appeared as an Austrian banker named José Bruschenthal in the Spanish court under Mendizabal. He later appeared in Brazil during the reign of Dom Pedro I as José de Bouschental, presumably of French origin. After losing a Brazilian fortune, he established a bank in Montevideo with the help of Palmerston in 1848. Also see Lucio V. Mansilla, ed., *Retratos y recuerdos*, p. 169.

[14] *Registro oficial*, no. 3441 (1855), III, 207.

[15] Ibid., no. 4297 (1895), October 30, 1857, IV, 72.

the construction of a railway between Caldera and Copiapó, Chile, in 1850. Above all, he thought in terms of the total commercial picture of Latin America. Like Henry Meiggs and other developers who characterized the mid-nineteenth century, he dreamed of the seemingly impossible. He wanted a canal across the Isthmus of Panama. Later, he hoped to compete with the isthmus by developing a trans-Andean railway from Caldera, Chile, to Rosario, Argentina. That line, he believed, would make a quicker, more reliable route from New Zealand and Australia to Europe than the Panamanian voyage.[16]

In all his undertakings Wheelwright had solicited the help of local British merchants and capitalists. In so doing he had established important financial contacts in London. Perhaps for that reason Mariano Fragueiro, the Confederation's minister of finance, suggested Wheelwright's appointment as a joint concessionaire with Buschenthal. Fragueiro knew of Wheelwright's previous work and used his influence with President Urquiza to have the concession awarded to the Yankee.[17] Wheelwright lent valuable assistance to the project. Both his experience and his reputation attracted attention to the Argentine enterprise in England.

Wheelwright did not have immediate success. British money remained tight in the aftermath of the crash of 1853. British investors showed little confidence in both the Confederation and Wheelwright. The break between Buenos Aires and the Confederation virtually froze the credit of the latter. Even doubling the land grant in 1857 did not attract enough capital to begin construction. Buschenthal soon dropped out of the picture.[18] As sole manager of the enterprise, Wheelwright continued his attempt to raise the funds. He deserves credit for his persistence. On numerous occasions he promised would-be investors that they could make their fortunes in Argentina. His railway would cross another Texas, he promised, rich in cotton and cattle: "England may indeed look with interest to that beautiful region, where the

[16] Fawcett, *Railways of the Andes*, pp. 26-31; Juan B. Alberdi, *The Life and Industrial Labors of William Wheelwright in South America.*
[17] Alberdi, *Life of William Wheelwright*, Appendix, pp. 1-20.
[18] Ibid., p. 139.

Anglo-Saxon labourer pursues his toil without the fear of an Indian sun, the fevers of Africa or the West Indies, and with his family enjoying health and abundance."[19] Investors remained unmoved. British merchants and capitalists continued to show an understandable preference to deal with Buenos Aires rather than with the more remote and impoverished Confederation.[20] For the time being Wheelwright had to admit failure, but not defeat.

While the Confederation attempted to attract foreign capital, the province of Buenos Aires pursued a policy of isolation in hopes of remaining economically independent of foreign capital. With the leading port city of Argentina within its confines, the province earned a self-sustaining income through the export of livestock and agricultural products and the revenue of the customhouse. Had the leaders of Buenos Aires remained regional rather than national in outlook, the province might have maintained itself indefinitely without the assistance of large foreign loans.[21] But the short-lived isolation soon gave way to a more liberal policy. Two factors stand out in the metamorphosis of Buenos Aires into a free-trade center. First, the representatives of British economic interests there used considerable influence to undermine the isolationist spirit. They induced the already pro-European leaders of Buenos Aires to open their doors to foreign enterprise and capital.[22] Second, the *porteños*, like their Spanish ancestors, were gripped with an endemic land fever that left very little private domestic capital for such public works as railways.

Not surprisingly, the first Argentine railway ran in Buenos Aires. It began as a combination of a successful land speculation venture with a not-so-successful private-investment enterprise. A group of Buenos Aires merchants and landowners founded the Sociedad de Camino de Hierro de Buenos Aires al Oeste in September, 1853.[23] On January 9, 1854, the provincial government of

---

[19] Wheelwright, *Introductory Remarks*, p. 2.

[20] Scalabrini Ortiz, *Ferrocarriles argentinos*, p. 84.

[21] Ferns, *Britain and Argentina*, pp. 313-315. Scalabrini Ortiz (*Ferrocarriles argentinos*, p. 22) suggests that the Rosas antiforeign attitude lasted until 1854 in Buenos Aires.

[22] Ferns, *Britain and Argentina*, p. 335.

[23] Gergorio Etcheguía, *Los ferrocarriles argentinos vistos por ojos argentinos*, p. 11; "Ferro-

Buenos Aires enfranchised this organization as an autonomous society with the privilege of constructing a railway six miles between downtown Buenos Aires and a western suburb. Physical factors partly explain their decision to build the railway; torrential rainstorms often rendered the densely populated western district a virtual island.[24] But the entrepreneurs also wanted to increase the value of real estate they owned there, as well as tap new markets. The railway builders had long-range designs. They considered the first six miles, completed in August, 1857, symbolic of greater things to come. The nomenclature of their first locomotives gives an idea of their larger aspirations. By 1860 the company owned locomotives with suggestive names, such as "Voy a Chile," "Progreso," and "Luz del Desierto," in spite of the fact that it owned little more than twenty-three miles of track.

The company's slow growth emphasizes the refusal of Argentine capitalists to invest in native industries. At first the society tried to solicit subscriptions from *porteños* only. Although many promised to buy subscriptions, very few actually paid up their capital. Only through the support of the provincial government, which paid one-third of the cost of the project and provided a free right of way, did the Oeste complete its six-mile run by 1857. Without indigenous capital, the Oeste had to look abroad for capital.[25] In so doing the company led Buenos Aires out of its isolationist policy.

The process of financing and constructing the Oeste gave the first Argentine railway an English accent. The company's first vice-president, Daniel Gowland, also served as chairman of the Committee of British Merchants in Buenos Aires. From the beginning, British members of the *porteño* commercial community supported railway construction as a means of extending their markets. They also wanted to improve the facilities for shipping products from

---

carriles," *Gran enciclopedia argentina*, ed. Diego A. de Santillán, II, 313. The founders of the society included Jaime Llavallol, Mariano Miro, Manuel de Guerrico, Bernardo Larrondi, Norberto de la Riestra, Adolfo von Praet, and Daniel Gowland.

[24]*Herapath's*, October 6, 1888, p. 1120.

[25] Rebuelto, "Historia del desarrollo de los ferrocarriles argentinos," p. 134; Ferns, *Britain and Argentina*, p. 313.

their own *estancias*.[26] An Englishman by the name of William Bragg managed the building of the line with the aid of 160 British workmen.[27] As Allen Campbell had pointed out in his study of the Córdoba-Rosario railway, Argentine laborers could easily grasp the essentials of railway construction. Like the *rotos* of Chile, the Argentine worker followed directions well and worked hard. Nonetheless, the founders of the Oeste felt it wiser to have the job done correctly. Their countrymen could learn about building railways by observing Englishmen who knew their business.

Topping off the English aspects of the Oeste, its first locomotive, rolling stock, and tracks came from England. A popular legend states that the first locomotive to run upon the Oeste's tracks, "La Porteña," was a broad-gauged veteran of the Crimean War built originally for service on a British-owned railway in India. The legend maintains that, after they had used the locomotive on the Balaclava railway during the siege of Sevastopol, the British sold the worn-out locomotive to the Oeste as "scrap iron."[28] For many years Argentines have used this episode to explain the Oeste's decision to use the broad gauge of 1.676 meters rather than the standard British gauge of 1.435 meters. But recent studies have proven this account fictitious.[29] The legend resulted from an attempt by Argentine nationalists to exaggerate British avarice in the post-1890 period.[30] More likely, the Argentines chose the wider gauge because Spain and Paraguay had already adopted it. The level Argentine terrain lent itself to the use of the heavier rolling stock of broad-gauge railways.

The Oeste got off to a rather inauspicious start. On the evening before its inauguration a group of *porteño* dignitaries made a trial run. On returning, their carriage skipped off the track, over-

---

[26] Colin Lewis, "Problems of Railway Development in Argentina, 1857-1890," *Inter-American Economic Affairs* 22, no. 2 (Autumn 1968): 68-70.

[27] Rebuelto, "Historia del desarrollo de los ferrocarriles argentinos," p. 135.

[28] For instance, see ibid., and Scalabrini Ortiz, *Ferrocarriles argentinos.*

[29] See Michael Robbins, "The Balaklava Railway," *Journal of Transport History* 1, no. 1 (May 1953): 41-42; and Pendle, "Railways in Argentina."

[30] According to *Railway Gazette*, May 25, 1910, p. 16, the rails used by the original Oeste were made out of Sebastopol cannon purchased from Britain. These myths might also have resulted from national pride. Argentines could boast that they built a prosperous business from British "scrap iron"—a tribute to Argentine ingenuity and enterprise.

turned, and dumped the officials in a ditch at the side of the track. Fortunately, none of the passengers sustained serious injuries. Swearing themselves to secrecy, the politicians and merchants helped put the train back on the track and resumed their trip back to the city.[31] At the inauguration ceremony the following day, Dr. Valentín Alsina, governor of Buenos Aires province, tried to reassure a doubting constituency of the efficacy of government support of the railway. He called the railway the first stone in a vast edifice. Alsina, like other liberals, felt that the line would open new horizons for the development of the nation. He believed that the Oeste demonstrated the benefits Europe had to bestow upon Argentina, for "those industries, . . . sciences, and their application are not indigenous to the new American states. No, all of this originated in other countries, on other continents." Argentina, he concluded, must look forward to the day on which "it will be possible to delete from the pages of public law the disagreeable word 'foreigner.' "[32]

Despite Alsina's optimism, many Argentines still doubted the advisability of supporting railway projects. Most Argentines had lived in provincial isolation. Few had visited Europe or the United States. Those who had knew the marvels of the locomotive. But the majority remained uncertain. Civil conflicts took up much of their time as Buenos Aires and the Confederation continued their rift. By 1860 the nation had only 23 miles of railway, all built by the enterprising Oeste. Even that railway had to prove its ability to make profits. When the provincial government voted in 1858 to help finance the extension of the Oeste another 238 miles, one deputy remarked, "I do not think we do wrong in voting for this railway, but I believe that it is a piece of precocious legislation to authorize a work which may be begun in the century which follows."[33]

[31] "Ferrocarriles," *Gran enciclopedia argentina*, II, 313.
[32] Etcheguía, *Los ferrocarriles argentinos*, p. 17.
[33] As quoted in *Herapath's*, October 6, 1888, p. 1120.

2. The First Steps

Politics more than any other single factor explains the slow growth of railways in Argentina before 1880. Railway building could not begin on a larger scale until the political unification of the country, which started in 1862. With Urquiza's unexpected withdrawal from national politics after the indecisive battle of Pavón in 1861, the schism between Buenos Aires and the Confederation began to heal. There remained some friction between the two regions, but at last they had a common government. Buenos Aires joined the provinces of the Confederation in creating the Argentine Republic under the Constitution of 1853. For the twelve years between 1862 and 1874 two exceptionally able presidents, Bartolomé Mitre and Domingo F. Sarmiento, headed the Argentine Republic. Both had previously championed *porteño* interests which they now gave broader national scope. With the economic resources of Argentina's richest province at their disposal, they started to construct a railway system like that envisioned by Alberdi, Campbell, and Wheelwright.

Alberdi's prophecies took shape under the leadership of Bartolomé Mitre. A consistent supporter of railway construction in the province of Buenos Aires since the overthrow of Rosas, Mitre planned a nationwide rail network. As governor of Buenos Aires he had encouraged the provincial congress to support the construction of the Great Southern Railway (Ferrocarril Sud) by members of the British commercial community.[1] That railway, which confined most of its activities to the province of Buenos Aires, became one of the most successful in the nation. Upon assuming the presidency in 1862, Mitre set about the task of inducing foreign-owned concerns to build railways on a national scale. The Oeste, built entirely within the well-developed province of Buenos Aires, had proven profitable on a limited scale. The railways of the new order called for running long lines through areas of low population density. They would incur heavy losses for many years. Foreign capital made such undertakings feasible since they were beyond the capacity of an extremely conservative and cautious Argentine financial community.[2]

Various developments in Europe, especially in Britain, made Mitre's task an easier one. Growing industrialization and urbanization created markets for the agricultural and pastoral products of Argentina. Britain had recently gone over to free trade. The British Company Act of 1862, the year of Mitre's inauguration, made it possible for British investors to form joint stock companies on a firm legal basis. This aided the establishment of organizations equipped to pool capital and spread the risks involved in financing enterprises in underdeveloped countries.[3]

On the Argentine side, the Mitre administration implemented the policy of free trade called for by the Constitution of 1853. As one of his first steps, Mitre removed internal trade barriers by replacing provincial tariffs with grants to the provincial governments from the revenues of Buenos Aires customs.[4] Mitre also prepared the Argentine Republic for the flood of foreign capital

---

[1] Gaston H. Lestard, *Historia de la evolución económica argentina*, p. 139.
[2] Henry S. Ferns, *Britain and Argentina in the Nineteenth Century*, p. 314.
[3] Ibid., p. 325.
[4] Ibid.

that he and his supporters anticipated. Although capital only trick-
led in during the 1860's, British capital accounted for building two
of Argentina's major railways, the Central Argentine and the
Great Southern. Britons also received concessions from the Mitre
administration to build the Buenos Aires Northern and the Boca
railways.

Rivalries between competing railway factions delayed the construction of foreign-owned railways in Argentina. The most
serious conflict took place during the early 1860's when the
Yankee William Wheelwright tried to block the building of the
Great Southern Railway by a British group, led by Edward Lumb.
Wheelwright refused to cooperate with Britons who planned to
construct competing lines. He also felt that the British group had
gotten better terms in the concession to build the Great Southern
than he had to build the Central Argentine. This led him to delay
the construction of both railways while he took legal action to improve the terms of his own concession.

After the Argentine Confederation made its last unsuccessful
effort to procure the funds for undertaking the Córdoba-Rosario
railway in September, 1861, Wheelwright took the project to
Mitre in 1862.[5] At that time, Wheelwright set the cost of construction at six thousand pounds sterling per mile. Although well above
the four thousand estimated by Campbell in 1855, the Mitre administration considered Wheelwright's request a moderate one.
Argentine leaders believed that Wheelwright would soon give
them cheap railway transportation through unpopulated areas of
the nation. Several government spokesmen supported Wheelwright's bid. According to Minister of Finance Norberto de la
Riestra, "one of the most common mistakes made by engineers is
to underestimate the actual cost of this type of work."[6] As he
pointed out, Wheelwright had built the cheapest railway in Latin
America between Copiapó and Caldera, Chile, at 6,400 pounds

---

[5] *Registro oficial*, no. 5522, September 26, 1861, IV, 413-414; no. 5668, September 5, 1862, IV, 473-474.

[6] Argentine Republic, Cámara de Senadores, *Diario de sesiones*, July 12, 1862, p. 199. Hereafter cited as Senadores, *Diario*.

sterling per mile, during the 1850's.[7] The price of materials had increased since then. Although the Argentine pampas offered level roadbeds, the construction of the Central Argentine necessitated the hauling of wood ties and stone ballast over long distances. This made the permanent construction between Rosario and Córdoba more expensive.[8] In a similar manner, Senator Angel Navarro of Catamarca defended the concession on the ground, "We want a thing that is well made, not only because it would be absurd if we constructed a railway inferior to that of the Republic of Chile, but because the Argentines should not put themselves behind anyone, but always be, if possible, in the vanguard."[9]

On September 5, 1862, the national government granted Wheelwright a concession to build the Central Argentine Railway from Rosario to Córdoba. The most conspicuous provision of the new contract guaranteed investors an annual dividend of 7 percent on a capital investment of 6,000 pounds sterling per mile. Similar provisions appeared in railway concessions in India, Russia, and Canada. British investors expected such safeguards. When Wheelwright returned to Buenos Aires in January, 1863, he suggested some changes in the concession to Mitre's minister of interior, Guillermo Rawson.[10] On March 19, 1863, these two signed a second contract which raised the capital value of the railway to 6,400 pounds sterling per mile.[11] The government guaranteed an annual profit of 7 percent for a forty-year period, with the stipulation that the railway would repay the government when profits exceeded 7 percent. At Wheelwright's insistence the government extended the grant of land from one and one-half miles to three miles on both sides of the right of way. Wheelwright wanted the land in order to establish colonies at ten-mile intervals. Since land near

[7] Raúl Scalabrini Ortiz (*Historia de los ferrocarriles argentinos*, pp. 92-93) claims this figure is wrong. He states that the Oeste built its main trunk at about five thousand pounds sterling per mile. But the Oeste crossed flatter terrain, had fewer bridges, and did not have to transport fill long distances.

[8] The cost of stone ballast was estimated at eleven hundred pounds sterling per mile by *Railway Gazette*, May 25, 1910, p. 16.

[9] Senadores, *Diario*, July 12, 1862, p. 201.

[10] Scalabrini Ortiz, *Ferrocarriles argentinos*, p. 85.

[11] *Registro oficial*, no. 5899, V, 29. Congress approved the contract on May 23, 1863.

Rosario cost only a little over two shillings per acre in 1863, the grant did not amount to an extravagant gift to the Central Argentine.[12] The Argentine government also subscribed to fifteen hundred twenty-pound shares of the company. In return, the company agreed to provide gratuitous mail transport and to carry troops and war matériel at half price. The latter two provisions had been used in the United States, where they had already begun to offset the cost of land grants and loans to private railway companies. They promised to do the same in Argentina once the railways gained a proper footing.

Almost simultaneously, the province of Buenos Aires awarded an even more generous concession to Edward Lumb to build the Great Southern Railway seventy-two miles southward from Buenos Aires to Chascomus.[13] Lumb's contract contained provisions similar to the Central's. As approved by the provincial legislature on November 12, 1862, the concession granted the railway free land, tax exemptions, and a guarantee that the government would not interfere in rate fixing. The government also guaranteed an annual profit of 7 percent on a capital investment of 10,000 pounds sterling per mile, or 3,600 pounds more per mile than that promised to Wheelwright.[14] Although the amount of land granted to the Great Southern was less than that given to the Central Argentine, the higher-estimated cost per mile assured the Great Southern concessionaires larger profits. The matter probably would never have received much attention from *porteño* officials had Wheelwright supported his British colleagues in their venture. He chose, however, to protest the discrepancies in the contracts. Wheelwright aspired to control the total Argentine railway scene. His reaction soon ran him afoul of influential British merchants, especially David Robertson and Frank Parish. Wheelwright's intransigence cost him important allies, who could have helped him in the British money market. At the same time, his machinations delayed building the Great Southern and the Central Argentine.

---

[12] Thomas J. Hutchinson, *The Paraná with Incidents of the Paraguayan War and South American Recollections from 1861 to 1868*, p. 167.

[13] William Rögind, *Historia del Ferrocarril Sud, 1861-1936*, p. 9.

[14] Ibid., pp. 15-16.

The governor of Buenos Aires refused to sign the contract for the Great Southern until the matter was settled. Work on the Great Southern did not begin until Robertson paid some 22,000 pounds sterling in bribes to Buenos Aires officials in 1863. As for Wheelwright, his difficulties with the British merchants of Buenos Aires finally forced him to resign from the Central Argentine's syndicate in 1865. Until then the Central Argentine made no significant progress.[15]

In spite of the delay caused by Wheelwright's squabble with the British, foreign interests led the railway industry. British merchants in Buenos Aires played an especially important role. Men like Edward Lumb, Frank Parish, John Fair, and David Robertson represented Britons who invested in Argentine railways to extend the hegemony\of their own commercial interests. They understood the mercantile possibilities the railways offered. With railways they could control the markets of the province. Their commercial houses would provide the interior settlements with imported goods and serve as clearinghouses for the shipment of wool, hides, and agricultural products from interior *estancias*. They also viewed railways as a profitable investment if well run under generous concessions.[16]

A great deal of vocal support for railway building came from the Argentine landed interests. Though they desired railways, they contributed little financial aid to their construction. The Argentine financial community proved unwilling, if able, to provide the necessary capital. According to H. S. Ferns, the British historian of Britain's economic relations with Argentina during the nineteenth century, "an inspection of the share lists of the Central Argentine Railway ... suggests that Argentines were not concerned whether to invest in or to gain control of such undertakings, no matter how freely they might criticize their activities in the newspapers and in the halls of Congress."[17] Land speculation also deter-

---

[15] Colin Lewis, "Problems of Railway Development in Argentina, 1857-1890," *Inter-American Economic Affairs* 22, no. 2 (Autumn 1968): 60-61.

[16] Ibid., pp. 68-71.

[17] Ferns, *Britain and Argentina*, p. 334.

mined Argentine participation in railway development. Large land-owners looked upon the railways as a means of increasing land values. Nominal profits did not interest them. They wanted to boom the price of land. Railways made new lands available for settlement and exploitation. Railways also made the land more attractive to prospective buyers because they assured ready access to markets. As in the United States, speculators bought land cheaply, then skyrocketed its value by encouraging unwary investors to build railway lines through their newly acquired holdings. Often landholders provided free land for stations and marshalling yards. Huge profits resulted from selling land to settlers who desired land next to railways. Between 1865 and 1890 speculators regularly made profits of over 350 percent from the sale of land along railways. Few resisted the temptation to speculate on land if they had the capital. Many notable Argentines made fortunes through land speculation. Bernardo de Irigoyen, for example, sold an estate in Santa Fe for five times the sum he paid for it, only six years after purchasing it from Edward Lumb.[18] As a rule, the typical Argentine landowner let the national or provincial governments and foreign investors take the major risks involved in building the railways. The speculator reaped profits by investing a fortune in land.

In this situation Mitre and his associates made what seemed to them the best possible compromise between national interests and the interests of foreign investors. Railway companies built lines where the state desired them. The management remained private. Through state-planned programs the Argentine government took on the important role of guaranteeing foreign investors minimum profits. At the same time, the government remained out of the free enterprise system in that it allowed foreigners to manage the private railways with very little state control.

Mitre's backing of the Central Argentine proved a wise political maneuver. At last a *porteño* administration supported an interior

[18] Julio Velar de Irigoyen, *Bernardo de Irigoyen*, p. 89. For more on speculation see Ferns, *Britain and Argentina*, p. 338; James Scobie, *Revolution on the Pampas*, pp. 5, 45-46; Mark Jefferson, *Peopling the Argentine Pampa*, pp. 177-178; Scalabrini Ortiz, *Ferrocarriles argentinos*, p. 29; and J. Fred Rippy, "Argentina: Late Major Field of British Overseas Investment," *Inter-American Economic Affairs* 6, no. 3 (1952): 3-13.

project. Even Alberdi, one of the leading critics of the *porteño*
regime, complimented Mitre and added, "By assuming the
patronage of it [the Central Argentine], as well as by adopting the
national constitution, neither one nor the other being original with
him, he gave a striking proof of his political sagacity."[19] The railways drew together isolated commercial regions of the republic.
They also played a significant military role. As Mitre pointed out
at the ground-breaking ceremony of the Central Argentine at
Rosario on April 20, 1863, "Everyone must rejoice on the opening
of this road, for it will tend to give riches where there is poverty
and to institute order where there is anarchy."[20] Military men like
Mitre deemed railways necessary both to defend the nation's frontiers and to establish domestic order and security which *caudillos*
and Indians continued to threaten through the 1870's. As one
deputy optimistically put it when discussing, the advantages of
building the Great Southern, railways would permit the government to carry authority to the remotest regions of the nation as
quickly as "a flash of lightning."[21]

Mitre believed that railways alone would bring about a social
and economic revolution in the Argentine Republic.[22] To his
generation the railways also played an important role as symbols of
nationalism. The railways expressed national progress, pride, and
power. The nationalism of Argentine leaders in this period looked
more to the future than the past. Their watchword was progress,
their goal the creation of a new and better Argentina, and their
chief instrument a great railway network.

In an attempt to attract railway lines to their provinces, interior
spokesmen consistently used nationalistic arguments. Their nationalism differed very little from that of the *porteños*. Whereas the
latter looked upon railways as a means of bringing "civilization"
and centralized authority to the interior, residents of the interior

[19] Juan B. Alberdi, *The Life and Industrial Labors of William Wheelwright in South America*, p. 145.

[20] Ibid., p. 146.

[21] Rögind, *Historia del Ferrocarril Sud*, p. 10; and Gregorio Etcheguía, *Los ferrocarriles argentinos vistos por ojos argentinos*, p. 141.

[22] Bartolomé Mitre's annual message to Congress of May 1, 1866, in Heraclio Mabragaña (ed.), *Los mensajes*, III, 213.

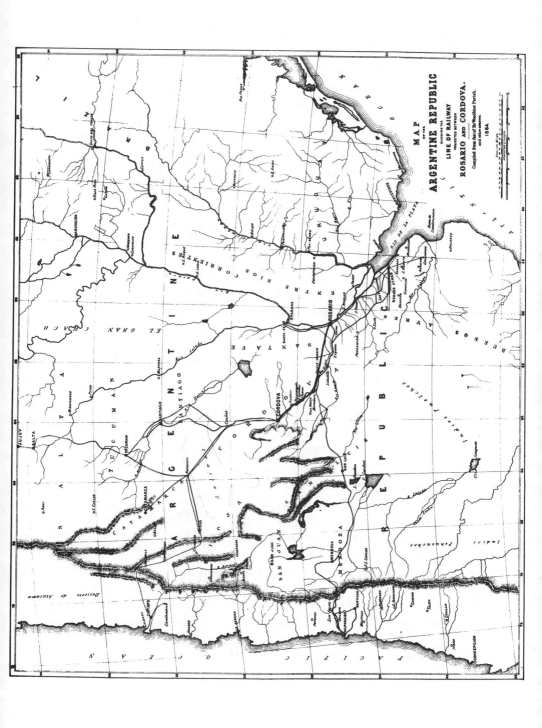

looked upon the railways as a means of creating a social and economic unity between the diverse regions of the country. They saw their position as equal to that of Buenos Aires in the new order. The need of the interior provinces for better trade outlets gave further impetus to their support of large-scale railway building. After the barren decade of the 1850's, representatives of the interior wanted to connect their remote cities with the ports of Argentina, especially Buenos Aires. Isolated cities like Córdoba, Tucumán, Mendoza, Catamarca, and San Juan needed railways as life lines in a changing world. Unless they progressed out of the ox-cart age and established rapid transportation to the markets of the east coast they faced certain economic decay. Of course, this policy led to importing foreign goods, which effectively destroyed the remnants of local industries. It also led to the establishment of a national market, which subordinated the interior to the port cities of the east coast. Nonetheless, farsighted interior politicians advocated railways as a means of economic salvation. They hoped to turn the "deserts" of the interior into prosperous and populated areas of production. In so doing they believed that the whole nation would benefit and that the economic predominance of Buenos Aires would end.

Provincials wanted to develop their own areas, but to do so they had to appeal to the national government for assistance. Interior provinces lacked the resources to build railways. For that reason they welcomed the subsidies offered to foreign corporations. During a debate over the concession granted to the Central Argentine, two distinguished members of the interior elite spelled out their position. On the one hand, Dalmacio Vélez Sársfield, from Córdoba, reflected the narrower goal of increasing the productivity of the interior. He supported the building of the Central Argentine because "it will create a great commercial center in Córdoba to which all the people who currently trade with Chile will come."[23] He emphasized that the railway would divert interior goods then flowing toward Chilean ports. Córdoba would develop into a market for goods from the ports of Rosario and Buenos Aires and

[23] Senadores, *Diario*, July 12, 1862, p. 195.

thus benefit the national economy. Turning the deserted interior into populated centers of production best served the interests of the nation. During the same debate, Angel Navarro, from the more removed province of Catamarca, fit the railways into the traditional *porteño*-interior struggle. He believed that railways offered a peaceful solution to the conflict. Railways, he argued, created a national sense of awareness and cooperation through the simple means of travel and commercial exchange. "The *porteños,* who have prejudices and do not know the people of the interior, will travel because of their curiosity to know them, and they will encounter an estimable society and a degree of richness that perhaps they did not know existed. The provincials, . . . who also have prejudices, will come to Buenos Aires, become intimate with its society, abandon the bad habits of their provinces, . . . and establish a brotherhood between people who have the desire to live united. Then all of the prejudices will disappear, and the mutual distrust between these people will cease."[24]

Regionalism typified the expressions of early advocates of railway expansion in Argentina. Most regionalists couched their rhetoric in national terms. Usually, provincial representatives argued that the entire nation benefited from the development of their own provinces. A statement by Senator José M. Cullen of Entre Ríos in September, 1864, offers an extreme example of this phenomenon. According to Cullen, the national government had an obligation to build railways in his province and in Corrientes. These provinces had willingly subscribed to shares of the Central Argentine. Moreover, these provinces contributed notably to the national treasury, although it cost the national government nothing to defend their frontiers. Finally, he continued, "We must not forget, in making a decision of such vital importance, that these were the provinces, and especially Entre Ríos, that contributed the most to the overthrow of General Rosas." The nation owed it to the northeastern provinces to finance railway construction there. The whole nation would benefit, the senator claimed,

[24] Ibid., p. 197.

"for it is due to acts like this that we are rapidly creating a second United States."[25]

Although Argentines expressed considerable interest in building railways during Mitre's administration, few companies began activities during the 1860's. Argentine railways built only 260 miles of new track between 1862 and 1868, bringing up the total distance to 343 miles at the end of his term.[26] Mitre, preoccupied with the protracted Paraguayan War (1865-1870), could give neither much time nor energy to railways during the latter half of his six-year administration. In 1867 work on the important Central Argentine slowed and finally stopped until the government loaned the company 1.7 million pesos.[27] The following year, Mitre admitted his disappointment that the war had kept his government from giving adequate support to railway construction. He expressed pride, however, that his administration had worked for progress by beginning railway construction, improving education, and increasing the prosperity of the nation.[28]

In 1868 Domingo F. Sarmiento came to the presidency dreaming of a new age in which Argentina would duplicate the achievements of the United States. Although he differed with Mitre on some points, he believed in the soundness of Mitre's railway policy and continued to follow a similar pattern of stimulating the development of foreign investment and enterprise in this field. Sarmiento dedicated his life to progress.

Sarmiento's background explains his attitude toward progress. Born in the interior province of San Juan, he knew from personal experience the poverty and backwardness of the remote areas of the Argentine Republic. Forced by Rosas, for political reasons, to leave Argentina, Sarmiento experienced long periods of exile before 1852. Outside Argentina he discovered another world. From his reading and from his travels in Europe and North

---

[25] José M. Cullen's address to Congress on September 10, 1864, as quoted in Neptalí Carranza, *Oratoria argentina*, II, 387-390.

[26] Argentine Republic, *Tercero censo nacional*, X, 405. Hereafter cited as *Tercero censo.*

[27] *Herapath's*, November 30, 1867, p. 1200. Also Scalabrini Ortiz, *Ferrocarriles argentinos*, pp. 115-119, and Alberdi, *Life of William Wheelwright*, p. 152.

[28] Senadores, *Diario*, May 18, 1868, p. 10; *Herapath's*, April 11, 1868, p. 372.

America he came to know the three countries—France, England, and the United States—that were most advanced in civilization as he defined it. Of these three, the United States easily stood first in his estimation. He spent most of his political life in trying to bestow upon Argentina the advantages of this civilization. More exactly, he wanted to "North Americanize" Argentina.[29]

Railways formed an important part of Sarmiento's civilizing crusade. He first became aware of steam locomotion while in Chile. Much impressed by the potential of the steam engine, he wrote from Chile in 1842, ". . . the application of steam to the means of transportation has so revolutionized commerce . . . that it would appear like the tool of the devil or a work of enchantment to people who are little accustomed to the spectacle of the progress of civilization."[30] The Argentine convinced himself that steamships and railways were necessary instruments of progress. He even switched from the liberal faction to support the Chilean conservative Manuel Mont because the latter promised, among other things, to begin railway building in Chile during the 1840's.[31]

After his return to Argentina in 1852, Sarmiento continued to support railway construction. As a member of the provincial senate of Buenos Aires, he became a leading proponent of railway expansion. Here he once stated that "to increase the numbers of railways is to reconquer for civilization, industry, and liberty the land that has been snatched away from us by barbarians."[32] On another occasion, members of the Buenos Aires Senate laughed at his excessive defense of railway building by foreign-owned concerns. Infuriated, Sarmiento protested. Livid with rage, he demanded the secretary to record that laughter in the minutes: "It is

[29] The best biography of Sarmiento's life in English is Allison W. Bunkley, *The Life of Sarmiento*. Another, though briefer, English work is Madeline W. Nichols, *Sarmiento: A Chronicle of Inter American Friendship*. The leading biographies by Argentine historians are Manuel Gálvez, *Vida de Sarmiento*; Alberto Palcos, *Sarmiento*; and Ricardo Rojas, *El profeta de la pampa*. See also Domingo F. Sarmiento, *Estados Unidos*, and his famous statement on his concept of civilization and barbarism in *Life in the Argentine Republic in the Days of the Tyrants*.

[30] Juan Francisco Castro, *Sarmiento y los ferrocarriles argentinos*, p. 21.

[31] Bunkley, *Life of Sarmiento*, pp. 151-152.

[32] Castro, *Sarmiento y los ferrocarriles*, p. 35.

necessary that future generations know that in order to aid the progress of my country I have had to acquire irrevocable confidence in its future. It also is necessary to record this laughter in order that it will be known what class of fools I have had to fight."[33] Later, as governor of his native province of San Juan, Sarmiento worked to bring the benefits of "civilization" to the interior between 1862 and 1863. His program called for the construction of roads and railways, but it met with little success in the backward province. In spite of this setback in San Juan, his fervor did not wane. Sarmiento continued to believe in the future greatness of Argentina and in the importance of railways for its development.[34]

Upon assuming the presidency in 1868, Sarmiento began a program intended to North Americanize Argentina. Among its first accomplishments, his administration completed the construction of the Central Argentine between Rosario and Córdoba. The railway had taken sixteen years to build since the granting of its original concession in 1854. Its construction had cost the national government millions of pesos in subsidies and expropriated land. Most modern Argentines felt the cost justifiable. In his annual message to Congress in 1870, Sarmiento spoke for the modernizers when he heralded the arrival of the railway at Córdoba as "a monument of honor for the Republic."[35] The inauguration of the Central Argentine Railway at Córdoba on May 17, 1870, received national attention. In compliance with a presidential decree, all public buildings displayed the national flag, and as soon as the telegraph from Córdoba announced the completion of the ceremony, a battery in Buenos Aires fired a twenty-one-gun salute. Thanks to the telegraph, the entire nation simultaneously received the benediction of the bishop of Córdoba as he closed the celebration.

Pressing matters of state made it impossible for Sarmiento to attend the inaugural ceremonies. He sent Minister of Interior Dalmacio Vélez Sársfield as his official representative. For Vélez

---

[33] Rögind, *Historia del Ferrocarril Sud*, p. 11.
[34] Bunkley, *Life of Sarmiento*, p. 399. Also Stuart Edgar Grummon (trans.), *A Sarmiento Anthology*, p. 20.
[35] Mabragaña, *Los mensajes*, III, 304.

Sársfield it meant returning to his home by rail after a prolonged absence.[36] One of Sarmiento's chief critics, Juan B. Alberdi, accused the president of lukewarm support to railway building, in spite of the pomp and official rhetoric. Yet the evidence does not support Alberdi's bitter accusation. Sarmiento had advocated railway building since the 1840's, for much the same reasons that Alberdi had. He believed that railways would unify and civilize the nation. He constantly made railway construction an important part of his reform programs. Indeed, he noted in his first annual message to Congress in May, 1869, that his party took as its symbol "a school, a telegraph, and a railway, agents of pacification and order that are much surer than cannon and penitentiaries." He supported railway construction because they "removed the desert, barbarism, and other obstacles and enemies of liberty and progress."[37]

In spite of the many obstacles that he faced as president, Sarmiento began important railway projects. In 1870, his government arranged a six-million-pound loan in London to extend the Central Argentine from Córdoba to Tucumán.[38] Although termed "an act of economic madness," the extension of a narrow-gauge line did stimulate the growth of the sugar industry in Tucumán upon its completion. Also, it helped the petty local industries which had languished for nearly half a century. Like the Canadian Pacific, built between 1873 and 1886, the Córdoba-Tucumán extension contributed to the peaceful building and settling of the nation. The similarity of the two lines goes further. Both resulted from calculated risks taken by government officials and private investors. Even though neither railway provided immediate profits as investments, both dramatically altered the economic development of the areas they served and helped to open new regions for exploitation.

In a law passed on November 5, 1872, the Sarmiento adminis-

[36] R. C. Kirk to SecState Hamilton Fish, June 6, 1870, Department of State, National Archives, Record Group 59, microcopy 69, roll 19. Hereafter material in the National Archives will be cited as NA, RG; Department of State will be cited as DS.

[37] Mabragaña, *Los mensajes*, III, 291.

[38] Ferns, *Britain and Argentina*, 331; and Alberdi, *Life of William Wheelwright*, p. 159. At the age of 74, Wheelwright no longer served on the board of directors of the Central Argentine. Nonetheless, he helped secure the loan to build the extension to Tucumán.

tration gave further support to railway expansion by establishing concessions for five new railways. These lines would link the capitals of the provinces.[39] Although actual work on these lines did not begin during his term, they demonstrate the support he gave to railway construction. Sarmiento took considerable pride in these accomplishments. He liked to think that the railways in Argentina were more successful than those in other countries. He also believed that their growth and the growth of industry they stimulated would encourage further investments in Argentina. On one occasion he claimed that a map of all the railways built, planned, and discussed during his administration "reveals that we are not far behind the most advanced nations in railways." In his farewell address he added that, "in railways, telegraph lines, and highways, our country marches in the vanguard of this part of America."[40]

For all his dreams of "progress" and his efforts to build railways, Sarmiento left very little material change. Only 406 miles of track were constructed between 1868 and 1874.[41] Undoubtedly more railway construction could have taken place under his direction if he had not been preoccupied with the tag end of the Paraguayan War, a series of civil revolts, and the beginning of an economic depression that originated with the panic of 1873. As one of his Argentine biographers has written, the period of Sarmiento's presidency amounted to "six years of disorder, blood and misery . . . that would have broken any man who did not possess the courage of Sarmiento."[42] He had expected changes to take place during his term in office that could be accomplished only over a long period. Allison W. Bunkley succinctly described the tragedy of Sarmiento's career: "He expected to spend six years in the presidency and leave his nation transformed. There was an element of magic in Sarmiento's method. The magic words (education, immigration, etc.) would be pronounced, and presto! The pumpkin

[39] Juan José Castro, *Treatise on the South American Railways and the Great International Lines*, p. 181. The five railways were the Buenos Aires to Mendoza and San Juan; San Juan to Totacalegos; Tucumán to Jujuy; Mercedes to Corrientes; and Transandine to Chile.

[40] See Sarmiento's annual messages to Congress of May 1, 1870; May, 1873; and May, 1874, in Mabragaña, *Los mensajes*, III, 303, 349, and 364.

[41] *Tercero censo*, X, 405.

[42] Rojas, *Profeta de la pampa*, p. 517.

would be turned into a carriage—the gaucho would be turned into a citizen, the Argentinean would be turned into a twin of his North American brother."[43]

It fell to Sarmiento's handpicked successor, Nicolás Avellaneda, to keep Argentina's overall economic development on an even keel during difficult years. This Avellaneda did by continuing the laissez faire policy of his predecessors toward foreign concerns while also considering the need for government-subsidized projects to encourage improvement of the nation. His efforts prepared the nation for the economic boom of the 1880's. Born at Tucumán and educated at the University of Córdoba, Avellaneda, like Sarmiento, typified the swing from *porteño* to provincial supremacy that characterized the political evolution of late-nineteenth-century Argentina. Youthful when he assumed the presidency, he belonged to the second generation of post-Rosas politicians. His anti-Rosas ties did not stem from his exile and struggle to overthrow the dictator, but from the fact that Rosas had executed his father during one of his many purges.

In many ways Avellaneda represents a transitional figure in Argentine political history. Thomas F. McGann has commented, "By his years he belonged to the new generation of the *ochenta*; by his work he was of the age of the organizers, whose achievements he capped."[44] Among the young president's accomplishments the following stand out. First, following a policy of retrenchment, he guided Argentina through the crisis of the world depression of the mid-1870's. In so doing he established the nation's credit abroad on a firm basis. Second, he opened the rich pampas by supporting General Julio A. Roca's campaign against the Indians of the pampas and of Patagonia. Third, he chose to stand by the election victory of Roca in 1880 and finally signed the legislation that made Buenos Aires the federal capital of the Argentine Republic. He refused to concede to *porteños,* who attempted an abortive revolution before they accepted Avellaneda's dictums. In all three cases he

[43] Bunkley, *Life of Sarmiento,* p. 471.
[44] Thomas F. McGann, *Argentina, the United States and the Inter-American System, 1880-1914,* p. 7.

worked to eliminate the causes of civil war that had kept the interior and *porteño* groups at odds for nearly three decades.

Above all, Avellaneda spoke for the free trade element. As a free trader he gave continuity to the policy begun by Mitre and later followed by the Generation of 1880, who effectively ruled Argentina between 1880 and 1916. A backer of individual enterprise, Avellaneda believed that foreign capital had transformed Argentina in twenty years, and he called it the "primary agent of our progress."[45] Because Argentina's economic policy depended upon a steady supply of foreign capital, Avellaneda kept one eye on the London stock exchange throughout his term in office. In fact, his annual messages to Congress reveal his deep concern with protecting the nation's foreign credit. To him the stakes were high because "the obligations of foreign credit are customarily represented by the anonymous sentiment of national honor, and by the public powers."[46]

Avellaneda's triumphal return to his home town of Tucumán in late 1876 symbolized much of the excitement of the era. He came home to dedicate the opening of the Córdoba-Tucumán railway. Previously the people of that city had had little communication with the outside world. They lived principally on what they produced. Now the president of the nation stood in the same plaza in which Rosas had executed his father. He told his audience: " ... sixteen years ago I left this City with a few books under my arm in a 'Bullock-Cart.' I return today for the first time, since that period, in the carriage of steam, as your Chief Magistrate."[47] The transformation of the interior had begun. In the mind of the president, a nine-hundred-mile railway journey from Buenos Aires epitomized progress. To the residents of Tucumán the fact that one of their own sons had achieved the presidency signalled a new future.

A new era of economic prosperity dawned for Argentina under Avellaneda. In retrospect, his administration appears pivotal. The

[45] Avellaneda's annual message to Congress of May, 1877, in Mabragaña, *Los mensajes*, III, 449.
[46] Ibid.
[47] Osborn to SecState, November 19, 1876, DS, NA, RG 59, microcopy 69, roll 22.

steady economic development of the 1860's and 1870's gave way to the unrivaled boom of the 1880's. The appearance of wheat as a lucrative export commodity gave incentive to tremendous growth and to outbursts of optimism unparalleled in the Western Hemisphere. Already whetted by the successes of the previous two decades, the appetites of English speculators, investors, and banking firms became insatiable. Argentine landed and political interests joined the foreigners to augment the nation's growth. With the recovery from the depression of the 1870's Argentina moved into a period of rapid development. Railways sprang up throughout the nation as an era of railway fever began.

Dissent loomed on the horizon. To date, Argentina had met all its financial obligations. After 1874 it became increasingly difficult to do so. Due to pressures caused by the depression that began in 1873, many Argentines began to resent the preponderant role foreign companies enjoyed in Argentina. The railways, especially, came under attack because of the large guaranteed profits they received from the national and provincial governments. From the start some opposition to foreign economic penetration had existed. This gained strength in the 1870's when voiced with special reference to the foreign-owned railways by the Entre Ríos *caudillo* Ricardo López Jordán and by the young Leandro Alem of Buenos Aires, future leader of the Radical party. For the most part the criticism was voiced by individuals who were not motivated by xenophobia, but rather by a desire to cut the government's expenses in promoting railway building.

Specifically, critics attacked seemingly irresponsible company officials who abused the terms of their concessions. Many British companies did not make enough profit to cover the minimum guarantee. In most cases these railways had not attempted to push forward. They accepted the guaranteed dividends from the government as satisfactory revenue. This led sensitive Argentines to protest. "All we do is send capital to London," one deputy exclaimed in objecting to a new railway concession. According to him the government had no need to give railways guarantees in the first place. The railways would make fortunes for their investors if they really earned the profits their exponents claimed they would.

Such criticism was commonplace. Though tinged with nationalism, it was not directed against foreigners. It resulted from the fact that private enterprise often proved inefficient and negligent in railway undertakings.[48] The critics wanted reforms in the existing system.

President Avellaneda joined critics of the British-owned railways. He accused them of taking advantage of the government's payment of minimum profits, whether the railways were efficiently run or not. By 1877 the violators had become so flagrant that Avellaneda promised to investigate the situation. With justified indignation he reminded recalcitrant railway directors, "We have paid everything to this moment, and we have paid it without tedious investigations, and even without any examination, because good or bad, this is one of the features of our national character."[49] But the president had only limited patience. He could not stand by and watch poorly managed railways take money from the government for services not rendered. He had begun a program of retrenchment, and he expected the railways to comply with his attempts to improve the Argentine economic scene. As a result, he refused to continue paying guarantees to companies that did not check their expenditures. He wanted private capital to join public companies in cutting their operating costs in order to hasten the economic recovery of the nation.[50]

Although Avellaneda publicly promised direct action, his administration did little to force the railways to improve their service. Laissez faire concepts prevailed. In the final analysis, Avellaneda feared pushing foreign capitalists too hard. He did not want to risk Argentina's foreign credit standing. His inaction led to increased

[48] Argentine Republic, Cámara de Diputados, *Diario de sesiones*, September 29, 1875, pp. 1298-1303; July 5, 1876, p. 528. Hereafter cited as Diputados, *Diario*. Also see Scalabrini Ortiz, *Ferrocarriles argentinos*, p. 39.

[49] Mabragaña, *Los mensajes*, III, 457; and Avellaneda's message to Congress of May 5, 1818 ibid., p. 397. There were those who felt that the railways and telegraphs should be owned by the state, but they were not critical of foreign ownership. Rather, they preferred state ownership to private ownership of important public utilities. For an example, see Diputados, *Diario*, July 5, 1876, p. 528.

[50] Scalabrini Ortiz, *Ferrocarriles argentinos*, pp. 39-40. Scalabrini Ortiz states that the Oeste was "an example of what the Argentines were able to do in the management of railways."

public hostility toward the inefficient British-owned railways. The fact that the provincially owned Oeste continued to make profits led many to believe that government ownership would assure better operation of the railways at lower costs. Many favored the expropriation of all private railways. In general, railway investments in Argentina were not self-liquidating. Most railways continued to burden the national income. Only the Oeste and the Great Southern had operated successfully from the beginning, and these railways ran within the confines of the rich province of Buenos Aires.

Talk of expropriation of the British-owned companies reached a peak in 1880, when it became known that the provincial legislature of Buenos Aires contemplated the expropriation of the Great Southern. Though it was only a rumor at the time, the directors of the Great Southern took steps to avert the possibility of expropriation. During July of that year Frank Parish and C. O. Barker, two company directors, traveled from London to Buenos Aires. They immediately began negotiating a new contract with the governor of the province, Dardo Rocha. On October 19, 1881, a new agreement stipulated that the government could not expropriate the company until May 27, 1902. In return, the Great Southern agreed to construct new lines and "to work for the general welfare of the nation." The action taken by Great Southern officials assured British investors that large-scale expansion of the British-owned railways would provide a safe investment.[51] Argentine leaders appeared reluctant, at least for a while, to take any strong measures against foreign concerns for fear of cutting off an important source of capital, despite public opinion.

By 1880 Argentina stood at the crossroads of economic development. In retrospect, little actual railway construction had taken place before that year. Some 343 miles had existed at the end of Mitre's administration in 1868, and by 1880 that total had risen to only 1,388 miles. The period remains important for other reasons than the construction of tracks. Mitre, Sarmiento, and Avellaneda set the pattern for future railway expansion in Argentina. They

[51] Rögind, *Historia del Ferrocarril Sud*, pp. 64-66.

used the resources of the state to encourage private foreign-owned companies to build the railways. Their policy guaranteed comfortable returns on foreign investments designed to convert Argentina into a large-scale exporter of agricultural goods and other primary materials. In this situation it became impossible for Argentina to develop a well-rounded national economy through industrialization. It balanced its payments by further agricultural and pastoral development. The social and economic revolution that Mitre had anticipated, and that was to a considerable extent realized by the end of the century, may have tamed the wild *gaucho*, enriched the country, and helped to give it political stability. As pointed out by H. S. Ferns, however, "Argentina was obliged to export or go bankrupt and this meant concentration upon a limited range of exportable staple products with all the social and political, not to mention moral and intellectual consequences, of intense specialization in an agricultural and rural setting."[52]

[52] Ferns, *Britain and Argentina*, p. 315.

3. The Golden Years

Argentina experienced its golden age of economic development between 1880 and 1916. Its material growth in this period was phenomenal. Social and political changes took place as well. Immigrants, mostly Spaniards and Italians, flocked to the nation in amazing numbers. The number of urban and rural laborers swelled. More important, these immigrants gave rise to a burgeoning middle class of merchants, professionals, and small industrialists. Along with the rapid increase in the foreign-born population, the amount of railway construction that took place offers one of the most notable signs of progress. As the famous traveler James Bryce wrote in 1912: "The best evidence or illustration of the swift progress of the republic and of the confidence which European investors feel in its resources is to be found in the development of its railway system. . . . Most of these railways, many of which are of a gauge broader than those in the

United States or Great Britain, have been built and are worked by British companies, a few by the government."[1]

Thanks to British investments, the Argentine railway network stretched from 1,388 miles in 1880 to 22,251 miles by 1915.[2] Although unimpressive by United States standards, Argentina claimed the third longest railway system in the Western Hemisphere, behind the United States and Canada. It had the largest in Latin America, comprising more than 40 percent of the total railway mileage on the continent of South America, and it ranked eighth in the world. More impressive, it had more miles of track per capita than the United States. Clearly the railway system of Argentina stood as a major accomplishment for a nation whose population numbered only a shade over 5.5 million in 1914.[3]

The years between 1880 and 1916 also mark the high point of an Argentine ruling elite known opprobriously as the oligarchy. Argentines have defined the term *oligarchy* as used in the 1880's and after as "the political organization composed of the president and his associates, the provincial governors and their supporters, the national representatives who obeyed the behests of the executive, whether national or local, and the economic interests, mainly landowners, which allied themselves with these men."[4] According to José Nicolás Matienzo, a distinguished member of the oligarchy, it included representatives of a directing class which corresponded approximately to the highest social stratum, formed by members of the traditional families, by the rich, and by the educated.[5] The members of this directing class shared common opinions and established a moral code by which they reciprocally lent services and favors without distinction or party politics.

The oligarchs carried their moral code into the public administration. They managed the interests of the country as if it were a

[1] James Bryce, *South America*, p. 337.

[2] *Tercero censo*, X, 405-406.

[3] Ibid., II, 124. The official number of Argentines was set at 5,527,285. This does not include 2,357,952 people listed as "foreigners" (League of Nations, Economic and Financial Section, *International Statistical Yearbook of the League of Nations, 1926*, pp. 121-122).

[4] Thomas F. McGann, *Argentina, the United States and the Inter-American System, 1880-1914*, pp. 32-33.

[5] José Nicolás Matienzo, *El gobierno representativo federal en la República Argentina*, p. 322.

large *estancia*. Their paternalistic attitude toward governing led one historian to liken the Argentine ruling elite to the antebellum plantation class of South Carolina and Georgia.[6] Although the oligarchy formed a basically homogeneous body, it embraced many different personality types. The austere habits of Bartolomé Mitre contrasted greatly with the ostentatious manners of many of the ruling elite, who concerned themselves primarily with self-enrichment and material gain through economic power.[7]

Above all, the Argentine ruling elite looked to Europe and North America for intellectual and political inspiration, as well as for economic guidance. By nineteenth-century standards they considered themselves liberal leaders who based their concept of government upon precepts held in Britain, France, and the United States. As José Luis Romero has noted in his study of Argentine political history, "the oligarchy worked for the material progress of the country, but oriented their action towards the satisfaction of their own interests."[8] The elite used liberal doctrines to protect their own conservatism. They became benevolent despots who wanted to bring economic progress to the nation and establish political order for their own benefit. They either feared or mistrusted the masses and kept political power as a class privilege. Increasingly, they came to consider public power as theirs by right. Most of them considered it patriotic not to place the government in the hands of the *criollo* and immigrant masses.[9]

Many political and intellectual leaders of Argentina during the last two decades of the nineteenth century adhered to the concepts of Spencerian positivism. They read works of Auguste Comte, Charles Darwin, and Karl Marx, but found in Herbert Spencer a prophet of their own age. Unlike the *científicos* in Mexico under Porfirio Díaz, positivists in Argentina never associated with one specific group. Nor did all the members of the "Generation of 1880" hold positivist tenets. Thus the political unity of those who followed Spencer did not match that of their Mexican counter-

[6] Arthur P. Whitaker, *The United States and Argentina*, p. 12.
[7] José Luis Romero, *A History of Argentine Political Thought*, trans. Thomas F. McGann, pp. 181-182 and 187.
[8] Ibid., p. 196.
[9] Ibid., p. 182; McGann, *Argentina*, p. 43.

parts. Nevertheless, positivism did play a determining role in the course of economic development followed by Argentine leaders. Spencer blended the scientific philosophy of Comte with the biological observations of Darwin. Like other English positivists, Spencer encouraged a liberal and democratic philosophy based on man's ability to apply science for progressive purposes. His concept of liberal progress well suited the Argentines, who had undertaken the task of building a nation.

Argentine positivists did not accept industrialization as a panacea. Rather, they advocated a policy of fitting Argentina into an international free-trade structure as a leading producer of foodstuffs. They subverted industry to a supportive role which would complement the important pastoral and agricultural sectors of the economy. In keeping with this line of reasoning, they borrowed from Spencer arguments that reinforced their self-aggrandizing modernization programs. They desired European immigration in order to assure an adequate supply of industrious rural laborers. They measured progress in narrow terms of miles of railway, numbers of public buildings, and the volume of commerce. The positivists say no contradiction in getting richer while the poor languished, since they reasoned that only the strong would survive.

Following the nationalization of Buenos Aires as the capital of Argentina, a new political faction came to power. Led by the young General Julio A. Roca, conqueror of the desert Indians and victor over rebellious *porteños,* the new leaders came from the interior. They formed the so-called Córdoba block, or Governors' League, which exercised a preponderant influence in Argentine politics during the last quarter of the past century. Politically, they attempted to bring law and order to Argentina by assertion of their well-organized political strength. They believed in internal order and political stability and had unbounded economic optimism. By putting the economic resources of Buenos Aires to work for the interior interests, they continued the steady expansion of the economic hegemony of the very city they had sought to dominate. Like many other provincials who moved to Buenos Aires, they became *porteños* in economic thought. Buenos Aires continued to be successful in any venture.[10] Although he represented the provincial element, Roca did not adhere to the old Federalist tradition of decentralized government. Soon after his ascension to office he revealed his belief in a strong central governing power. He used the *porteño* economic stranglehold to maintain strict political control over the nation and a strong army to keep peace and order in the provinces.

Roca liked to think that no other president had ever served in an epoch of greater prosperity and success. "Order and Progress" was the slogan of the day. Profit became the motivating force as Argentina began an era of unprecedented growth. Roca's administration opened Argentina to foreign capital. At last railways bound together the distant areas of the nation. Roca interpreted the growth of railways as a leading sign of progress. During his administration, between 1880 and 1886, the total railway mileage expanded from 1,388 miles to 3,850 miles.[11]

Steady growth between 1870 and 1880 had completed the basic trunk lines of Argentina's railway system. Only three major companies had operated in 1870, all tying areas of agricultural and pastoral production to eastern seaports. To the north, the broadgauged Central Argentine stretched from Rosario to Córdoba. Farther south, the lines of the provincially owned Oeste and the British-owned Great Southern fanned out across the province of Buenos Aires. During the 1870's these railways limited the bulk of their construction to the pampa region. Many railway planners dreamed of completing a trans-Andean link with Chile, but none had begun the enterprise. In an independent act, the Argentine government helped push a narrow-gauge line from Córdoba to Tucumán by 1875. Begun before the work ended on the wide-gauged Rosario-Córdoba section, the extension of a narrow-gauge track typifies the lack of coordinated planning that went into much

[10] McGann, *Argentina*, pp. 14-15; Ismael Bucich Escobar, *Los presidentes argentinos, 1826-1918*, p. 118.

[11] Statistics on railway profits are found in *Tercero censo*, X, 405-407. For the British response to increased profits see Henry S. Ferns, *Britain and Argentina in the Nineteenth Century*, pp. 392-393. Also see Julio A. Roca's annual message to Congress of May, 1883, in Heraclio Mabragaña (ed.), *Los mensajes*, IV, 65, and May, 1884, IV, 101.

of the nation's early railway construction. It is not that Argentina claimed any uniqueness in developing railway networks of various gauges. Austria, the United States, and Russia suffered even more from mismatched railway gauges in their major systems. Actually, the Córdoba-Tucumán extension reflects a current predilection of railway builders the world over to use the economical meter gauge. Experiments with the narrow gauge, seen in many parts as the "railway of the future," took place in western and southern United States and in Australia. As in the case of the Córdoba-Tucumán line, none of these railways suited the long-range needs of the areas they served. They could not carry heavy loads. Indeed, they often compounded the national transportation problems by necessitating the expensive and time-consuming transferal of goods where lines of two different gauges met.

The construction of pampa railways flourished between 1875 and 1890. At least five lines crossed the province of Santa Fe running to Córdoba by 1890. More and more lines emanating from Buenos Aires laced the western and southern reaches of the fertile pampa. By 1884 the port of Bahía Blanca became the coastal terminus of an important southern system. Through cattle and wheat exports Bahía Blanca became the nation's third largest port. In 1886 the two leading ports, Buenos Aires and Rosario, were linked for the first time by rail. Few lines extended beyond the pampa, but by 1882 an Andean branch of the Pacific railway reached San Luis, and in 1885 it arrived at Mendoza and San Juan. Between 1884 and 1889 the Central Argentine constructed trunk lines to Santiago de Estero and Catamarca. During the next two years other important links opened up as the Central Argentine finished a direct broad-gauge route between Rosario and Tucumán, and the Central Norte lengthened its line from Santa Fe to Tucumán farther north as far as Salta. The conquering of the Andes in 1910 capped the expansion of Argentina's railways beyond the pampa. In that year Argentine and Chilean miners, working from opposite sides of the Andean mountain range, completed the amazing Cumbre tunnel, over two miles long.[12] Direct rail traffic with

[12] Brian Fawcett, *Railways of the Andes,* pp. 87-109; Pierre Denis, *The Argentine Republic,*

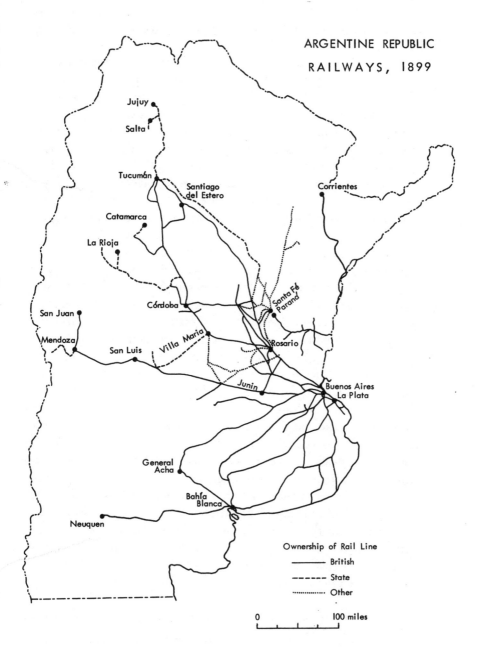

ARGENTINE REPUBLIC
RAILWAYS, 1899

Jujuy

Salta

Tucumán

Santiago
del Estero

Corrientes

Catamarca

La Rioja

Córdoba

Santa Fé
Paraná

San Juan

Mendoza

San Luis

Villa Maria

Rosario

Junin

Buenos Aires
La Plata

General
Acha

Bahía
Blanca

Neuquen

Ownership of Rail Line

——————— British

– – – – – State

·············· Other

0   100 miles

Chile at last became a reality after nearly fifty years of planning and hard labor.

Steel rails began an era of colonization and agricultural expansion on the pampas by opening new land for development. As Alberdi had predicted in 1852, railway construction and colonization of unpopulated regions of the nation by European immigrants went hand-in-hand. Railways became both a cause and an effect of what James Scobie has called the revolution of the pampas during the boom years of the 1880's. Towns sprang up along the railways in agricultural areas, usually near watering places. Cultivation increased rapidly as the railways created traffic with amazing results.

Changing world markets forced major changes in Argentina's export trade after 1870. Tallow and hides, the two staple export items of the earlier period, lost value in the world market. Tallow exports suffered as a consequence of oil production in North America. The market for dried and salted meat also diminished, although Cuban and Brazilian slave plantations still purchased large quantities. In an effort to save their pastoral economy, Argentine *estancieros* turned to the exportation of surplus meat to an expanding European market. The invention of chilled and frozen meat processes and refrigerated boats sped up the transition to raising cattle and sheep for prime meat rather than for their by-products. New methods of raising cattle and sheep appeared on the pampas with the founding of the Sociedad Rural and its subsequent sponsorship of improved stock raising. Argentine cattlemen began to import new stock from Europe. Enterprising breeders brought the famous shorthorn cattle from England in order to produce a better quality of beef. Sheepherders introduced new breeds, replacing the Merino with the Lincoln. The latter produced wool as well as better meat. With these innovations and others, including the use of wire fences to enclose large tracts, the leading pastoral enterprises underwent a basic metamorphosis from backward, haphazard undertakings to integrated, scientific, and efficiently run businesses.[13]

---

trans. Joseph McCabe, pp. 220-223; James R. Scobie, *Argentina*, p. 140; Mark Jefferson, *Peopling the Argentina Pampa*, pp. 161-164.

[13] Scobie, *Argentina*, pp. 115-117; and Aldo Ferrer, *The Argentine Economy*, trans. Marjory M. Urquidi, pp. 77-132.

Land, cattle, and wheat dominated the economic revolution of
the 1880's. Political, social, and economic status depended upon
ownership of land. To land, grains, and cattle the oligarchs added
increased railways, harbor facilities, and immigrants to effect their
brand of progress upon the pampas. Distinct land tenure patterns
evolved in the province of Buenos Aires, where the cattle industry
predominated. *Porteño* cattlemen used land for pasturage, breeding,
and for raising alfalfa to fatten cattle and sheep. The land-rich
porteño cattlemen jealously maintained their ownership of the soil.
This policy discouraged immigrants from moving into rural sections of the province. By refusing to subdivide their properties, the
cattle producers limited the role of the agricultural immigrant in
the province to that of tenant farmer. As such, large numbers of
Italian farmers contracted to work land owned by cattlemen,
usually for a three-year period. The average farmer broke up the
soil, planted his fields with wheat, and hoped for favorable weather
and good market conditions. At the end of the third year the tenant moved on to a similar plot on similar terms, having sown the
fields with alfalfa for pasturage. If all went well he made a
relatively comfortable sum. If not, he joined the number of broken
and indebted agricultural laborers in poverty. In both cases, the
estanciero lost nothing and gained valuable new pasturage in the
process.

By contrast, the major wheat and grain cultivation centered in
the provinces of Santa Fe and Entre Ríos. In the former province,
Italian immigrants spearheaded a series of colonization projects
sponsored by the Central Argentine Railway and by local land
speculators. Upon arrival in Santa Fe, the immigrants began to
plant wheat on marginal lands, previously considered incapable of
sustaining pastoral enterprises. By subdividing their land and selling
portions on installment terms to immigrants, the landowners
realized substantial profits. Land usually sold at three to four times
its original value. The value of the remaining land increased, too,
due to its proximity to cultivated lands.[14] With any luck the immigrants soon paid off their debts and became owners of the land

---

[14] James R. Scobie, *Revolution on the Pampas*, p. 45; and Denis, *Argentine Republic*, p. 190.

they farmed. Railways facilitated their task by considerably reducing the cost of transporting their produce from previously isolated areas to river ports. Cheap land and transportation enabled the colonists to make a comfortable living from wheat production, first in central Santa Fe, then in the southern part of the province as well. Argentina, which had imported wheat throughout the colonial epoch and continued to do so until the 1870's, exported the grain by the end of that decade. With the passing of the century, Argentina sent nearly 70 percent of its wheat production to Europe. Agricultural exports, which had represented only 1 percent of the nation's exports in 1870, reached 20 percent by 1890. By the first decade of the present century they almost equaled livestock exports.[15]

Although conveying livestock and agricultural products for export comprised the bulk of the British railways' carrying trade, other important sources of revenue existed. A growing home trade complemented the outward flow of goods serviced by the major networks. The railways carried building materials, such as bricks, lime, and stone, along with minerals, particularly salt. In the north a thriving timber trade gave the Central Norte and the Central Argentine considerable traffic. Sleepers (railway ties), fence posts, and charcoal all represented important domestic needs. The wines of Mendoza accounted for substantial receipts for the Pacific railways. Both the Central Argentine and the Central Córdoba carried large amounts of sugar from Tucumán. To this, the railways added the transportation of livestock and cereals for domestic consumption in the densely populated regions of Buenos Aires and the pampas. Finally, the railways provided a steady flow of foreign goods, which dealt deathblows to the stagnant regional economies of the interior. No longer isolated from European competitors, many interior producers could not face the onslaught of cheap imported products. As a result, self-sufficient subsistence economies gave way to a national economy controlled by eastern pastoral and banking interests.[16]

As the strength of the dominant eastern export sectors grew

---

[15] Ferrer, *Argentine Economy*, p. 100.
[16] Ibid., p. 131.

they placed the weaker areas in an increasingly dependent position. Railways permitted some interior sections to survive the foreign threat through increased efficiency and specialization. Wines in Mendoza and Cuyo, sugar in Tucumán, yerba maté in the northeast, cotton in Chaco, and fruits in the upper valley of the Río Negro offer examples of this process. These areas paid a high price for their prosperity. By the close of the century the interior provinces depended upon tax support from Buenos Aires and the coastal provinces.

In spite of the seeming success of the railways in transforming the economy of Argentina, there remained several sources of friction between Argentine economic interests and the management of the British-owned companies. On the one hand, the Argentines wanted to speed their products toward external and internal markets at the lowest possible cost and with the greatest haste. On the other hand, the British desired immediate returns on their investments. The British often hesitated to provide services that did not promise quick results. A continuing clash between these philosophies underlay a rising current of antirailway feeling during the last quarter of the nineteenth century. In particular, three issues caused the most serious rifts between Argentine and British interests: (1) lack of adequate rolling stock at harvest times, (2) abuses of the guarantee system, and (3) high freight rates charged by the companies.

During the 1880's and 1890's the increased production of marketable wheat created seasonal problems for the railways. Harvests took place January through April. During these months farmers and merchants expected the railways to supply enough rolling stock to carry the grain to markets without unnecessary delays. This meant that during the rest of the year cars lay idle. Few companies could afford the expense of maintaining seasonal rolling stock. The marketing process itself complicated matters further. Usually, farmers carried their wheat in bags to the nearest railway siding, where agents of shippers or millers bought it on the spot. Immediately there arose a problem of storing the wheat before shipment. Though most railways in wheat regions existed primarily to ship grain, they supplied surprisingly few facilities for handling it. Since the railways had no direct financial stake in the grain, they took few precautions to protect it. As a result, the 160-pound bags of wheat that farmers hauled from their *chacras* to the railway depots lay exposed to the elements, only covered by tarpaulins supplied by the merchants. By conservative estimates merchants lost thousands of pounds of wheat annually to weather and vermin. To avoid losses, grain agents naturally demanded rapid handling of their property by the railways. Shortage of rolling stock caused delays. The loading and unloading of the unwieldy bags created an equally vexing problem. Loading the bags required a large labor force and tied up cars for considerable time. Lack of adequate harbor facilities further compounded the railways' dilemma. Neither Rosario nor Buenos Aires could unload cars fast enough. Rosario began to build grain elevators late in the century. But even so, rolling stock lay idle for days until strong-backed peons unloaded them bag by bag.[17]

In Canada and the United States the introduction of bulk-handling techniques solved these problems. In both nations efficient grain elevators cleaned, classified, and stored wheat at local depots before shipment. In Argentina primitive conditions persisted. Argentine producers refused to sort and grade their produce. Most observers attribute the unwillingness to adopt bulk handling to the obstinacy of marginal farmers and to the merchants' lack of concern. Despite the added expense of bags, the farmers still thought it better to employ a system that facilitated the rapid sale of their produce. They needed quick cash to pay off their debts. Also, most farmers distrusted the merchants and remained suspicious of the railway agents. Working on low marginal profits, they opposed any scheme that might depress the price of wheat. Merchants, for their part, did not want to pay for storage facilities. They discounted their losses in the low prices they paid farmers for the wheat. Of course, the railways bear some responsibility for continuing the old system. In the first place, they used old English cars with capacities of only ten to eighteen tons. Not until the present

[17] Jefferson, *Peopling the Argentine Pampa*, pp. 136-137; Scobie, *Revolution on the Pampas*, pp. 71-113; W. P. Rutter, *Wheat-Growing in Canada, the United States and the Argentine*, pp. 163-198.

century did they adopt larger, four-wheeled bogie cars from the United States which could carry thirty to forty tons. The companies did not feel compelled to build grain elevators, neither in the interior nor at seaports. In fact, the companies seldom felt it necessary to provide warehouses for the safe storage of grain in spite of legislation which required them to do so.

Because of their poor service, a great deal of controversy surrounded the profits railways made during the 1880's. To men like President Roca, handsome profits made by the Central Argentine and the Great Southern exemplified the excellent results foreign capital could expect from investments in Argentine utilities.[18] Both of these lines abandoned the guarantee system before 1890 and paid dividends out of their own earnings. Other lines failed to live up to their expectations and continued to rely upon government payment of guarantees. Bad management, as in the case of the East Argentine and the Northern, explains most of the poor performance. Well run or not, the British-owned railways became targets of increasing public criticism. The money-making railways were attacked because they apparently made excessive profits from high freight rates. The unsuccessful companies received criticism because they relied on the guarantees paid by the government and purposefully failed to provide proper service.

Public officials and newspapers attacked avaricious British investors for threatening Argentina's economic development. As the principal British-owned railways increasingly monopolized transportation in Argentina, they became the focus of the same kind of criticism aimed at railways in the United States by the Western Grange and Farmers' Alliance groups at that time. In Argentina, however, the agrarians who controlled the government were not of the granger type. They represented the large landowners who had encouraged building these foreign-owned railways, had profited greatly from them, and had bound themselves to the foreign owners by a permanent alliance. Hence, criticism of the railways in Argentina proved largely ineffectual. The Argentines passed no equivalent of the granger laws or the Interstate

[18] Roca's annual message to Congress of May, 1884, in Mabragaña, *Los mensajes*, IV, 101.

Commerce Commission Act as in the United States during the same decade.

From their London headquarters, the British directors of the railway companies paid little attention to the mounting criticism. Their stocks had only recently become widely held in Britain, and they did not consider their profits high. Railways in Brazil paid dividends of at least 5 percent, and those in India and Russia annually guaranteed as much. Argentina had to compete in a world market, which left very little choice in the matter as far as English investors were concerned. With the exception of the 1880's, the successful British-owned railways in Argentina rarely declared dividends higher than those paid by home companies.[19] The railways' profits never matched those made by banks, such as the Bank of London and the River Plate. Thus railway directors ignored any criticism of their operations. In fact, they prided themselves upon the civilizing contributions their "English" companies made to Argentina's rapid growth and never tried to hide the origin of their capital, locomotives, or control.

If the British directors ignored criticism, they did not overlook threats to their well-being. In a classic case of disregard of public opinion, the directors of the Central Argentine successfully defied the efforts of the national government to collect a large sum between 1883 and 1885, owed to it by the company. The company's original concession guaranteed it an annual profit of 7 percent on an estimated value of 6,400 pounds sterling per mile. It also stipulated that whenever profits exceeded that amount the railway would reimburse the government for the guarantees paid to it in the past.[20] When that contingency occurred, the directors of the Central Argentine simply refused to pay. When the government insisted, the directors stopped the flow of freight. They also refused to put further capital investment in the important arterial routes across the northern pampas. Frank Parish, then chairman of

[19] Colin Lewis, "Problems of Railway Development in Argentina, 1857-1890," *Inter-American Economic Affairs* 22, no. 2 (Autumn 1968): 71.

[20] The struggle between the Central Argentine and the national government is discussed at considerable length by Raúl Scalabrini Ortiz, *Historia de los ferrocarriles argentinos*, pp. 129-132; and briefly by Ferns, *Britain and Argentina*, pp. 404-406.

both the Central Argentine and the Great Southern, demanded that the government cancel the debt. At the same time he asked to have the guarantee terms dropped from the company's concession. Then, through clever book work, the Central Argentine eliminated its past obligation to the government by raising its capital value by the amount of the debt.[21]

The Central Argentine's highhanded action precipitated a loud outcry in the press and Congress for the expropriation of the railway. Notably, the majority of the protestors attacked the monopoly aspects of the company. The Central Argentine had long controlled the traffic of northeastern Argentina with little or no regard for public sentiment, and did so until a competing branch of the Buenos Aires and Rosario railway reached Tucumán in 1890. Advocates of expropriation believed that state ownership best suited public needs by providing better service at lower rates. A few attacked the foreign ownership of the company, but these blatant nationalists formed a minority. On the other hand, apologists for the British-owned Central Argentine cited the foreign ownership of the line as a justification for yielding to the company's demands. They argued that the government should give the company free rein, in order to assure an uninterrupted flow of foreign capital into Argentina for investment purposes. Expropriation, they warned, would dry up the source of funds needed to build a new Argentina.[22]

The Argentine elite lacked the desire, even if they could find the resources, to take over the railways. They eschewed state ownership of the railways as contrary to their laissez faire precepts of administration. Minister of Interior Bernardo de Irigoyen expressed this opinion succinctly, "The majority favor the private form of enterprise because the state lacks the capacity to put companies into operation with any efficiency."[23] From the beginning the government played an important role by encouraging railway construction, and by 1886 it even owned 1,126 miles itself.[24] The

[21] Ferns, *Britain and Argentina*, p. 404; Scalabrini Ortiz, *Ferrocarriles argentinos*, pp. 130-132.

[22] Ferns, *Britain and Argentina*, pp. 405-406, 414.

[23] Julio Velar de Irigoyen, *Bernardo de Irigoyen*, p. 164.

[24] See Roca's annual message to Congress of May, 1886, in Mabragaña, *Los mensajes*, IV, 158.

oligarchs, however, wanted the government to plan and stimulate the development of the economy by private investors. They chose to impose only minimal restrictions upon foreign investors and businessmen active in Argentina.

Unfortunately for Argentina and its foreign creditors, Miguel Juárez Celman succeeded Roca as president in 1886. Arriving at the presidency after a relatively successful political career in Córdoba, Juárez served an abbreviated term which ended in 1890. He first acquired national prominence when elected governor of Córdoba in 1880. Four years later he served as national senator from the same province. Besides these credentials, he was Roca's brother-in-law, although Roca did not choose him as a successor. Juárez easily won the election of 1886 with the help of the powerful Governors' League.[25] Like Roca, Juárez believed in a strong executive power. Historians generally consider these two men the most eminent representatives of the *unicato*, or one-party system, that prevailed in the late nineteenth century. Under the *unicato* the president enjoyed nearly absolute power and exercised a decisive influence in all political affairs of the nation, whether national or local.[26] The similarity between the two men ends there. Juárez and his followers nearly undid all that Roca had worked for. If Roca bullied the nation in the name of peace and strong central administration, Juárez exploited it in the name of profits. Where Roca used his power to put down political opposition and subdue the wild elements of the more remote provinces, Juárez used his position with less discretion and followed a course of exploitation which permitted political debauchery in Buenos Aires and the provinces and soon led to economic disaster.[27]

Juárez has taken the lion's share of blame for the financial debacle of 1890. Actually, he inherited a critical financial situation when he came to office. Under his predecessor the national and provincial governments had contracted foreign loans far beyond their capacity to repay. Unwise speculation and soaring land prices quickly overextended Argentina's credit. Furthermore, inflation-

[25] Bucich Escobar, *Presidentes argentinos*, pp. 116-118.
[26] Romero, *History*, pp. 188-189.
[27] McGann, *Argentina*, pp. 28-29.

ary practices had flooded the nation with paper money which lacked gold reserves.[28] *Estancieros*, agricultural producers, and exporters may have found the inflationary spiral of the peso to their advantage on the short term. They received pounds sterling for their produce yet paid off their local expenses in paper. Between 1884 and 1890 the value of the peso dropped from 100 to 350 to the gold ounce. Accordingly, the value of land-mortgage bonds and loans held abroad depreciated rapidly. After 1886 Europeans no longer regarded Argentina as a safe credit risk.

For the most part, Argentines simply refused to acknowledge that they faced an increasingly serious economic crisis. They had unbounded faith in their ability to pay off their debt. The boom under the Roca and Juárez administrations demonstrated their optimism. Few were alarmed in Argentina. To the contrary, an official report on the public debt, drawn up in 1887 by Pedro Agote at the request of Minister of Finance Wenceslao Pacheco, expressed surprise that in 1886 the London Stock Exchange listed official Argentine quotations lower than those for Chile.[29] Agote saw no plausible explanation for Argentina's inferior credit position on the London market. According to him, Argentina had always served its debt at home and abroad and continued to progress at a rate "which outsteps the most sanguine anticipation."[30] Argentina could hardly be inferior to any of its neighbors, he added, because "no South American state has a greater trade, nor a more considerable extent of railway lines, the greatest element of progress that has been placed within a nation's reach. With no wish to be unjust to Chile, there is no doubt that she is very far from having reached such a stage, which places her in a position of inferiority as compared with us."[31]

The British did not base their decision to cut down Argentine investments upon the latter's relative status among Latin American nations. As *The Economist* of January 9, 1886, explained, British capitalists believed that Argentines had tried to develop their

[28] *The Economist*, January 9, 1886, p. 37.
[29] Pedro Agote, *Report on the Public Debt, Banking Institutions, and Mint of the Argentine Republic*, trans. L. B. Trant, IV, 7-8.
[30] Ibid., p. 8.
[31] Ibid.

country too rapidly.[32] When the Argentine government arranged a large loan from Berlin later in the same year, *The Economist* observed, ". . . the wisdom of this feverish desire to develop the country is extremely questionable, but with the commercial outlook improving, as it is at the present, and with Germany so freely proffering her assistance, the voice of prudence is scarcely likely to make itself heard."[33]

These were prophetic words. During the next four years Juárez blindly led the nation toward financial ruin. Among other things, he became an enthusiastic supporter of railway expansion in an age when the axiom of the day held that "all railways are good; the only bad ones are those that have not been built."[34] The national and provincial governments granted railway concessions without rhyme or reason. Between 1886 and 1890, national and provincial authorities approved over eleven thousand miles of new railway projects, the majority of them with generous guaranteed profits. They called for some six thousand miles in 1889. On one day alone the national Congress acted on as many as thirty-three new concessions. Many of the proposed lines rivaled existing companies, and many others were put forward only as a means of increasing land values. Scheming politicians and landowners saw concessions as shortcuts to fortunes, although this seems a dangerous practice in retrospect.[35] Neither railway promoters nor foreign investors escaped the fever of speculation in Argentina that prepared the way for the crash of 1890. The national Congress proved a willing accomplice by sanctioning railways as soon as the concessionaires found supporters to finance them.

The rampant extension of poorly conceived railways had its Argentine critics. Among them, the leading *porteño* newspaper *La Prensa* warned its readers in late 1887 that "the Congress of 1887 is suffering from railway delirium." According to this prestigious

[32] Ibid., p. 37.

[33] *The Economist*, October 30, 1886, p. 1351.

[34] Juan Balestra, *El noventa*, p. 12.

[35] Gregorio Etcheguía, *Los ferrocarriles argentinos vistos por ojos argentinos*, p. 36; William Rögind, *Historia del Ferrocarril Sud, 1861-1936*, p. 151. According to *Tercero censo*, X, 405, only 2,303 miles were actually built between 1886 and 1890, bringing the total to 5,552 miles. But many thousand miles of new construction were planned.

newspaper, the rash of railway concessions would soon have serious repercussions in Europe. "What is the meaning of such a policy?" it asked. "Is it intended to persecute, urge war, and destroy railways constructed anterior to the year of our Lord 1887? A country which is developed by railways built by foreign capital is bound to afford the amplest security for such capital, not only in the direct interests of the country, but from a sense of honor and honesty toward the foreign investors who send their money three thousand leagues to be employed in enterprises which may not enjoy a very prosperous present, but which abound in flattering prospects for the future." As *La Prensa* noted in closing its commentary, "Englishmen are not such madmen as to create competition with their own money against themselves."[36] Some nine months later, the *Buenos Aires Standard* voiced a similar protest: "The country is suffering from railway on the brain. Like measles and whooping cough, it is, perhaps, an unavoidable complaint, and not very dangerous; but it requires treatment."[37] Within a month the *Buenos Aires Herald* phrased the same sentiments in sharper language: "Railway schemes continue to fall in showers on Congress. We do not have enough interest to keep them all in mind, because most of them are not designed to be built, but to serve as a pretext and cover for wheedling capital out of confiding foreigners, We are in the full swing of South Sea bubbleism, wherefrom is to come a cyclone of wisdom learned in the costly school of experience."[38]

In the Argentine Congress, Aristóbulo del Valle, a distinguished senator from Buenos Aires and a leading opponent of the Juárez administration, vehemently attacked reckless spending by the government. Called the Daniel Webster of Argentina because of his gift for oratory, del Valle represented a key political figure of the late nineteenth century. At the time he led an opposition party, the Partido Republicano, which he later deserted in order to help establish the Unión Cívica in 1889. He probably made his chief

---

[36] *La Prensa*, November 11, 1887.

[37] *Buenos Aires Standard*, June 23, 1888. The *Standard* is also quoted by *Railway Times*, July 28, 1888, p. 107; and *Herapath's*, August 11, 1888, p. 923.

[38] *Buenos Aires Herald*, August 18, 1888.

contribution to Argentine politics and nationalism as political mentor of the growing body of young politicians, such as Lisandro de la Torre, Juan B. Justo, and Hipólito Yrigoyen, who later became the most outspoken critics of the oligarchy and of foreign enterprise. Del Valle's incessant criticism of the Juárez administration did not go unnoticed. In principle, he opposed the government's lavish award of handsome guarantees to new railway companies without first studying the territory through which they would pass. He took the moderate and reasonable position that no advantage could come from the extravagant building of ill-planned railways. Del Valle did not take an antiforeign stance. In fact, he realized the need for European capital to finance legitimate railway construction, but he believed that the state should control the railways. In this regard he contrasted notably with the prevailing laissez faire attitudes expressed by the president.[39]

One of the most forceful laissez faire statements made in the 1880's appears in President Juárez Celman's annual message to Congress of May, 1887.[40] In that address Juárez touched upon two related problems. He refuted the idea of nationalizing the private railways. At the same time, he criticized foreign-owned companies which continued to misuse the guarantee system. The speech reflects the oligarchs' desire to have excellent service at low costs. It also expressed their aversion to state operation of the railways. According to Juárez, the state had two alternatives. First, Argentina could follow the lead of Italy by nationalizing the lines. Second, it could enact legislation allowing for increased public regulation of the railways. While recognizing that, theoretically, nationalization of the railways would seem to result in improved service at lower and more uniform rates, Juárez did not feel that this would occur in practice. The arguments in favor of nationalization were fallacious, he maintained. State ownership of the railways would not reduce the costs of operating them. Rather, nationalization meant that the public, which the government wanted to protect,

[39] Mariano de Vedía y Mitre, *La revolución del 1890*, pp. 29-30; Aristóbulo del Valle, *La política económica argentina en la decada del 1880*, pp. 29, 162-200; Aristóbulo del Valle, *Discursos políticos*, p. 126.

[40] Mabragaña, *Los mensajes*, IV, 179-187.

would pay for the railways' deficit by other contributions, namely taxes. In the final analysis, the president felt that sound business principles governed the private companies. They would prove more progressive and economical in the long run. Consequently, he preferred the second alternative, more effective state regulation of private railway activities.[41]

As a corollary to his argument against nationalizing the private railways, Juárez expressed his commitment to sell the major state-owned railways to private enterprises: "In my opinion it will be to the best interest of the nation to entrust to private enterprise the construction and development of public works that by their disposition are not inherent in its sovereignty, and to reserve to the government the construction of such as cannot be carried out by private enterprise."[42] Juárez proposed the sale of the state-owned Andino Railway to a British firm. Then, in May, 1888, he asked Congress to authorize the sale of 39,135 shares of the Central Argentine Railway belonging to the state. Ostensibly he did this in order to use the receipts to pay back loans from foreign banking firms, but primarily he objected to the state's direct participation in free enterprise.[43]

In a similar manner, the provincial government of Buenos Aires sold the Oeste railway in 1889 to a British concern known as the Buenos Aires Great Western Railway Company. Under Argentine ownership and management the Oeste had expanded from its original 6 miles to more than 726 miles in 1889. In the process it had developed into one of the most prosperous railways in Argentina.[44] Yet in 1889 many *porteños*, imbued with the laissez faire doctrine of the 1880's, called it a harmful state-controlled monopoly. They considered it distasteful, anti-Argentine, and detrimental to the development of free enterprise. Governor Máximo Paz even attacked the Oeste on the ground that as a monopoly it charged lower rates than private railways, to the

[41] Ibid.
[42] Ibid.
[43] Ibid., IV, 244. Also Hanna to SecState, January 16, 1887, DS, NA, RG 59, microcopy 69, roll 22.
[44] Scalabrini Ortiz, *Ferrocarriles argentinos*, pp. 42-47.

detriment of the latter.[45] Another supporter of the sale expressed the same attitude in even stronger terms: "Today the Ferrocarril al Oeste is a regrettable monopoly, harmful to the progress of the province, to the progress of the same area that it serves, and a permanent offense against the freedom of industry. Since the Ferrocarril al Oeste has existed as a state company it has blocked the construction of all other railways by maintaining its monopoly." The same speaker went on to justify the sale of the Oeste because "politically it has been, and is, a conspirator against public liberties; because economically it is the negation of the doctrine of free enterprise that prevails in America; and, finally, because constitutionally it is an absurdity."[46]

Proponents of the sale hoped the sale would bail the province out of financial difficulties. In announcing the government's decision to sell the railway, Governor Paz suggested that the forty million pesos that the sale might bring would enable the government to begin new public works. Capital currently tied up in the operation of the Oeste would be freed for public use.

The above reasons do not fully explain the sale of the prosperous Oeste. The sale also removed one of the major obstacles to the expansion of the British-owned railways operating in the province of Buenos Aires. It put an end to an immediate threat to the Great Southern. Between 1887 and 1889, the provincial legislature had authorized the Oeste to construct nine hundred miles of new lines in areas that would have brought it into direct competition with the Great Southern. The British saw the Oeste as a formidable competitor in areas they had formerly served without competition.[47] Immediately, the directors of the Great Southern took steps to block the expansion. They protested to the provincial government. In short order, Argentine citizens of British extraction, such as Parish, Drable, Coughlan, and Ainsworth, worked

[45] Juárez Celman's annual message to Congress, May, 1888, Mabragaña,*Los mensajes*, IV, 244. Also see Hanna to SecState, January 16, 1887; Scalabrini Ortiz, *Ferrocarriles argentinos*, pp. 42-44; Etcheguía, *Ferrocarriles argentinos*, p. 37; and Rögind, *Historia del Ferrocarril Sud*, p. 156.

[46] Etcheguía, *Ferrocarriles argentinos*, p. 188.

[47] Ibid., p. 137; *Railway Times*, November 12, 1887, p. 633; and Rögind, *Historia del Ferrocarril Sud*, p. 156.

to convince the provincial authorities against undertaking further construction of the Oeste. As a result, the government finally agreed to sell the railway to the London-based syndicate. Later generations of Argentine nationalists never forgave the provincial legislators for this act. Clearly, they had sold an Argentine institution to a British-owned concern. In so doing, the provincial government finally removed itself from direct control of a large railway company and left the British companies the rewarding, though difficult, task of constructing railways through the richest parts of the nation.

The British wasted no time in assessing the long-range effects of the sale upon their leading companies. To begin with, it saved them from "an unscrupulous competitor," which had invaded their territories. Also, as *The Railway Times* of May 24, 1890, stated, "it relegates to limbo the dread expropriation which has been begotten by the presence in their midst of a State railway." Now the British companies operated free from undue competition. They could actually rent the lines of their former adversary from the new syndicate. Thus assured that the provincial authorities would restrict state-owned railways to a supportive role, Frank Parish told those in attendance at the annual meeting of shareholders of the Great Southern in May, 1890, that the purchase of the Oeste disposed "now and forever of the vexed question of expropriation, which has so long been an element of disquietude, if not danger, hanging over our heads like the sword of Damocles."[48] The British now had a clear field to develop the major railways of the Argentine Republic without fear.

[48] *Railway Times*, May 24, 1890, p. 672.

4. Railway Regulation

Although the Argentine oligarchs advocated private management of the railways, they also felt it necessary to impose strict regulations upon the industry. As large public utilities, and as monopolies in the field of rapid long-distance transit during the nineteenth century, railways made natural targets for regulation. But a universal pattern of public control never developed. In France and Italy the governments took strict measures to nationalize the railways. Despite the clamor for public control in Argentina, the government followed a more irregular pattern. As in the United States, where the government reluctantly enforced public control after the belated passage of the Interstate Commerce Commission legislation of 1887, the Argentine authorities declined to interfere directly in the operation of the industry unless necessary to protect their own interests.[1]

[1] As a result of irregular control Argentine railways used a variety of gauges. The major railways followed the Oeste Railway in using the broad gauge of 1.676 meters in width commonly used in Russia and India, as compared with the British standard gauge of 1.435

In spite of their desire not to oversee day-to-day operation of railways, the elite would not tolerate shoddy service. They could not afford to. Good railway service became a matter of economic life or death for the producers on the pampas. Paying minimum profits to inefficient companies bothered them, but not half as much as having their cereals rot at local sidings for lack of adequate rolling stock. In this spirit, President Miguel Juárez Celman, chief spokesman for the oligarchs, launched a campaign against the leading offenders of the guarantee system. In his annual message of May, 1888, he bluntly stated his case: "I cannot find adequate terms to describe the conduct of those companies which collect their guarantee at the end of each quarter and yet pay little or no attention to traffic, which is allowed to languish and decrease. On the slightest pretext they call attention to the necessity of paying the guarantee punctually in order to maintain the credit of the country abroad, but I do not see how the credit of the country could suffer when it is proven that the state is compelled to take coercive steps against companies that have converted government protection into a criminal and iniquitous exaction."[2]

Avellaneda had expressed similar sentiments under similar circumstances in the late 1870's. The companies, fearing that government meddling would limit their profits, chose to resist Juárez as they had Avellaneda. Juárez's insistence on improved service had special justification. The government guaranteed handsome profits in thirteen out of seventeen railway concessions granted between 1887 and 1888. In 1889 the sum paid by the government in guarantees came close to four million pesos.[3] According to Juárez, the government should not pay such a large amount, especially since the companies could easily have trebled their traffic if they had

---

meters. But railways built in Corrientes and Entre Ríos used the standard width, while the Transandine Railway and numerous short, provincial lines used the narrow one-meter gauge. In fact the first rail system between Rosario and Tucumán comprised two sections; one, between Rosario and Córdoba, was of the broad gauge, while the section from Córdoba to Tucumán was a narrow-gauge line.

[2] Heraclio Mabragaña (ed.), *Los mensajes*, IV, 220-221; and Hanna to SecState, July 29, 1888, DS, NA, RG 59, microcopy 69, roll 22.

[3] Figures are based upon Juárez Celman's annual messages to Congress of May, 1888, and May, 1889, in Mabragaña, *Los mensajes*, IV, 220-221, 266. Also see Juan José Castro, *Treatise on the South American Railways and the Great International Lines*, p. 253.

enough rolling stock. As a result of relatively low railway returns for 1887-1888, the president felt it necessary in May, 1888 to warn the companies that, unless they "strained every nerve to increase their traffic and earnings, the government would have sufficient ground for the withdrawal of the guarantees." A year later he repeated the same warning and announced that the government had taken definite steps to modify the guarantee system in order to give the government the right to intervene directly in the operation of the railways.[4]

In late October, 1888, Juárez informed the Argentine Great Western Railway that it had two months to get adequate rolling stock or else face a reduction of government guarantees. According to the *Buenos Aires Standard*, Juárez had good cause to make the threat. As that newspaper explained: "It is as difficult to keep up with the traffic without rolling stock as it is to breathe without air. The London Board are, perhaps, unaware that the State does not pay a guarantee with a view to fill the pockets of a handful of shareholders who have a dim idea that the Argentine Great Western runs somewhere in the northern regions of Brazil. If the State guarantees a certain percentage on capital, it is merely with a view to enable the line to more fully meet the requirements of an ever increasing traffic. This fact has been repeatedly emphasized by Minister [Eduardo] Wilde, and even by the President in his inaugural message to Congress. Yet the London Board remained steeped in their customary indifference and seemed to smile incredulously at the just threat of Dr. Wilde."[5]

Other British observers had little sympathy for the openly corrupt Juárez regime. The Buenos Aires correspondent for *Herapath's* made a particularly harsh judgment of the Argentine government. Above all, he felt that the railways should not receive blame for the financial problems that confronted Juárez. Rather, he maintained that Juárez tried to use the guaranteed railways as a scapegoat for the financial chaos that the reckless spending of his

[4] Mabragaña, *Los mensajes*, IV, 179-187, 220-221, and 226. Also Castro, *Treatise on the South American Railways*, p. 253.

[5] As quoted by *Railway Times*, October 20, 1888, p. 543.

administration had brought to Argentina. Among other things, the writer claimed that the president had completely ignored reference to the report of a special commission which had studied the state-owned railways. That report had revealed that the state-owned railways' rolling stock was not greater, nor was it in better condition than that of the private companies.

Yet it is a peculiar feature of the President's Message, and one which reflects a strong national tendency, that the evils produced by its own incompetent interference are indiscriminately laid to the charge of foreign mismanagement. The same peculiarity marks another part of the Message, where, speaking of the financial conditions of the country, the President dwells with exaggerated self-complacency upon the fact that the increasing number of fortunes made by private individuals reflects the solid financial prosperity of the nation. Anyone conversant with the true state of affairs knows that there is no greater fallacy—that it is only by heavily taxing imports, by pawning the country, mortgaging its future, and selling its great public works that the Government is enabled to carry on a hand-to-mouth existence, hoping perpetually that "something may turn up" to keep the supply of fuel. In the evils brought about by official interference the Government seeks to shift the whole blame on foreign mismanagement. In the good results achieved by individual energy and enterprise it loudly lays claim to the whole merit.[6]

The British-owned railways and the agrarian oligarchs often worked at cross-purposes to protect their respective interests. Juárez meant to clean up the railway industry. At least he wanted to increase their receipts to the fullest. To accomplish this goal he threatened to withdraw guarantees. He did not make idle threats. A presidential decree suspended the payment of guarantees to the East Argentine Railway Company in November, 1889, "until this line is placed in the conditions prescribed by law, as regards rolling stock, its working expenses, and the method of keeping its accounts."[7] The decree called for a complete audit of the company's books by the National Railway Board, which would file its full report with the minister of the interior following the investigation. Juárez did not intend to limit his interference in railway affairs to

[6] *Herapath's,* June 9, 1888, p. 653.
[7] *The Economist,* January 4, 1890, p. 7.

the East Argentine. He contemplated overhauling the whole
guarantee system. Before he resolved the problem, however, the
nation's financial structure fell. Soon thereafter an abortive political revolution forced Juárez out of office.

The crash of 1890 did not come as a surprise to knowledgeable
observers of Argentina's economic development. *The Economist*
had long predicted such a disaster and greeted it by stating simply
that "the long-anticipated collapse of the River Plate has at long
last taken place."[8] For a number of years British financiers realized
that a prolonged course of reckless borrowing for varied projects—a few of them good, but most of them bad or indifferent—had led the nation into a precarious financial condition.
Only absolute cessation of the borrowing mania and rigorous
retrenchment in every department of the state could have averted
utter collapse. Among other things, Juárez had encouraged inflation and issued illegal, clandestine, and fraudulent money to the extent of 60 million pesos.[9] For this, most historians have dismissed
him as too shortsighted and ignorant to have averted the disaster
of the Baring crash. One of his milder critics summed up his administration as "sterile."[10] Juárez's failure also resulted from his optimistic belief in his country's ability to meet its financial obligations under any circumstances. He spoke for his class. On the very
eve of the economic crash of 1890, which spelled political disaster
for him, Juárez said, as he had on previous occasions, "the Nation
will always be rich enough to meet its obligations and to provide
great profits for investors."[11] The frenetic boom had to end, as it
did when gold reserves ran out in 1890. When the crash of that
year carried the British firm of the Baring Brothers into ruin and
shook the whole British financial structure, the economic dependence of the Argentine Republic upon foreign capital became
painfully clear.

The almost simultaneous occurrence of the economic crash and
the political revolution of 1890 had a sobering effect upon the

[8] Ibid., July 12, 1890, p. 890.

[9] Ibid., August 2, 1890, p. 983.

[10] Mariano de Vedía y Mitre, *La revolución del 1890*, p. 25.

[11] Mabragaña, *Los mensajes*, IV, 267.

Argentine oligarchs. Their foreign credit, which had dwindled during the past years, disappeared. Former Vice-President Carlos
Pellegrini, the new president, faced the unenviable tasks of settling
the large public debt and trying to restore Argentina's economic
equilibrium. For a number of reasons Pellegrini ranks with former
Presidents Julio A. Roca and Bartolomé Mitre as the most influential politicians in Argentina during the late nineteenth century.
Not a man of the people by nature, he nonetheless became a leading orator of his day. The son of an Italian immigrant who made a
fortune in banking, Pellegrini represented the new plutocrats.
Because of his family background and personal fortune, the upper
classes of Buenos Aires held him in high esteem.[12] As president,
however, he did not succeed in solving the nation's economic problems. He mistakenly proclaimed that increased production would
provide the perfect cure for the financial ills of the nation.
Furthermore, he resorted to new issues of inconvertible paper
money, which only brought the currency to new lows and made it
impossible for the government to meet payments on its foreign
debt at the end of 1890.[13]

In attempting to return the nation's financial situation "back to
normal" Pellegrini tried to resolve several problems related to the
British-owned railways. His administration had to deal with the
question of guarantee payments and had to establish a viable
system of governmental controls over private railways. The
Argentine public, embittered by the Baring crash and the subsequent hardships it faced, demanded measures to restrict the activities of the British companies. The latter added fat to the fire by
operating as in the past with no concern for the needs of the nation. In a highly critical article the *Buenos Aires Herald* tried to
make the Argentine case clear to Britons. In straightforward terms
the *Herald* stated that the companies could no longer operate their
lines without having managers in Buenos Aires who could make
decisions without referring them to their London offices, some

---

[12] Vedía y Mitre, *Revolución del 1890*, p. 26.
[13] See Pellegrini's annual message to Congress of May, 1891, in Mabragaña, *Los mensajes*,
V, 7.

seven thousand miles away. To the average Argentine, the *Herald*
pointed out, it appeared as though the London-based director
"despises the South American and counts him as a good-natured
profligate who is indifferent to what service he gets or what is demanded for it."[14] For years the major British-owned companies
had appointed prominent oligarchs to their local boards. Local
board members gave the companies ready access to the president
and the Congress. Board members served an important political
function for the British companies but played only a nominal role
in the operation of the lines. They did little to improve the public
image of the foreign-owned utilities since they remained subser-
vient to the absentee British directors who made all the decisions
regarding operation of the railways.

In spite of mounting tensions, the British-owned companies continued to ignore their public responsibilities. They still charged
seemingly high rates, did not maintain sufficient rolling stock, and
lacked any sensitivity to the needs and desires of the general
Argentine public. Their growth slowed down as a result of the
crash, and in some parts of the nation it could be reported as late as
1891 that the bullock cart "rolls slowly alongside the rails and successfully competes with them."[15] However, the irresponsible days
of the 1880's had ended. As *Railway Times* spelled out to its British subscribers, "No company can antagonize public opinion successfully, no matter what power is given by its charter, and Argentine railway companies, in general, with perhaps one or two
exceptions, must make a very radical change of policy, or they will
encounter an angered public opinion, which will find a way of making its anger felt."[16]

Public pressure led to the swift enactment of the General Railway Regulation, Law 2873 of October, 1891, which supplanted the
older and highly ineffective regulation of 1872. The previous
General Railway Regulation, Law 531 of September 18, 1872, had
subjected railways to the control of a vaguely structured National

---

[14] As quoted by *Railway Times*, August 29, 1891, p. 242.
[15] Ibid.
[16] Ibid.

Railway Board. But the duties and responsibilities of that office had long been forgotten. Intended to supplement the provisions found in each company's concession, the 1872 law gave national authorities few regulatory powers by which to coordinate the nation's entire rail network. For the most part the law was ignored; no administration had enforced it strictly. As President Pellegrini admitted in 1892, the law, like many others, "had been forgotten by the state and railway companies alike during the prosperous years."[17]

The promulgation of the General Railway Regulation of 1891 followed a congressional investigation of the guaranteed railways that took place during 1890 and 1891.[18] In the course of that study members of the Congress heatedly debated the question of government control over all railways in Argentina. Several representatives expressed antiforeign sentiments, especially men from the interior provinces who felt they had become victims of foreign monopolies. Provincials assumed a hostile position and led a growing attack on railway directors who maintained headquarters in London, not Buenos Aires. Most of their resentment resulted from the usual complaints against high rates, inadequate service, and abuse of the guarantee system. On more than one occasion they expressed strong anti-British feelings. These nationalists resented the British for treating Argentines like a "nation of inexpert fools."[19] They attacked the British openly and severely. According to one nationalist, "[the directors] have believed, without doubt, that this country is destined exclusively to satisfy their special interests; and that the sums that were paid them through guarantees were strictly for expenditures by the directors and were not for satisfying the true and legitimate interests of the people of the country." Nationalists felt that Britons gained the money while Argentines did the work. Some even went so far as to blame their

---

[17] Carlos Pellegrini's annual message to Congress, May, 1892, in Mabragaña, *Los mensajes*, V, 52. Full texts of both railway laws are found in Alejandro Bunge, *Ferrocarriles argentinos*, pp. 41-77.

[18] Diputados, *Investigación parlamentaria de los ferrocarriles garantidos de la nación.*

[19] Ibid., p. 56.

country's financial plight upon British bankers because the latter, as men of experience, should have warned the Argentines of the dangers of overborrowing instead of forcing more money upon them than they could possibly repay.[20]

The anti-British feelings of the interior representatives made Congress too weak for President Pellegrini to depend upon. In spite of such a hostile climate of opinion, the law of 1891 did not contain antiforeign provisions. Nor did it do away with the troublesome guarantee system, the root of many of the doubtful activities of some British-owned railways. The law represented a compromise between the British-owned railways and the dominant agrarian and pastoral oligarchs. Both groups benefited by continuing the railway schemes created during the 1880's. At best the 1891 regulations merely reiterated laws and concession terms long in effect. The bill lacked uniformity. It did not attempt to place all the private railways under one set of unified regulations. Some companies continued their guarantee privileges, although by this time the most prosperous companies had found it more convenient and profitable to replace the guarantees with duty exemptions on materials imported for construction and operation of the railways.[21]

Several provisions of the General Railway Regulation of 1891 demonstrate the attempt by large agricultural producers to use laws to protect their interests at the expense of small farmers. For instance, the regulations paid strict attention to the question of rolling stock. One provision made it mandatory for railway companies to secure the approval of the director general of railways before discontinuing use of any worn piece of equipment in service. Another increased the government's right to control the rates charged by private companies. In the same vein, Article 67 made it illegal for companies serving the same area to enter into rate-fixing agreements or to agree to distribute the trade in a given region. Article 49 did permit the companies to offer reduced rates for large shipments, clearly to the advantage of the *estancieros* and

[20] *The Economist*, November 21, 1891, p. 1493.
[21] Raúl Scalabrini Ortiz, *Historia de los ferrocarriles argentinos*, pp. 355-363.

large agriculturalists who desired to legalize and institutionalize a practice already in effect. Now they could legally receive preferential treatment and favorable rates. Furthermore, they assumed that their products would not rot at the stations for lack of cars. Nothing in the law indicates that it guaranteed any advantages to the small users of the railways. They could still serve the rich with little concern for the poor. The railways did not have to alter their service much to meet the requirements of the new regulations.

Most of the presidents elected between 1892 and 1916 came to office in the spirit of compromise. Hence, Luis Sáenz Peña, a competent supreme court justice, became president in 1892 as a conciliation candidate after Mitre and Roca agreed that a nonpartisan president would avert possible civil war. The very nonpartisanship of the new president rendered him ineffective as a leader. His refusal to cooperate with those who nominated him soon caused a practical deadlock in the workings of the government. Sáenz Peña did not have a plan for the economic recovery of the nation. Protectionists dominated his cabinet, yet they followed a pacific concept that allowed large foreign-owned enterprises like the British-owned railways to operate with little interference.

In particular, Sáenz Peña faced a major problem in the guaranteed railways, which continued to demand annual tribute from the government. After some delay at the beginning of his administration, he did work out an arrangement by which the government agreed to pay nearly four million pesos in guarantees through gradual payments spread over an unstipulated number of years. The administration, however, refused to pay any of the guarantees unless the companies fulfilled the requirements of their concessions. They had to provide adequate rolling stock and build new extensions as promised. That the government agreed to pay even part of the guarantees in face of the large unpaid public debt reveals the preponderant influence of the British-owned railways at the time. Sáenz Peña justified the payments on the ground that "the railways are one of the principal agents of progress, as much in the political as in the economic order of things, because they permit the public authorities to act with all speed anywhere it is necessary; they exercise their civilizing action even in the remote territories, and they facilitate the development of the products of our favored soil."[22]

Sáenz Peña could only effect a stopgap solution to the guarantee problem. He did not please British investors. The latter protested the protectionist tendencies of Sáenz's minister of finance, José A. Terry, especially when Terry introduced a bill to transfer the provincial debts to the nation. To quote *The Economist*, ". . . why in the name of common financial sense and honesty has the National Government 'generously,' as Dr. Terry says, come forward to assume fresh burdens to favour the creditors of the provinces while leaving its own guaranteed railway creditors unsettled with, seeking to keep them silent by a yearly sop of one-fourth their just dues?"[23] Terry supported the pet delusion of Argentine protectionists—production—in an effort to make Argentina independent of foreign trade. In a speech given in December, 1894, he asserted his conviction that the government should expropriate all the railways in the country in order to favor production by cheap freight.[24] Since the state had just sold several of its railways, and the last two presidents had urged the sale of the Andino, Terry probably did not seriously contemplate expropriation as a serious way out of the railway-guarantee difficulty. More likely, he hoped to bluff the worst offenders into complying with government regulations. Whatever his intentions, the sudden resignation of Sáenz Peña in January, 1895, left both the guarantee question and public-debt issue in the hands of José E. Uriburu.

Uriburu, who became president upon Sáenz Peña's resignation, continued Sáenz Peña's plan to unify the provincial and national debt. The plan finally met with defeat in late 1895 through the efforts of Carlos Pellegrini, who favored full payment of the national debt and dropping of the provincial debts.[25] Although the debt continued unsettled and the nation struggled under a misguided protectionist policy, the major British-owned railways fared

---

[22] Luis Sáenz Peña's annual message to Congress of May, 1894, in Mabragaña, *Los mensajes*, V, 163. *The Economist*, June 3, 1893, p. 663; September 29, 1894, p. 1195.

[23] *The Economist*, September 29, 1894, p. 1195.

[24] Ibid., January 12, 1895, p. 44.

[25] Ibid., December 14, 1895, p. 1618; January 11, 1816, p. 39.

well.[26] As a senator from Buenos Aires, Pellegrini earned the reputation of an Argentine Alexander Hamilton because of the protectionist inclinations he manifested since the founding of the Club Industrial in 1875. Since that time he served as a leading supporter of high tariffs. While he defended native industries against foreign competition by advocating high tariffs, he showed unusual tolerance toward the large British-owned railways, which continued to receive benevolent treatment from Argentine governments. The companies especially benefited from concessions which excluded them from paying duties on materials they imported for maintaining and operating their lines. Pellegrini's somewhat ambivalent attitude owes in large part to his curious and highly flexible protectionist philosophy. This he once summed up in a speech delivered to the Senate on December 12, 1899, in which he stated, "It is my aspiration, and that of all protectionists, neither to live in protection, nor to have protection as an end in itself, but rather we desire protection as a means of arriving at free trade."[27] By this, he explained, he meant that protection would develop Argentine industry and agriculture to a point where the nation could bargain effectively for any market in the world.

Argentina's protective tariffs did not have the results Pellegrini desired, mainly because administrations employed the tariffs as a means of acquiring revenue. Often they charged exaggerated rates on raw materials, while collecting liberal duties on finished products, thereby eliminating the margin of difference for the local manufacturer. On other occasions, the tariffs arbitrarily forced up the prices of local manufactured products, to the disadvantage of indigenous consumers. At any rate, the tariff system did not give substantial impetus to industrialization. The tremendous development of the cattle and agricultural industries, along with more speculative ventures, such as land, absorbed the bulk of native capital investments, to the detriment of native industry. The lack

---

[26] The major British-owned railways had no guarantees in 1895. These railways were the Great Southern, Buenos Aires Western, Buenos Aires and Rosario, Buenos Aires and Enseñada Port, Buenos Aires Northern, Central Argentine, and Central Córdoba.

[27] Senadores, *Diario*, December 12, 1899, p. 1013.

of capital to establish large, new industries presented a major
obstacle to more advanced industrial growth in Argentina.
Furthermore, as one Argentine observer noted, "the preference of
the public for foreign products is a characteristic of this country,"
which the Argentine consumers sustained by their lack of confidence in domestic industries.[28]

British-owned railways did not foster Argentine industrialization. Rather, the British-owned railways opened up commercial
opportunities to Britons far more valuable than the dividends they
paid. Supplying coal, locomotives, rolling stock, rails, and standard
equipment for the daily operation of the lines meant steady
employment for numerous British workers and profits for British
firms. In turn, the working class of England consumed a relatively
inexpensive diet that contained large quantities of Argentine beef,
lamb, and cereals. In this situation Argentina could not develop a
well-rounded national economy. Railways did not spawn large steel
complexes, as they had in Britain and the United States. The majority of the industries that the railways helped to create concentrated upon processing raw materials for export and producing consumer goods and foodstuffs.

Increased agricultural traffic accounted for an upswing in the
fortunes of the British-owned railways in the mid-1890's. Even the
guaranteed railways improved, having set their houses in order
after the Uriburu administration threatened to publish highly unfavorable data on the methods that railways used to run up the
guarantees.[29] Most of the companies shared the government's
desire to settle the guarantee issue. They finally reached a solution
in late 1895, when the companies reduced their fixed costs, thereby reducing the amount covered by the guarantees. At this
juncture, the government set aside two million gold pesos for
guarantees, but it settled them individually with each company by
separate negotiations, rather than jointly, as the companies had
wanted.[30] The accord thus reached satisfied both the companies

[28] See Eusebio E. García's introduction to *Tercero censo*, VII, 23-24.
[29] *The Economist*, December 28, 1895, pp. 1678-1679.
[30] Ibid., p. 1679.

and the government. On that note *The Economist* happily assured its readers that 1895 had been a year of progress.[31] By the end of Uriburu's term in 1898 the country appeared well on the road to economic recovery. Rumors even circulated that various plots existed in England to "boom" Argentina again.[32]

In 1898 Julio A. Roca returned to the presidency for the second time. His victory was well received among the British, for he was a noted Anglophile and known as a moderate on the tariff issue.[33] Increasingly wealthy, Argentina was far from becoming an industrial state. By 1902 the nation had again reached a favorable balance of trade due to its exports of cattle and agricultural products.[34] With foreign credit restored, the Argentine leaders embarked upon another series of large public works in which foreign capital played an important role. Oligarchs enjoyed a prosperity that derived from economic alliance with Europe. As Roca stated in his annual message to Congress in 1902, after serving as president in a prosperous and progressive period of Argentine development for the second time, "the country is filled with confidence in its own strength and has given itself up energetically to new works. Capital has returned in considerable proportions, and we see with satisfaction that the European markets have completely restored the credit of Argentina, which is the most powerful agent of our wealth and civilization."[35]

The extension of the British-owned Great Southern from Bahía Blanca along the Río Negro to Neuquén, at the foot of the Andes near the Chilean border, offers an example of the mutual benefits that derived from the Anglo-Argentine alliance. The new construction began at the request of President Uriburu in 1895 to give the Argentine army rapid access to the western frontier at a time

[31] Ibid. According to Henry S. Ferns (*Britain and Argentina in the Nineteenth Century*, pp. 444 and 480), railway profits dipped from 1,193,000 pounds sterling in 1889 to 943,000 in 1891. In 1891 the Great Southern paid only 3 percent and the Central Argentine .75 per cent.

[32] *The Economist*, May 7, 1898, p. 689.

[33] Ibid., November 19, 1898, p. 1655.

[34] Mabragaña, *Los mensajes*, VI, 45.

[35] Ibid.

when war with Chile seemed imminent. By the time the Great
Southern completed the line in 1899 the war crisis had passed,
at least for the moment. Nonetheless, Argentine officials hailed
the addition as a significant accomplishment. Both Argentines
and Britons termed it a successful joint effort. One observer even
likened it to a second campaign of the pampa. At the inauguration
of the new extension to Neuquén, President Roca praised the
directors of the Great Southern for having spared neither money,
time, nor work in building the railway during a grave national
crisis. He called the railway a "new and wonderful testimony of
the benefits given to the country by English capital and enterprise." If the nation received important benefits from the
line, so did the British-owned company. First, the national government paid the Great Southern fifteen million pesos to extend its
railway across the fertile pampas. Second, the government used its
right of eminent domain to procure all the land necessary for the
right of way to Neuquén and gave it to the railway. Third, the
company received a forty-year exemption from import duties on
all equipment used in the construction and subsequent operation of
the branch line. This exemption in itself amounted to a large loan
of an indeterminable amount. Indeed, these generous provisions
helped to make the Great Southern the most prosperous railway
in Argentina at the turn of the century.[36]

Roca's immediate successors to the presidency, Manuel Quintana and José Figueroa Alcorta, two relatively obscure figures
in Argentina's political history, reflected the moderating influence
of a new generation of oligarchs. Although they enthusiastically
encouraged the expansion of the British-owned railways, they
pressed for increased regulation of the private companies. Like
their predecessors, these men wanted the companies to provide
better service at lower costs. They did not have quite the same at-
tachment to laissez faire economics that Roca and Juárez had.
Quintana began a campaign to gain closer governmental supervi-

---

[36] William Rögind, *Historia del Ferrocarril Sud, 1861-1936*, pp. 196-207. According to
The Economist, July 8, 1899, the Great Southern paid a 6 percent dividend in 1898 and could
pay 7 percent in 1899.

sion of the private industries. He recognized the contributions that the British railways had made to Argentina's progress, but he felt that the state should have the ultimate control over the nation's transportation services. He did not advocate state ownership of the entire railway system, nor did he object to the fact that foreigners owned the major lines. Rather, he sought legislation that would enable the government to intervene directly in matters, such as rate fixing and supervision of operation.[37]

Under José Figueroa Alcorta, Congress finally passed such legislation. The Mitre Law of September 30, 1907 (Law 5315), applied uniform regulations to Argentina's 13,690-mile railway network and brought to an end the anarchy of the railways. The law derived its name from its author, Emilio Mitre, who introduced it in the Chamber of Deputies after two years of careful research. Basically, the law clarified and defined the government's regulatory privileges. It also revised the types of incentives offered to the companies to encourage future building. To achieve the right balance between public and private control of the railway industry, the law stressed three major points. First, it resolved the question of the right of the government to interfere in rate fixing. Second, it abolished the troublesome guarantee system. Third, for the first time in their history, the private railways had to pay a tax to the national government. Proponents of the bill wanted to protect the interests of both the government and the private railways. Two articles in particular achieved this goal. Article 8 abolished the old guarantees and replaced them with a forty-year duty exemption upon all equipment and materials imported by the companies. This provision extended until January 1, 1947. In return for the privilege of importing equipment at reduced rates, the law obligated the railways to pay an annual tax of 3 percent of their yearly profits for the purpose of constructing and maintaining feeder roads to railway stations and ports throughout the nation. The second important provision, included in Article 9, established the right of the executive power to interfere in fixing rates whenever a company earned profits of over 17 percent for three consecutive years. This

[37] Mabragaña, *Los mensajes*, VI, 149.

article (and the fact that the Mitre Law made the General Railway Act of 1891 applicable to all railways) gave the central authorities tighter control over all phases of private railway operation, even those planned and built under the auspices of the provincial governments.

In introducing the bill, Emilio Mitre stated the government's objectives. According to him, the railways had made important contributions to the progress of the nation and would continue to do so. At the same time, he defended the liberal treatment accorded the railways by past administrations in their efforts to stimulate growth. By 1907 he believed that the major private companies would not endeavor to extend their lines unless the government worked out some new and uniform system of incentives. As for the 3 percent tax, he felt that, "without departing from the policy of stimulating and fomenting these companies, which have contributed so much to the progress of the country, it would behoove us to make the same fiscal demands upon them that are placed upon all taxpayers in the nation, by making them contribute part of their profits to the support of the public administration."[38] He thought the 3 percent tax a modest one, no more than the equivalent of the income tax collected in England. Furthermore, this revenue would build roads to the railways' advantage. Undoubtedly, the 3 percent tax amounted to very little when compared with the value of import exemptions granted to the railways. Because private companies imported all their heavy equipment and fuel, the duties quickly outweighed the tax. Typical of the Argentines' optimism, Mitre defended the arrangement on the ground that Argentine railways were "still in their cradle, in their infancy." Someday they would reach the same proportion as those in the United States. At that time the tax they paid would provide the nation with an enormous income.

Some members of Congress doubted the efficacy of the Mitre Law. Conservatives feared that it would drive foreign capital out of Argentina. They maintained the nineteenth-century concept that foreign capital equalled progress, and they did not want to do anything that might disturb the flow of foreign investments.

[38] Diputados, *Diario*, August 5, 1907, pp. 680-682.

Replacing the guarantee system with duty exemptions seemed especially risky to this group. Foreign investors might ignore Argentina completely, they felt, if antagonized. As one of their spokesmen, Mariano Demaría led the opposition to the law. He feared that lowering tariff duties would not provide enough inducement to foreigners, because "the situation is difficult today and is going to become worse if we do not stimulate foreign capital that is now so suspicious. If our own resources are insufficient for the demands of our progress, as everybody knows, we must attract foreign capital. The only way to do this is to assure good remuneration to the capital presently invested in the country."[39] Ponciano Vivanco of Córdoba expressed a similar opinion, although he believed that the exemptions would achieve the Argentine goal. "After all," he reminded his colleagues, "antagonism of foreign capital is something that has not existed, does not exist, and never will exist for reasons that all the world knows."[40]

The conservatives' fears proved needless. In the next decade the Mitre Law sparked the resurgence of railway construction. Between 1907 and 1914 the railways expanded their lines at an average of some 1,100 miles per year—more than any European nation during the same time—bringing Argentina's total mileage up to 22,066 miles at the outbreak of World War I in 1914.[41] Since the companies had the option of adopting the terms of the law or not, until their original concessions terminated, the fact that all the British-owned railways immediately agreed to accept the law indicates that they welcomed it. In fact, rumors circulated in Buenos Aires for years thereafter that the major British firms had paid large bribes to facilitate quick passage of the law. At any rate, the Mitre Law removed the basic areas of friction between the Argentine government and the British-owned railways. The government continued to encourage railway building by private railways whenever possible. It did begin a railway program of its

[39] Ibid., p. 1018.
[40] Ibid.
[41] *Tercero censo*, X, 406. Also Gregorio Etcheguía, *Los ferrocarriles argentinos vistos por ojos argentinos*, p. 40.

own under Law 6757 in September, 1909, but the state-owned railways called for by this legislation went to the more remote regions of the country that private companies had neglected. The railway program of President Figueroa Alcorta (1906-1910) separated the areas served by private companies from those in which the state took charge to eliminate wasteful competition between state and private railways. This program, continued by his successors, not only emphasized building state railways in sections that did not attract the foreign investors, but also included the sale of state-owned lines that served the same regions as the British-owned companies. As a result of the government's position, the British-owned railways no longer faced the threat of competing with state-owned lines. The British built new lines and brought new areas into contact with port cities. Argentine agricultural production made significant advances, which encouraged further railway expansion. It seemed as though an era of good will would prevail. In 1916, however, Argentina's golden age came to an end. With its demise the British-owned railways began a long process of steady decline and eventual failure.

5. End of the Golden Age

For narrow purposes the Argentine elite encouraged the growth of a large British-owned railway network during the quarter century preceding the outbreak of World War I. Repeatedly, members of the oligarchy publicly defended the British enterprises as agents of progress, order, and modernization. Oligarchs served on the companies' local boards and as lawyers and advisers to the British firms. This they did for both profit and prestige. Oligarchs defended the railways because they continued to equate prosperity with the expansion of the Anglo-Argentine trade alliance. To their way of thinking Argentina had become a prosperous nation or, simply, the oligarchs themselves had become rich men. As the railways grew, their export industries flourished. Land prices continued to rise. The oligarchs believed that they had nearly realized the dreams of the generation of Alberdi, Mitre and Sarmiento.

At the same time their Argentine dream had its seamier side. The practices of the positivist-inspired oligarchy of the late nine-

teenth century had done more than transform the nation's economy. It altered the social and political life of Argentina. Open support of European immigration introduced thousands of
agricultural laborers who pioneered the pampa between 1890 and
1916. The same policy also had a radical effect upon the urban
population. Cities attracted more immigrants than did rural areas.
In Buenos Aires nearly 50 percent of the population were foreign-
born by 1914. Foreigners swelled the ranks of the nation's urban
proletariat. Many immigrants turned their energies to commercial
ventures. Syrians, Lebanese, and East European Jews joined enterprising Italian and Spanish businessmen in starting new businesses.
Hardworking, frugal, and ambitious, these immigrants attained
economic success. As their commercial and industrial ventures
prospered, they began to form an important faction of a growing
urban bourgeoisie. Seldom considered gentlemen by the *criollo*
elite, immigrant entrepreneurs comprised a wealthy but alienated
segment of the Argentine population. They built considerable
wealth by introducing new businesses to Argentina. Employing
European techniques, foreigners opened new channels of economic
opportunity in Argentina. By the world war, immigrants controlled nearly 72 percent of the commercial firms in Argentina. As a
result of their financial position in a land of opportunity, the immigrant middle class actively pursued political and social rewards in
a closed society.[1]

Several conflicting currents produced a turbulent social and political situation between 1890 and 1914. The nation suffered
cultural chaos. As in the United States, a multitude of ethnic
groups lived together and competed with each other in the cities
of Argentina. Social assimilation went slowly. Argentines feared
that immigrants would subvert their nation, but Argentines had
not yet defined what it meant to be Argentine. The Argentine elite
continued to rule the nation after the Baring crisis with little concern for the masses. They led cosmopolitan lives, often isolating
themselves from the realities of day-to-day existence in their own
nation. They did not understand poverty, nor did they comprehend

[1] Carl Solberg, *Immigration and Nationalism*, pp. 3-64.

the forces that drove immigrants to work industriously in Argentina in hope of making fortunes. Despite their aloofness, the oligarchs could not ignore several threats to their position. On the one hand, dissident *criollo* groups challenged their right to govern. New parties, such as the Radicals, the Socialists, and the Liga del Sur of Santa Fe, made important inroads into the oligarchs' exclusive powers. On the other hand, the immigrant middle and working classes threatened to undermine the cultural and economic base of the oligarchs' rule. Foreign-inspired labor unions began to alter the classic employer-employee relationships in Argentina. Although the elite tried to pass off this phenomenon as the work of foreign-born anarchists and revolutionaries, the labor movement gained an important foothold in Argentina by the turn of the century. Strikes increasingly disrupted the economic life of the nation.[2]

Before the turn of the century a number of complex antiforeign attitudes appeared in Argentina. The oligarchs' fear of the masses heightened, especially of the foreign-born element. They resented the success of enterprising immigrant commercial and professional men. They despised the union activities of the foreign proletariat and intellectuals. The masses, in turn, hated the domination of the nation by an elite working hand-in-hand with foreign-owned monopolies, such as the British-owned railways. Antiimperialism often merged with antitrust movements. Immigrant and *criollo* merchants, industrialists, and small farmers protested the activities of large foreign-owned trusts, not because the trusts exploited Argentine workers but because they made it impossible for small businesses to operate on an equal footing with large international corporations. Railways seldom served the interests of the small operators. The same class opposed with increasing fervor the government of the oligarchs, which protected the foreign trusts at the expense of nationals.

Xenophobia became increasingly popular on two planes during the last decade of the past century and the first decade of the pres-

[2] Ibid., pp. 65-131; Samuel L. Baily, *Labor, Nationalism, and Politics in Argentina*, pp. 9-27.

ent. On an intellectual level, Argentine writers expressed anti-foreign sentiments. They hoped to define an Argentine culture while at the same time eschewing all foreign ideas they found uncongenial. Many resented the materialism of the positivists. Others attacked immigrants, especially Jews, and attributed to foreigners many of Argentina's vices. Yet others attempted to revive the Rosista image of Argentina. At a political level, struggling middle-class political parties turned against foreigners as part of an attack on the elite. As owners of monopolies and as non-Argentines, foreign businessmen made good targets for political attacks. Middle-class politicians often joined the oligarchs in attributing most of Argentina's growing pains to immigrants and foreign capitalists. Rising crime rates, prostitution, overcrowded housing, under-employment of *criollos*, and a multitude of urban and rural sins were blamed upon foreigners.[3]

Cultural nationalism manifested the antiforeign nationalism of the post-1890 decades. The arts often serve as an indicator of change for a society. Artists and writers who expressed antiforeign sentiments reflected the thoughts of a larger populace. They depicted the confusion of *criollos* in a multiethnic nation. Cultural nationalists wanted to hasten the assimilation of immigrants. They also encouraged proliferation of antiforeign nationalism and anti-imperialism. Many members of the Generation of 1880 became discouraged with Argentina's economic and cultural dependence upon foreigners.[4] As Leopoldo Zea expressed it: "Sarmiento's dream of Argentina as the United States of South America seemed to be a fact. But this generation, like others of its kind in all parts of Hispanic America, did not know how to realize or could not put into effect such a dream. Just as they had done in all Hispanic America, the great European bourgeoisie made the Argentine bourgeoisie mere bookkeepers for their business. Railways began to cross the pampa, industries flourished in the cities, banks began

---

[3] Solberg, *Immigration and Nationalism*, pp. 65-131.

[4] As used by Thomas F. McGann (*Argentina, the United States and the Inter-American System, 1880-1914*), the term "Generation of 1880" included such leading politicians as Julio A. Roca and Carlos Pellegrini, who dominated the political scene during the late nineteenth century.

to multiply, and wealth seemed to increase; but the firms that owned these railways, industries, and banks were foreign."[5]

Disillusioned Argentine intellectuals began to search Argentina's past to discover its glory. By 1910, leading cultural nationalists, such as Ricardo Rojas and Manuel Gálvez, attempted to define *argentinidad*. They wanted to create national pride in the population, yet rejected the materialism of their own age. Nationalists often avoided discussing contemporary economic and political problems in order to emphasize the nation's cultural achievements. They also glorified the role Argentina played in the independence movement of South America. Revival of the Rosas tradition characterized the post-1890 period, as well. Such political leaders as Leandro Alem and Hipólito Yrigoyen began to popularize reactionary xenophobia of the Rosas type. Culturally, a movement began to resuscitate the Rosas image. A leader of this movement, Adolfo Saldías, believed that Argentina's golden years had occurred during the Rosas regime. In writing about Rosas, Saldías came into direct conflict with liberal historians led by Bartolomé Mitre, who wrote about the dictator from the point of view of those who had overthrown him.[6]

More direct in their criticism of the generation's foreign-inspired materialism were Julián Martel (pseudonym used by José María Miro) and Juan Agustín García. In *La bolsa* Martel wrote one of the bitterest anti-Semitic and antiforeign novels of the nineteenth century. In that work he attacked the materialism of the age, especially what he considered the "avarice" of unethical Jewish financiers and businessmen. García launched a more direct

[5] Leopoldo Zea, *The Latin-American Mind*, trans. James H. Abbott and Lowell Dunham, pp. 217-218. Two articles on Argentine historiography have been referred to for this section. They are Joseph R. Barager, "The Historiography of the Río de la Plata Area," *Hispanic American Historical Review* 39, no. 4 (November 1959): 588-642; and Edberto Oscar Acevedo, "Situación actual de la historia argentina," *Estudios Americanos* 60, no. 43 (May 1955): 353-396. Also helpful were Juan José Hernández Arreguí, *Imperialismo y cultura* ; Luis Alberto Sánchez, *Nueva historia de la literatura americana*.

[6] Adolfo Saldías, *La evolución republicana*. The liberal historians of the second half of the nineteenth century wrote anti-Rosas, pro-European histories, characterized by a call to civilize the barbarian parts of the nation that had not been touched by the modern institutions of the United States and Western Europe.

attack on the Spencerian positivism expressed by his contemporaries. In *Sobre nuestra incultura* (1900) he assailed the bastion of positivism and lamented its effects upon Argentina. García criticized what he felt to be a false definition of progress by the ruling elite. He felt that as a result of positivism Argentina had become nothing but a colossal *estancia* crossed by railways and canals, filled with packing houses, populated cities, and abundant riches of all types, but without one wise man, artist, or philosopher.[7] He professed that he would prefer living in the most miserable place on earth if the sentiments of truth and goodness still prevailed rather than allow Argentina to be transformed by the materialism of his age.

In 1910 nationalism received a new impetus from the writings of young *criollos* commissioned to write for the centennial celebration of that year. Members of the Generation of 1910, as the new intellectual group came to be known, presaged a new era of Argentine nationalism. Such writers as Ricardo Rojas and Manuel Gálvez joined José Ingenieros and Leopoldo Lugones as the most influential Argentine literary figures of the immediate post-1900 period. Rojas and Gálvez played instrumental roles in creating an antiforeign atmosphere. Both had come to Buenos Aires from interior provinces. Like Sarmiento they represented the *criollo* who migrated to the nation's capital and there came in contact with contemporary European and foreign literary currents. Each reacted against the cosmopolitanism and materialism of their elders and soon directed attacks against the non-Argentine aspects they found in Buenos Aires. The works of Gálvez, one of Argentina's most gifted novelists, reveal a deep concern for the political, economic, and social problems of Argentina. Based on Hispanicism and Catholicism, his writings became increasingly antidemocratic between 1910 and 1930, as he urged his countrymen to turn from materialism and skepticism toward the spiritualization of a national conscience.[8] Rojas, called "the pre-eminent Argentine cultural na-

---

[7] Juan Agustín García, *Sobre nuestra incultura*; and Alejandro Korn, *Influencias filosóficas en el evolución nacional*, p. 200.

[8] See Otis H. Green, "Manuel Gálvez, 'Gabriel Quiroga,' and *la maestra normal*,"

tionalist" by one biographer, remained within the tradition of liberal nationalism set by Sarmiento and continued to accept the country's democratic precepts.[9] He not only agreed with Sarmiento that Argentina's destiny lay in her future, but also shared the latter's faith in democratic institutions. Although he continued Sarmiento's political philosophy, he broke sharply with his cosmopolitanism. Rojas believed that the valuable aspects of Argentine culture stemmed from the encounter between the Spanish and the indigenous races of Argentina. He further believed that the nation's youth needed to be inculcated with a spirit of *argentinidad*, or national identity, so that foreign and *criollo* elements could blend into one.[10] He welcomed foreigners to Argentina as human beings, but not as Britons, Frenchmen, Italians, or Jews.

The same atmosphere that created nationalistic discontent within Argentine intellectual circles also generated antiforeign economic nationalism among the middle and laboring classes. Small farmers and commercial interests from the interior provinces, especially, felt hostile toward the British-owned railways. They felt that the railways worked to subvert the interior to Buenos Aires. They also felt exploited by the railways. Interior interest groups had traditionally been reluctant to accept an economic alliance with Britain, although at an earlier stage many of their leaders had spoken in favor of foreign-owned railways as a means of developing their regions. The fact that large British-owned railways squeezed them financially gave the provincials cause for opposing them. Although no interior politician attempted to incorporate an-

---

Hispanic Review 11 (1943): 221-252; idem, "Manuel Gálvez, 'Gabriel Quiroga,' and 'El mal metafísico,' " ibid. 11 (1943): 314-327; and idem, "Gálvez's 'La sombra del convento' and Its Relation to 'El Diario de Gabriel Quiroga,' " ibid. 12 (1944): 196-210. For discussions of Gálvez's nationalism, see Hernández Arreguí, *Imperialismo y cultura*, pp. 80-81; McGann, *Argentina*, p. 291; and Arthur P. Whitaker, *Nationalism in Latin America*, pp. 45-47.

[9] Earl T. Glauert, "Ricardo Rojas and the Emergence of Argentine Cultural Nationalism," *Hispanic American Historical Review*, 43, no. 1 (February 1963): 1-13.

[10] Rojas's early nationalism is to be found in his first three major works, *La restauración nacionalista* (1909), *Blasón de plata* (1910), and *La argentinidad* (1916). In *La restauración nacionalista* (p. 342) Rojas was distressed by a recent book which revealed that "in addition to the Jewish and British capitalists, who are accustomed to considering us as an industrial colony, the Italians are also beginning to view us as an Italian colony."

tiforeign nationalism into a well-defined political ideology, the seeds of economic nationalism grew unchecked in the interior. Futile attempts to break the power of foreign-controlled monopolies frustrated citizens of the interior. Interior citizens frequently attacked the railways and grew to distrust and despise the government of the oligarchs, which consistently protected the foreign-owned corporations.

Most provincial dissidents turned to reactionary nationalism of the Rosas type. They did not appreciate the radical progress made in wealthier parts of the nation. It meant little to the average provincial that Buenos Aires had become a Paris of the Western Hemisphere in appearances and culture. Their lot had changed little. They still depended upon Buenos Aires and vagaries of world markets for their raw materials. The provincials never methodically developed their nationalism. Usually provincials limited their feelings to spontaneous outbursts of rage when individual spokesmen criticized the preeminence of British-owned monopolies. Nonetheless, such outbursts precipitated the type of xenophobia that has dominated Argentina since the 1920's. Antimonopolistic activities strengthened the arguments of xenophobes. Railways refused to cut down on their expenses, yet the government continued to support them. In times of financial crisis Argentines who suffered most felt the injustice of a government policy that favored foreigners at the expense of nationals.

The sale of the Oeste railway to the British syndicate in 1889 provoked an example of these isolated outbreaks of antiforeign nationalism. Proponents of the sale argued that the Oeste had become a dangerous monopoly. Opponents agreed in part, but they feared a foreign-owned monopoly far more than they did a state-owned monopoly. Opponents to the sale did not want to assist in extending the British economic hegemony over the entire republic. Debates in the provincial legislature of Buenos Aires reveal a diversity of economic theories. These theories show that opponents to the sale maintained an antiforeign spirit and willingly expressed distaste for the ruling elite. Many *porteños*, like their provincial brothers, did not want foreigners to dominate the nation's economy. Accordingly, one outspoken critic of the sale warned, "I do not want to see my country overrun with railways owned by foreigners, and I do not lack the foresight to see that within eighty to ninety years it will be totally traversed by the locomotive, but the locomotive of the foreigner, acquired with foreign capital." The same critic advocated state ownership of the railways. He felt that it offered the "sole means . . . of raising the Republic to a place among the top nations of America." He felt it was neither necessary nor desirable to encourage foreign owner-ship of the railways. He thought that competent administrators could be found in Argentina. "We do not need to go to England to find railway directors as one would go in search of a pure-blooded Durham bull."[11]

Similar attacks against foreign ownership of the major railways followed the Baring crash of 1890. The harmony between the Brit-ish-owned railways and the Argentine public had ended. Oligarchical protection buffered the companies from the public wrath for the time being. Opponents of the pro-European oligarchy became increasingly vocal during the last decade of the nineteenth century. Anti-British feelings reached a peak in 1890 and 1891, after the Mortoribus-Rothschild loan prevented the un-popular Baring Brothers firm from going bankrupt. English banks and utilities became the targets of numerous popular demon-strations, some of them genuine manifestations of Argentine na-tionalism, others political protests against the existing regime. As one observer recorded, the disposition of the common Argentine toward British enterprise "seeks frequent angry expression, ap-pears in gross and often obscene caricatures of the English in several pictorial prints and gave its most recent vicious tokens in the concerted assault upon the London and River Plate Bank in order to wreck it."[12] On one occasion "well-dressed Argentines" tore down English flags from their standards at the Plaza Victoria, where they had flown in silent commemoration of the Tucumán Declaration of Independence.[13] Perhaps the best description of the

---

[11] Gregorio Etcheguía, *Los ferrocarriles argentinos vistos por ojos argentinos*, p. 187.
[12] Pitkin to Blaine, June 6, 1891, DS, NA, RG 59, microcopy 69, roll 24.
[13] Ibid. Also reported by the *Buenos Aires Standard*, June 5, 1891.

anti-British climate of opinion appeared in the *Buenos Aires Standard* of June 5, 1891, which stated: "It was English gold that helped South America, and especially Buenos Aires, to throw off the yoke of Spain. Nevertheless, the bare mention of English gold is now like hanging out a red cloak to a bull."

A product of his times, Juan Bautista Justo soon played a leading role as an Argentine economic nationalist. A young *porteño* surgeon who collaborated with del Valle and Mitre in the unsuccessful revolution of 1890, he helped to form the Socialist party in 1894. As leader of that party he established himself as a chief proponent of economic independence for Argentina. Throughout his political career, Justo campaigned against foreign capitalists. He became one of the first middle-class politicians to incorporate economic nationalism into his party's ideology.[14] Of course his economic nationalism reflected the antiimperialism expressed by all socialists. When he attacked capitalism, however, he primarily considered foreign capital bad. He wrote in 1895 that he did not oppose the extension of railways by capitalistic means, but Justo did believe that foreign capitalists had acquired too much control over the nation's railway network. For that reason it appeared that foreign capitalists, especially those from Britain, would soon become more powerful than the state. According to him, "the governing class is not the least bit alarmed about this. That which they desire is to increase the value of their land, and not being able to construct the railways themselves, they entrust the work to foreign capital."[15]

As a nationalist, Justo opposed the foreign-owned railways as instruments of foreign imperialists who dominated Argentina. He argued that the railways contributed very little to the welfare of the Argentine people. They would not benefit the masses as long as they remained in foreign hands. To his way of thinking, the millions of pesos that went to England in dividends and interest payments were of as much good to Argentina as if the money were

---

[14] José Luis Romero, *A History of Argentine Political Thought*, trans. Thomas F. McGann, pp. 193-196.

[15] As quoted by Dardo Cúneo, *Juan B. Justo y las luchas sociales en la Argentina*, p. 104.

thrown into the sea. More seriously, he charged that British-owned railways would not create a stronger Argentina; they provided a means by which the British would acquire another Ireland.[16]

Justo had some justification for his extreme position. The Argentine elite showed little evidence that they cared to resist a widespread invasion by foreign capital. Between 1889 and 1910 the government took steps to remove itself from major railway operation. Shortly after the turn of the century North American meat-packing companies, especially Swift and Armour, moved into Argentina. By 1912 they controlled a substantial portion of that industry, at the expense of the existing British firms. Nationalists, like Justo, feared similar developments in other industries, including petroleum and the railways. Throughout the period the oligarchs did nothing to limit the power of foreign trusts, whether British or North American.

In 1907 President José Figueroa Alcorta introduced a bill to sell the Andino Railway to a British concern. The bill resulted from the president's decision to continue a policy begun by Juárez Celman to remove the government from railway operation whenever possible. The Andino was the last major link of the state-owned railway system. Despite considerable opposition, the administration finally forced through the sale in 1909. As in the case of the sale of the Oeste in 1889, the sale of the Andino placated British capital. Selling the Andino to the British freed the latter further to develop their transportation trusts. By 1910 the so-called Big Four—the Great Southern, the Central Argentine, the Buenos Ayres and Pacific, and the Western—lionized the Argentine railway scene with the cooperation of the Argentine elite.

Prominent members of the oligarchy advocated sale of the Andino. Two well-known Anglophiles, Carlos Saavedra Lamas and Ezequiel Ramos Mexía, led debates in the Chamber of Deputies. Ramos Mexía, then minister of public works, had served as legal council for several of the large British-owned railways, a position he retained through the 1920's. These men mouthed the tradi-

16 Ibid., and Romero, *History of Argentine Political Thought*, p. 193.

tional belief that Argentina could not survive without British capital. They considered British-owned railways positive factors in the development of modern Argentina. Railways had transformed the nation from an underdeveloped wilderness into a food basket of the western world. Saavedra Lamas and Ramos Mexía typified the conservatives who convinced themselves that Argentina owed its material progress and future greatness to the British-owned railways.[17] Ramos Mexía also represented one of many Argentine professional men who received large retainers from the British companies. His interest in the railways' welfare went beyond national consideration.

Arguing in favor of the sale of the Andino, both Saavedra Lamas and Ramos Mexía refuted the popular charge that the British companies drained wealth from the nation by sending dividends to Europe. Saavedra Lamas maintained that the drain amounted to no more than expected in an international capitalistic system. The situation did not hurt Argentina, he claimed, since the Argentines could "nationalize" such capital through "the unique procedure of offering to the same old capital new incentives, by offering it the stimulation of new and useful applications, by nationalizing it, one would say, by perpetuating it in the life of the country through a series of new and consecutive undertakings."[18] Saavedra Lamas reasoned simplistically that by allowing British enterprises to make profits the Argentines stimulated further investment in building new railways and other large public works projects. These projects, in turn, generated more Argentine wealth.

The oligarchs wanted to maintain Argentina's credit abroad. As minister of public works, Ramos Mexía expressed special concern that unfriendly acts toward British firms might cut off the nation's foreign credit. "I say: if we wish to be sincere and serious, we must give consistent evidence that the purpose of the national government is to respect this capital, once it has reached the country, and defend it, as I defend it, exposing myself to irresponsible accusa-

[17] The debates are found in Diputados, *Diario*, September 1, 3, and 6, 1909, II, 43-146.
[18] Ibid., p. 72. Saavedra Lamas also stated: ". . . we do not maintain a railway for the mere love of tradition. We are not going to keep the Andino only in order to add it to the festivities of the centennial."

tions or insinuations that I am paid by the companies."[19] Paid or not, the minister claimed that he took great honor in championing the companies. He did not fear the results of "gossip." Adhering to the laissez faire doctrines of the Generation of 1880, he reiterated his conviction that the president and Congress ought to respect and protect private capital, "because it is ruinous business for a nation if foreign companies come here with a great deal of capital to invest and lose it."[20] Foreign companies should make profits. Profits gave the best proof of the potential wealth of the nation. As long as British-owned railways did not exploit the riches of the nation in "exaggerated excess" they should receive every encouragement from the Argentine government. Ramos Mexía believed that the British would never take advantage of their Argentine friends.

The proposed sale of the Andino met with bitter resistance. The profits referred to by Ramos Mexía benefited only a handful of Argentines. In 1907 the proposal came to an impasse in the Chamber of Deputies, where a majority opposed the plan to sell the state-owned line.[21] Emilio Mitre, author of the Mitre Law, felt it wiser to lease the Andino to the British-owned Buenos Ayres and Pacific than to sell the line outright.[22] Others argued that the sale went against the best interests of the Argentine Republic. They urged the government to reconsider the project and refused to approve it. Through delaying tactics the Congress embarrassed the government. Deputies refused to accede to the desires of the oligarchs and British railway tycoons. In desperation, the government introduced the sale of the Andino in August, 1909, as an article in a general irrigation law, whereby the proceeds of the sale were to be used to finance irrigation projects in the nation's interior.[23]

Opposition to the sale of the Andino resulted from two basic causes. First, a growing number of Argentines sincerely opposed

[19] Ibid., p. 115. Ramos Mexía often served as legal council to the British-owned railways, and after serving as minister of public works he advised the Entre Ríos and the North East Railway companies.

[20] Ibid.

[21] *South American Journal*, February 22, 1908, p. 216.

[22] Ibid., June 27, 1908, p. 728; and Diputados, *Diario*, June 5, 1908, pp. 180-182.

[23] Diputados, *Diario*, August 11, 1909, I, 970-972. Article 18, section *c*, of Law 6546, the

extension of foreign-owned industries. Second, a larger number publicly protested the establishment of transportation monopolies, regardless of nationality. Opposition to the Argentine elite also sparked some protests. The administration openly sided with the British railways in this issue, but it showed little evidence of having thought out its line of reasoning. Its spokesmen were particularly vulnerable to criticism by opponents of the sale. As one deputy reminded the Chamber of Deputies, Ramos Mexía had written a pamphlet in 1907 in which he praised the Andino and expressed his belief that selling the Oeste had been a mistake.[24] The deputy could not understand Ramos Mexía's rapid but inexplicable metamorphosis. Others saw more clearly the danger involved in removing the state from direct control of an important railway link. Private companies would benefit. Eventually they would raise their rates, for without competitors they would have a free hand. The public would lose. The government had demonstrated lack of concern for the public by introducing the sale in the first place.

Representatives of small farming interests of the coastal and interior provinces led the fight against sale of the Andino. Particularly outspoken, Celestino L. Pera of Santa Fe contended that the sale of the Andino would only help the British-dominated railway trust, which already strangled production and commerce throughout the interior of Argentina. According to him, the fact that London-based companies controlled that trust further aggravated the situation for the interior producers. The producers had no recourse, especially if the Argentine government refused to protect their interests. The fight against the foreign trust had proven fruitless, he lamented. "In vain the stock exchange of Rosario has made its protests heard through the lips of the deputies from Santa Fe; in vain the administrators of the Andino have demonstrated the desirability of extending the line to Rosario; in vain the former minister of public works, Señor [Emilio] Civit, discussed in his reports and memoranda all the advantages and benefits of extending the Andino from Villa María to Rosario; in

General Law of Irrigation, stated simply that the proceeds of the sale of the Andino would be used to finance irrigation projects in the interior.

[24] Ibid., September 6, 1909, II, 119.

vain Congress has dictated a law authorizing the construction of this branch." These voices had not been heard, Pera contended, because "greater than the voice of the deputies, greater than the stock exchange, greater than the counsel of the administrators of this railway, greater than the advice of the minister and of the Congress of the nation has been the omnipotent, preponderant, authoritarian will of the English!"[25]

The oratory of Eduardo Castex, from Buenos Aires, followed a similar line of attack. An opponent of the sale and of the administration, Castex maintained that establishing a state railway administration represented a legitimate and patriotic goal. He believed that the present opposition to the sale manifested a sincere and eloquent, though premature, expression of a nationalistic tendency. He said, "As our ancestors attained political independence when they had sufficient force to impose it, in the same manner our successors, at their own time, will attain economic independence, recovering the railways and other public works that are now in the hands of foreign capital when these same works have yielded to the inhabitants of the country the riches necessary for their acquisition."[26] Castex's prognostication proved fairly accurate; nationalism was instrumental in bringing about the purchase of the British-owned railways nearly forty years later.

The Andino Railway affair indicates the presence of extensive antiforeign nationalism during the first decade of the twentieth century. It also demonstrates the all-powerful rule of the oligarchs. The Argentine elite could still rule without giving serious consideration to the desires of the people. The elite governed for themselves. Under the circumstances, they found it advantageous to deal with British capitalists on the latter's terms, even if it meant establishing monopolies. The practice may have proved disastrous in the long run, but during the prosperous years before World War I the elite enjoyed the advantages of a strong Anglo-Argentine economic alliance.

The Big Four British-owned railways precipitated a new wave of antiforeign economic nationalism between 1909 and 1914. Dur-

---

[25] Ibid., September 1, 3, and 6, 1909, pp. 122-124.
[26] Ibid., p. 146.

ing those years the large companies attempted to absorb the smaller private companies into their systems. They also tried to combine many overlapping services, despite laws forbidding such practices. Ostensibly the mergers began in order to eliminate inefficient lines and to do away with redundant services. As in the case of the merger of the Central Argentine with the smaller Buenos Aires and Rosario in September, 1908, the Argentine Congress usually gave willing approval of mergers involving small companies.[27] Regional interests often opposed such mergers since they removed alternative transportation systems. Merchants in Rosario especially opposed the merging of competing British firms, for, as they correctly anticipated, the unions led to increased rates.[28] Such protests did not stop the mergers. The national government continued to sanction the process by which the Big Four bought up their competitors. The Argentine press carried very few unfavorable notices about the mergers, largely because of the universal conviction in the current Argentine administration that "with the unification of several of the railways the progress of the country will receive a vigorous impulse."[29]

In 1912 Argentines took a new look at the railway situation. Two developments radically changed it during that year. On the one hand, two British-owned giants, the Great Southern and the Western, announced their intentions to unite. At the same time, a North American syndicate headed by Percival Farquhar made an open bid to gain control of important sectors of the Argentine railway network.[30] Both developments disturbed a large portion of the Argentine public. As much as most Argentines resented the creation of a British-owned railway trust, they feared more the

[27] *South American Journal,* November 7, 1908, p. 506. The merger of the Central Argentine and the Buenos Aires railways had been approved seven years before by the British Parliament, but when this was announced to the Argentines the note was short and highly offensive to the latter, since it assumed automatic approval of the merger by the Argentine Congress. Partly because their pride had been wounded, the Argentines delayed the merger.

[28] *South American Journal,* January 16, 1909, p. 66, points out that the enlarged Central Argentine raised its rates substantially.

[29] *Review of the River Plate,* November 8, 1912, p. 1167.

[30] See Simon G. Hanson, "The Farquhar Syndicate in South America," *Hispanic American Historical Review* 17, no. 3 (August 1937): 314-326.

specter of Wall Street. The British made matters worse by taking advantage of the syndicate's threat to unify major Argentine railways.

The Farquhar syndicate did not attract widespread attention in Argentina between 1912 and 1913, mainly because it met with economic disaster in mid-1913. However, it did create quite a storm in Britain. British observers convinced themselves that Farquhar wanted to monopolize the transportation of South America by establishing a continental railway system in accordance with proposals made by the newly established Pan American Union.[31] For the most part, the North American threat never became very serious, although it did materialize in late 1912 when representatives of the Farquhar syndicate bought controlling interest in the Entre Ríos, the North Eastern, and the Rosario-Puerto Belgrano railways. The syndicate already owned railways in Brazil and Uruguay. It also offered to buy two state-owned railways, the Central Northern and the Northern Argentine, from the Argentine government for 250 million pesos. At the outset it appeared that the Argentine Congress would assent to the sale of the Central Northern and the Northern Argentine, in spite of strong resistance by representatives of the provinces served by the two railways. The Argentine government needed the revenue that the sale would provide. Furthermore, neither railway had made money for the state. Both suffered from poor management, and neither could extend its present system.[32] Both the *South American Journal* and the *Review of the River Plate* agreed that the transaction involved two "white elephants," whose sale would relieve the financial strain of the national government.[33] For years the railways had

---

[31] *Buenos Aires Standard*, October 20, 1912.

[32] *South American Journal*, October 12, 1912, p. 413; *Railway Times*, August 24, 1912, p. 207; Tower to Grey, October 12, 1912, Great Britain, Public Record Office, Foreign Office 368/649. Hereafter material from the Public Record Office, Foreign Office, will be cited as PRO, FO. Actually, the syndicate represented predominately European capital, but for a number of reasons was chartered in the state of Maine. Among other things, it could not attract North American capital to the scheme (see Hanson, "The Farquhar Syndicate in South America," p. 321).

[33] *South American Journal*, November 23, 1912, p. 607; also see *Review of the River Plate*, December 6, 1912, p. 1425.

served as political instruments. Their employees, from top to bottom, held their jobs as rewards for political services. "For similar reasons the tariffs have to be regulated in a manner satisfactory to the inhabitants of the districts through which the railways are carried."[34]

As much as the British may have favored the sale of the two poorly managed state-owned railways to private concerns, they violently opposed selling them to an American firm. In its November 30, 1912, issue, the *South American Journal* stated emphatically that, "if, as is asserted, there is any risk in such a transaction of delivering the country to the manipulations of a huge trust *à l'Américaine*, a proposal of this character may bear quite another complexion." It then went on to quote an article from the *Buenos Aires Standard* which attributed the worst features of Yankee wire pulling to the Farquhar syndicate and to forecast evil days for the Argentine public should the Americans succeed, because "these trusts have no country, no patriotism, and no compassion, insofar as concerns its dividends, but touching its political aspirations, the 'dynamos' operating in New York will have the power behind them necessary to make the countries concerned dance to New York time." In closing, the *Journal* played upon growing Argentine antipathy toward the United States by warning, "Once the Farquhar trust, which promises to be the biggest and most powerful of them all, establishes itself firmly in South America, it will drag down the United States on top of these little Republics."[35] The Argentine Congress, partly due to British pressures and propaganda, but largely due to anti-Yankee feelings, refused to deal with the Farquhar group. Before the Farquhar trust could construct a workable offensive it suffered the effects of overextension. Setbacks in Brazil and Uruguay swept the syndicate from Argentina.

Using the Farquhar threat as an excuse, the directors of the British-owned Great Southern and the Western announced plans to merge in 1912. That announcement received far more attention in Argentina than did Farquhar's activities. Public reaction against the

[34] *South American Journal*, November 23, 1912, p. 607.
[35] Ibid., p. 626.

merger surprised the British. Whereas limited opposition had met the absorption of smaller companies into the larger ones, uniting these two giants met with widespread hostility. Not only did Argentines criticize the monopolistic aspects of the two railways, but they also attacked the foreign nature of the railway trust. British directors did not help matters. They treated the proposed merger as a *fait accompli* and considered their application for union little more than a token gesture. As Sir Henry Bell, president of the Western and member of the board of the Great Southern, explained the situation, the majority of the Western's stockholders already owned a controlling share of the Great Southern. Four out of five directors of the Great Southern also served as directors of the Western. Surveying the scene from distant London, Bell considered the merger a natural economic measure. He did not pay attention to Argentine nationalism. Rather, he advocated the merger "not only for our own interests, but also for the interest of the country in which we labour and whose prosperity is so bound to ours."[36]

The proposal met with stiff resistance in Argentina. Bell's highhanded attitude offended many Argentines. Many more feared the economic consequences of a merger of this magnitude. According to Rogelio Araya, a Radical deputy from Santa Fe, the closeness of the two lines and their boards did not constitute a point in favor of merger. Araya thought that a congressional committee should study the subject. As he pointed out, the fusion already existed. The two companies worked together so closely, he charged, that their returns for June showed a difference of only one penny. Afraid that a railway trust would choke off the economic opportunities of his province, Araya stated, "I would not fear the trust if I did not know that the railways, like all industrial trusts and monopolies, exercise a depressive influence, especially upon the morale of a country."[37] Many shared Araya's fears. Some went beyond him in attacking the British railway monopoly. One, Rafael Castillo of

---

[36] William Rögind, *Historia del Ferrocarril Sud, 1861-1936*, p. 487. See also Tower to Grey, July 12, 1912, PRO, FO 368/649, in which Tower informed Grey that the details of the amalgamation leaked out prematurely.

[37] Diputados, *Diario*, September 22, 1913, III, 439-441.

Catamarca, spoke for small farmers, cattlemen, and merchants of the interior whose livelihood the railway trust jeopardized. He could not understand how the Argentine government could support the British position. Noting the ambivalence of British capitalists active in Argentina, he concluded that the British-owned railway companies not only "have faith that the Argentine government is going to combat the [United States] meat trust, but also have faith that the government is going to aid the [British] railway trust. Their contradiction is understandable, but ours is not."[38]

Congress imposed a number of obligations upon British railway companies in an effort to abort the proposed merger. Among the most imposing demands were that the companies (1) accept a pension law for employees, (2) make considerable rate reductions, and (3) build nine hundred miles of new lines in the province of Buenos Aires. The last stipulation posed a particularly difficult barrier. Such expansion would not have yielded a fair return on the capital invested for a long time. Furthermore, the new construction would have proven difficult to complete and more difficult to run equitably, since the provincial government of Buenos Aires proposed to build some three thousand miles of state-owned railway in areas presently controlled by the Western and the Great Southern.[39]

The issue came to a close on September 16, 1913, when the directors of the British companies withdrew their petition. Ostensibly the British did not promote the merger after 1913 because of obstacles imposed by the Argentines. The fact that the Farquhar syndicate withdrew from Argentina that year also explains the change in the British attitude. Without the Yankee threat the British did not have to legitimize what already existed in London. The companies could continue to work together, as they had in the past, without a formal merger. They had little to fear from the Argentines. The province of Buenos Aires did not have sufficient funds to construct three thousand miles of railway; it had bluffed to

---

[38] Ibid., p. 437.

[39] *South American Journal*, September 27, 1913, p. 350; October 25, 1913, p. 470; and Rögind, *Historia del Ferrocarril Sud*, p. 490.

halt the British railway merger.[40] With the support of the oligarchs the railways could weather public animosity. Furthermore, Minister of Public Works Meyer Pellegrini made clear in a speech to the Chamber of Deputies that neither he nor the president would take part in any scheme detrimental to the private companies.[41] The British-owned companies continued to work under the aegis of the national government. Argentines had come to hate the British because the latter formed an obstacle to social and economic mobility and a barrier to obtaining political power.

[40] Lullind to SecState, December 16, 1912, DS, NA, RG 59, 835.77/39. Lullind, chargé d'affaires ad interim for the United States, reported a conversation with an Englishman, A. W. Barrow, who was a representative of the Farquhar syndicate in Argentina, in which Barrow indicated that in spite of current difficulties the syndicate would eventually control all the railways in that part of the continent.

[41] Diputados, *Diario*, September 22, 1913, III, 4-5.

6. The Radical Interlude

To all intents and purposes, British railway expansion in Argentina ended with the outbreak of World War I in 1914. After that year the British-owned railways built few new lines. Economic difficulties resulting from the war and its aftermath combined with a changing Argentine political scene to bring a halt to the growth of the British enterprises. The railways continued to operate, often with comfortable profits through 1929. But they could not generate enough new traffic to warrant large-scale expansion. Railway owners feared new investments because of the appearance of the Radical party as the ruling party in Argentina. Under the leadership of Hipólito Yrigoyen the Radical party threatened to end the privileged position that British-owned railways had enjoyed since the 1850's.

Many historians have written about the election of Hipólito Yrigoyen as president of Argentina in 1916. In theory the Argentines turned their government over to potential xenophobes, whose middle-class nationalism had both antiforeign and antioligarchical characteristics. But Yrigoyen, the leader of the pre-dominantly middle class Radical party, presents a difficult political figure. A mystic, he never made his political or economic policies clear. Voted into office after the Sáenz Peña election reform of 1912 permitted free and secret elections, Yrigoyen headed a sup-posedly democratic faction of Argentina. Outwardly, he appeared nationalistic in his opposition to foreign enterprises and their allies among the Argentine oligarchy. He attempted to build a following among the nation's urban proletariat. As a self-professed leader of "the people," he ruled the nation as a *caudillo*. The government continued rife with corruption as it had during the heyday of the oligarchs. Labor gained few benefits, despite promises from the Radical administration. A shift in emphasis did occur in that the Yrigoyen administration showed traditional Radical hostility toward the oligarchy. It also accepted the principles of economic nationalism that had prevailed during the Rosas era. These Yrigoyen combined into a popular political doctrine which criti-cized foreign capital and repudiated the "fraudulent and dis-credited" regime of the oligarchs.[1] In actual practice, little chang-ed but the rhetoric.

Yrigoyen's election in 1916 represents an important point in Argentine history. After a long struggle the middle class finally achieved political power, but transferring power from the elite to the middle class did not constitute a broad social and economic revolution. The Radical party never planned to undertake major social changes. Its leaders, especially Yrigoyen, remained loyal to a nineteenth-century concept of political change. They had strug-gled for basic political reforms that would enable them to assume traditional power. This concept they adopted from the Unión Cívica, created in 1889. Political power, not broad social change, caused the abortive revolutions of 1890, 1893, and 1905. In spite of its proclamations supporting social change, the Unión Cívica had

---

[1] Ysabel F. Rennie, *The Argentine Republic*, p. 214; Peter G. Snow, *Argentine Radicalism*, pp. 16-45; Manuel Gálvez, *Vida de Hipólito Yrigoyen*; Gabriel del Mazo (ed.), *El pensamien-to escrito de Yrigoyen*; José Luis Romero, *A History of Argentine Political Thought*, trans. Thomas F. McGann, pp. 205-226; Federico Pinedo, *En tiempos de la república*, I, 45; Arthur P. Whitaker, *Nationalism in Latin America*, p. 48.

represented a *criollo* movement. Its leaders made no effort to win the support of Argentina's rapidly growing immigrant population. They never attempted to organize the new immigrant-dominated middle class and the growing urban proletariat into an effective political force. To win their struggle the leaders of Unión Cívica turned to the organized military. Furthermore, they did not state revolutionary objectives, other than promising new faces in the nation's governing bodies. The Unión Cívica attempted a coup in 1890, not a revolution. Its members wanted control of the same political institutions the oligarchs monopolized. Moreover, the Unión Cívica represented a movement, not a political party. When it failed to achieve its immediate objectives it disintegrated. Several organizers simply withdrew from politics. Others rejoined the ranks of the victors.

As for the middle class, no one political movement replaced the Unión Cívica after 1890. In many ways that year marks the beginning of the political fragmentation of the middle class, not its political baptism as a unified entity. By the turn of the century Argentina had neither a homogeneous nor a politically well-organized middle class. The middle class broke down into urban and rural factions with numerous subdivisions.[2] The appearance of a prosperous immigrant bourgeoisie created a serious rift in the middle-class structure. Even to the casual observer, the mass of immigrants remained outside the *criollo* mainstream; *criollos* wanted power kept in the hands of nationals. Their separate social, economic, and political aspirations weakened the middle-class movement considerably.

Middle-class political groups suffered from heterogeneity and from a tendency to follow personalities or strong leaders rather than ideologies. No one political figure tried to appeal to all these diverse middle-class groups. Leading middle-class politicians, in-

---

[2] See John J. Johnson, *Political Change in Latin America*, for an idealized treatment of the progressive role of the middle class. Johnson later reconsidered this role in "Whither the Latin American Middle Sectors," *Virginia Quarterly Review* 37, no. 4 (Autumn 1961): 508-521. For a thorough treatment of the composition of the Radical party see Gilbert W. Merkx, "Political and Economic Change in Argentina from 1870 to 1966," Ph.D. dissertation, Yale University, 1968.

cluding Yrigoyen, Juan B. Justo, and Lisandro de la Torre, followed separate tacks toward political power. They varied greatly in detail in their approach to politics. In leading independent movements of their own, they further debilitated the political impact of the Argentine middle class.

The Unión Cívica withered as its leading personalities left its ranks. Mitre and del Valle retreated to join their allies in the oligarchy, taking with them a number of followers. Leandro Alem, disillusioned by the failure of 1890, wasted and soon committed suicide. With his death he left leadership of the important Unión Cívica Radical movement in the hands of his nephew, Hipólito Yrigoyen. The latter, a pedestrian spokesman of the middle-class cause, followed a course destined to lead him to power. He advocated the same strong executive form of government practiced by the very elite he wished to depose. Quixotic and tempestuous Lisandro de la Torre, from a well-to-do provincial family, retired from the Radical movement in a fit of rage. After opposing Yrigoyen, he withdrew to Santa Fe and began an independent political career as a *porteño* in the provinces, provincial in Buenos Aires, Argentine in all parts. In Santa Fe he helped found the Liga del Sur. Unlike the Radical movement, the Liga del Sur had a definite ideology, sought immigrant support, and opposed the centralism of the oligarchs. De la Torre believed in strong local government. He assumed a *federalista* rather than a *unitario* position, in contrast to the majority of middle-class politicians. Finally, the young surgeon Juan B. Justo, moved by a blend of socialism, liberalism, Spencerian positivism, Marxism, and nationalism, helped organize the Socialist party, which he ran until his death in 1928. In leading this movement he made a concerted effort to identify the party with the needs of Argentina's immigrant population.

Although the middle-class movements found a common enemy in the oligarchs, middle-class politicians aligned themselves against neither the constitution nor the political system which the oligarchs represented. Popular politicians could not easily overcome the heritage of *caudillismo* and autocratic rule by the oligarchy. Sarmiento had reverted to *caudillo* methods in his haste to reform the nation, and Yrigoyen followed suit. Yrigoyen played the role of a middle-class social reformer with a concern for the laboring masses. He also appeared to be a staunch antiforeign nationalist and a friend of labor. Thanks to his urging, the Congress created the national oil monopoly, Yacimientos Petrolíferos Fiscales (Y.P.F.), that represented a positive step toward economic independence. He also represented an attitude that a more cosmopolitan Argentine observer considered regressive isolationism that "for moments became notoriously xenophobic."[3]

Yrigoyen made his name anathema among British economic interests. He did not go to the length that Cipriano Castro had in Venezuela when, a decade earlier, he provoked the British and German governments to blockade the Venezuelan coast in order to collect foreign debts. Yrigoyen did follow a decidedly anti-British policy, but not one designed to force British retaliation. President Baltasar Brum of Uruguay once described Yrigoyen for a British diplomat: "Of England he [Yrigoyen] has a holy horror. . . . He regarded England as a Power sunk in materialism and which, having grabbed half the world and not being sated, could now put on a hypocritical mask of generosity."[4] Brum may have exaggerated Yrigoyen's hostility toward the British, but Yrigoyen undoubtedly made life difficult and uncertain for the British-owned railways during his first administration between 1916 and 1922. As an exponent of economic nationalism he considered the principle of domination of the railways and their extension by the state "as fundamental for the social, political, and economic development of the nation," because "in countries of constant growth and progress, such as ours, the public utilities have been considered principally as instruments of the government."[5] Concomitantly, he wanted to end the political role of the British-owned railways.

Prior to 1916 the big British companies had taken great care to appoint the most respected Argentines to their local boards. In so doing they had assured themselves the cooperation of the Argen-

[3] Pinedo, *En tiempos de la república*, I, 45.
[4] Tower to Balfour, April 9, 1919, PRO, FO 371/3504.
[5] Mazo, *El pensamiento escrito de Yrigoyen*, p. 95.

tine elite. Men of wealth with high positions in Argentine society made useful agents in bargaining with the oligarchs. These men, mostly lawyers, bankers, and engineers, made the local boards powerful bodies. Their high salaries always proved a worthy expenditure since they gave the British-owned railways direct access to the Casa Rosada. With the ascension of Yrigoyen, the arrangement boomeranged. The local board members comprised political opponents of Yrigoyen. With justification Yrigoyen accused board members of using their positions for political reasons and refused to deal with them. The very men who previously wielded power now found themselves powerless, with no access to the president's mansion. The railways could now count them as liabilities.[6]

The British further offended the Yrigoyen regime by continuing to operate the railways through London-based directorates. To the Argentines, the British seemed responsible only to shareholders for the security of their capital and adequate returns. The British showed little concern for Argentine interests in forming their policies. Perhaps British reluctance to remove the London domination of the railways resulted from their traditional belief that only honest and efficient British administration ensured the security of their stake in Argentina. They did not trust the Argentines. They assumed, in keeping with previous policy, that Argentines should respect the virtue of upright British administration. As a result of these prejudices, they ran the railways in an atmosphere of superiority to the host country. The British directors ignored Argentine pride and self-esteem. Like most Britons, they shared the widespread opinion that most Argentines were corrupt and that privileges and services could be bought. Corruption did exist in Argentina. Argentines had traditionally used intermediaries to transact public and private business. Argentines considered personal contacts important in transacting business, and government salaries remained low. They could not understand the British attitude; the Briton's superior airs offended the sensitive Argentine.

Railway companies probably could have eased the situation by

[6] Tower to Balfour, May 9, 1918, PRO, FO 371/3131.

shifting their headquarters from London to Buenos Aires. Each company could have effected a basic change quite simply by delegating power to an official in Buenos Aires. Companies did not have to subordinate British interests completely to the Argentine point of view, but they did need someone to direct the activities of general managers and managerial organizations on the scene, who administered the technical aspects of the railway. The companies needed representatives who could make important policy decisions without referring the matters to London. Such modification in the railways' hierarchy could have altered Argentine official and public opinion. Outwardly the railways could have appeared as indigenous contributors to Argentine progress and prosperity. To improve their public image the companies needed to identify the railways as part of the Argentine national life by assimilating British interests with those of the Argentines.

The British failed to rectify this situation for a number of reasons. They refused to cooperate with the nationalistic Yrigoyen government. Evidently the British railway directors did not recognize the cause of their precarious status in Argentina after 1916, nor did they fully understand the growing intransigence of the new governing body in Argentina. Though World War I dramatically reduced the economic preeminence of Britain in Argentina, Britons knew that their economic influence had not ended. Perhaps Britons overestimated the potential for railway development in the post-World War I era. Some may have believed Yrigoyen, who informally led the British to believe that his government would encourage further British investment once the war ended. The British railway interests had little reason for optimism about their future under Radical rule.

British-owned railways faced a number of vexing problems between 1917 and 1921. First, the war itself halted railway growth the world over. It cut off the flow of British capital and merchandise to Argentina, taxing the resourcefulness of the British directors to continue operation of the major lines. Second, a series of labor disputes involving the railway unions of Argentina periodically disrupted railway service. Third, decreased commerce and increased costs of operation forced the railways to press for higher rates. In so doing the companies became involved in a prolonged conflict with the Yrigoyen administration. The rates struggle proved a lesson in futility to the companies. Yrigoyen refused to accept their claims as valid. On at least one occasion he even threatened to expropriate the British properties rather than raise freight charges. Finally, Yrigoyen's inimical position discouraged further development of the railways once the war ended. As a result, the British built only eighty-seven miles of new line between 1916 and 1923.[7]

The first serious crisis began in August, 1917, when a general railway strike broke out. The dismissal of two Argentine workers at the Pérez workshop of the British-owned Central Argentine Railway for disciplinary purposes precipitated the strike. No question of wages, hours of work, or labor conditions in general entered into the demands of the strikers. They simply demanded immediate reappointment of the two dismissed men. When the company failed to do this, the workers went on strike and urged other railway groups to join them. In short order, workers crippled rail transportation throughout the *litoral*. Some violence occurred. During the troubled months between August, 1917, and June, 1918, the most serious incidents took place in Rosario in the form of wildcat strikes. There the strikers committed every kind of outrage against the British-owned railways. Strikers seized telegraph offices, held up troop trains, blew up bridges, interrupted service, beat up non strikers, and destroyed British property on a large scale. Government troops, noticeably present but inactive, maintained an indulgent attitude toward the mobs. Police and national troops, commissioned to protect company properties, did nothing to restrain the strikers. On more than one occasion they watched as workers burned British property. Their presence made destruction of property easier by making it clear that the government would not arrest anyone for damage done to the British railway companies.[8]

---

[7] From figures in *South American Journal*, January 9, 1932, p. 35.

[8] For details on the strike see PRO, FO 371/3130, 371/3131, and 371/3504. See also *Railway News*, August 18, 1917, p. 160; September 22, 1917, p. 205; September 29, 1917, p. 280; October 6, 1917, p. 300; November 10, 1917, p. 422; February 16, 1918, p. 181; Febru-

Throughout the crisis Yrigoyen remained openly sympathetic and benevolent in his treatment of the unruly strikers. At the time he placed their aspirations above any other issue. He did nothing to ruin the workers' sport. He certainly paid no attention to charges by Allied diplomats that he followed a pro-Axis policy. Allied powers considered the transportation of foodstuffs essential to their war effort. The strikes halted the flow of much-needed wheat. Britons quickly accused Yrigoyen of pro-Axis sympathies, despite the lack of any Axis organizers of the strikes. Yrigoyen placed internal concerns, the plight of the workers and partisan politics, above international considerations. Obviously he knew the international consequences of his stance. Nonetheless, he ignored repeated British pleas to get the trains running.

Yrigoyen's behavior demonstrated his political sagacity and opportunism. With important elections scheduled for 1918, Yrigoyen worked feverishly to defeat the Socialists in Buenos Aires and the Progressive Democrats in Santa Fe. He could not afford to take repressive steps against labor on the eve of elections. By waiting until after the federal and provincial elections of 1918 to act against the strikers, he helped assure an important voting bloc his party ardently desired to win. Although such a position manifested anti-British and anticapitalist characteristics, it resulted from political expediency as much as from xenophobia. By this maneuver, he worked to replace the Socialists as leaders of the working class. The British had to bear the situation, for as one observer noted: ". . . the strikes which are being engineered are the result of the antagonism between Socialists and Radicals. And when politics enter into such matters, reason, law and justice are dead letters and have no force."[9]

Yrigoyen assumed the role of "the poorman's president" when the strikes ended to the satisfaction of the railway workers in June, 1918. Labor supported the Radicals. Moreover, the party gained control of the province of Buenos Aires. As a by-product of

---

ary 23, 1918, p. 213; June 8, 1918, p. 594. See also Juan B. Chitti and Francisco Agnelli, *La fraternidad*, p. 322-333.

[9] *Railway News*, September 29, 1917, p. 280.

the strike, the political power of the British-owned railways was broken. They never again attained the political dominance they had enjoyed during the latter half of the nineteenth century. British economic interests remained important, but the railways no longer carried much weight, either in London or in Buenos Aires.

Faced with increased operating costs and decreasing traffic during the immediate postwar period, the companies found it necessary to press for higher freight and passenger rates in 1919. The railways touched off Argentine rancor, which led the Yrigoyen regime to use the controversy for political reasons. Ensuing difficulties frustrated the railways' activities. Ostensibly the rates controversy centered on the ambiguous wording of Article 9 of the Mitre Law. According to the companies' interpretation of the law, they had the right to raise their rates without government permission whenever profits fell below 6.8 percent for three consecutive years. The British-owned railways estimated that the net average return obtained for the previous five years amounted to little more than 3.5 percent by 1919, far below the amount specified by the Mitre Law.[10] Several factors explained their low returns; however, the companies felt that the decline in revenue resulted primarily from the government's labor policy. They argued that their overhead charges had increased because the government obligated them to reduce working hours and to increase the number of employees. Increased cost of materials and a slacking off of traffic also motivated companies to seek higher rates. Additionally, most British railway experts felt that Argentina had derived immense benefits from the railways in the past, although few Argentines had invested capital in the companies. From their vantage point, they thought that Argentines owed the British a few favors.[11]

Yrigoyen did not deal with the rates issue on purely commercial lines, nor did he allow sentiment to affect his thinking. As in

[10] *Review of the River Plate*, February 28, 1919, pp. 68-70; White to SecState, January 10, 1922, DS, NA, RG 59, 835.773/11.

[11] For an example see Viscount St. Davids's report to the annual general meeting of the shareholders of the Buenos Ayres and Pacific Railway Company as it appeared in *The Financier*, October 25, 1921.

the case of the general railway strike, he reacted to partisan politics and public opinion. For obvious political reasons Yrigoyen could not permit rate increases. Like his nineteenth-century predecessors, he had to guarantee cheap transportation to the nation's agricultural interests. The Radicals could hardly have maintained their political supremacy in crucial provinces, such as Córdoba, if the rates had increased.[12] By opposing the large British concerns he also assumed a popular antiforeign stance, which served him well in continuing his political domination.

Yrigoyen scored a major victory over the British-owned railways on the rates issue. Throughout the struggle he held the upper hand. The Mitre Law and universally accepted technical principles ruled that rates be just and reasonable. A growing anti-British sentiment raised the specter of expropriation. With both moral and legal arguments weighing in favor of the Argentines, the companies had to accept the rulings of the Argentine government. To ignore the authorities involved either paying heavy penalties or possible expropriation. In order to weaken the British bargaining position further, Yrigoyen prolonged the rates crisis by dealing separately with each company. The added delay served to highlight his stand against foreign capitalists. It also put the companies in a poor light. Some of their shady activities caught up with them, especially their watering of stock. The Argentine government refused to recognize large quantities of ordinary stock which it regarded as "water." In so doing, the government reduced the recognized capital value of the British-owned railways. This action in turn allowed the government to limit the amount of profit the companies could make without invoking the government's right to interfere in fixing rates under a strict interpretation of Article 9 of the Mitre Law. Reducing the fixed capital value of the railways also reintroduced the possibility of their expropriation. In fact, the British railways operated in doubt as to their future until August, 1919, at which time the minister of public works flatly stated that

[12] White to SecState, January 10, 1922, DS, NA, RG 59, 835.773/11; and Chalkey to FO, June 27, 1922, PRO, FO 371/7170. According to the latter, once the Radical victory was assured, the Yrigoyen government issued a decree authorizing partial rate increases. Also see Ernesto Tornquist, *Business Conditions in Argentina*, no. 152 (October 1, 1921), p. 10.

reports of expropriation circulated by the London press had no foundation.[13]

Throughout the rates controversy the Yrigoyen administration maintained essentially anticapitalist and prolabor positions. These it combined into a potent brand of popular nationalism, a harbinger of the type of popular nationalism Juan D. Perón used so effectively after 1943. In arguing against rate increases government officials often couched their positions in nationalistic statements against "the pernicious British." The anti-British attitude became so strong that the British minister to Argentina, J. W. R. Macleay, complained in October, 1921, that the semiofficial government press, helped by Germans, had encouraged hostility among "the unthinking and ill-formed sections of Argentine opinion" by suggesting that the railways continued to make great profits.[14] Actually, the railways made only modest returns. Radicals directed most of their economic nationalism against the British-owned railways because they offered a large and convenient target.

Under Yrigoyen the Radicals encouraged a nationalism based upon a combination of economic independence and social justice. They did not break with the traditional capitalistic system as Perón did by creating his "third position" in the popular nationalism of the 1940's. The Radicals did take an anticapitalistic stance in opposing the British-owned railways. During the strike of 1917-1918 the unofficial party organ, *La Época*, accused the British capitalists of thinking with their pockets rather than "in accordance with the principles of Justice."[15] According to the same editorial, the British had mistakenly believed that Yrigoyen wanted to create a paradise for railway employees and workmen at the expense of British capital. *La Época* considered this position both "absurd and unjust." Two years later the same newspaper clarified the issue somewhat. The railways, it maintained, failed to see the prudent and politic at-

---

[13] *South American Journal*, August 16, 1919, p. 108.
[14] Macleay to Tyrell, October 13, 1921, PRO, FO 371/5526.
[15] *La Época*, November 9, 1917, as translated in enclosure with Tower to Balfour, November 14, 1917, PRO, FO 371/3130.

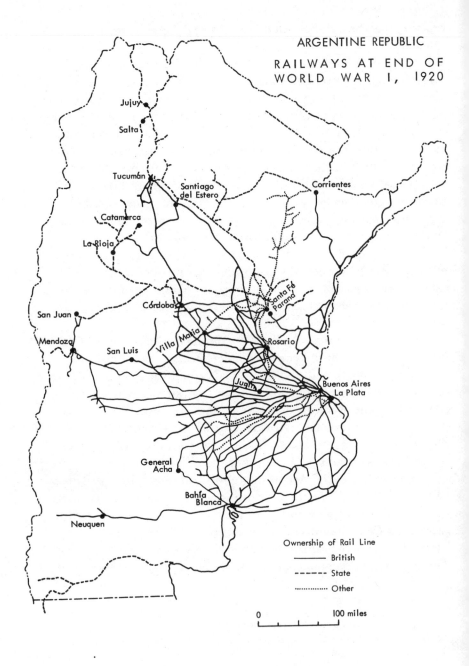

ARGENTINE REPUBLIC

RAILWAYS AT END OF
WORLD WAR 1, 1920

Jujuy

Salta

Tucumán

Santiago
del Estero

Corrientes

Catamarca

La Rioja

San Juan

Córdoba

Santa Fé
Paraná

Mendoza

Villa Maria

Rosario

San Luis

Junin

Buenos Aires
La Plata

General
Acha

Bahía
Blanca

Neuquen

Ownership of Rail Line

——————— British

- - - - - - State

· · · · · · · · · Other

0   100 miles

titude of the chief executive. "They accuse him of carrying out a prolabor policy hostile to capital; they do not see that . . . this is the wisest course in view of the phenomena which are now transforming the social and political structure of the world."[16] Despite their efforts the railways could not thwart Yrigoyen, who defeated candidates "generously supported by grants of railways and ship owners."[17]

The Yrigoyen administration planted the seeds of popular nationalism. Yrigoyen never followed a systematic attack upon the British, nor did he carry on a sustained anti-British policy. In fact, just before leaving office in 1922 he gave to the railways a rate increase of the amount they desired. When compared to the steady efforts of his neighbor, José Batlle y Ordóñez of Uruguay, Yrigoyen's nationalism seems minimal. Batlle effectively campaigned against foreign capital in his country and began a slow process of nationalizing the Uruguayan railway network as part of his economic nationalism.[18] In part, the difference between Batlle and Yrigoyen may have resulted from the fact that Batlle came from an aristocratic background and had effective control of the nation as president. Batlle's peaceful revolution in Uruguay came from the top down with little opposition. Yrigoyen, on the other hand, represented the first person of his class—comprising professional men, intellectuals, merchants, industrialists, engineers, and small farmers—to become president of Argentina. As a leader of a political machine, he failed to work a revolution from within. He won a narrow election victory. If Lisandro de la Torre, who ran for president as head of the Progressive Democrats of Santa Fe, had not given Yrigoyen his electoral votes, the latter would not have put an end to Conservative rule. Yrigoyen, the self-proclaimed leader of the workingman, had to share the government with the Conservatives. The Conservatives continued to hold the balance of power in the Senate and blocked Yrigoyen's legislation. As for the

[16] Enclosure in Tower to Balfour, April 4, 1919, PRO, FO 371/3504.
[17] Ibid.
[18] Robert J. Alexander, *Prophets of the Revolution*, p. 20. See also Jorge Batlle (ed.), *Batlle, su obra y su vida*; Simon G. Hanson, *Utopia in Uruguay*; and Milton I. Vanger, *Batlle y Ordóñez of Uruguay*.

working class, Yrigoyen and the Radicals followed a pragmatic program which paid token interest to the workers' desires and used popular nationalism rather than sincere reform as a political tool.[19]

The heterogeneous nature of the Radical party itself further qualified Yrigoyen's nationalism. Many new Argentines, whose families had not played important roles in Argentina's political history, joined the Radical party. In economic background and class they differed very little from the Conservatives.[20] While Yrigoyen ran the government in an autocratic *caudillo*-like manner, the everyday politician proved as corrupt as his Conservative predecessor. At the same time, the party included honest men of aristocratic background, such as Marcelo T. Alvear and Honario Pueyrredón. Many of these men held influential positions in the Radical administration. They also professed pro-British sympathies. Pueyrredón, a long-time Anglophile, had little previous political experience before becoming Yrigoyen's minister of foreign affairs.[21] On several occasions he countered the xenophobia of his chief executive by expressing his friendship for the British. Once, while in England on an official visit in December, 1920, he told representatives of the British press that he regarded England as his own country, next to Argentina.[22] Other high-ranking officials in the Yrigoyen government also identified their interests with those of Britain. They frequently reassured British colleagues that Yrigoyen's bark was worse than his bite. Many Radicals bound their interest with those of British enterprises, in spite of the president's inimical position. Such pro-British expressions obviously had a restraining effect upon the economic nationalism propounded by Yrigoyen.

[19] Snow, *Argentine Radicalism*, p. 31; Rennie, *Argentine Republic*, p. 214. For the most part, the Argentine press was friendly to the British railways. With the exception of *La Época*, most were fair in treating the central issues, such as strikes, rate increases, and service.

[20] Merkx, "Political and Economic Change," pp. 112, 135-136; Peter H. Smith, "Los radicales argentinos y la defensa de los intereses ganaderos 1916-1930," *Desarrollo Económico* 7, no. 25 (April-June 1967): 795-829; Tomás Robert Fillol, *Social Factors in Economic Development*, pp. 34-37.

[21] Tower to Balfour, April 19, 1919, PRO, FO 371/3504.

[22] *South American Journal*, December 25, 1920, p. 507.

A further explanation for the comparative ineffectiveness of
Yrigoyen's nationalism lies in the fact that he failed to control his
handpicked successor, Marcelo T. Alvear. Alvear not only proved
unmanageable but also opposed in general Yrigoyen's economic
nationalism. He also refused to accept Yrigoyen's personal control
of the Radical party. He represented the right wing of the Radical
party. Like many well-to-do and professional men in the party,
Alvear had a much more cosmopolitan outlook than the *criollo*
Yrigoyen element. He also favored the cattle and agricultural interests of the nation. Because of this the British welcomed Alvear's
election. They anticipated a brighter future. Yrigoyen had already
allowed their rate increases to go into effect. Now a known friend
became his successor. Thus the *South American Journal* heralded
Alvear's election by stating that he would probably "take a far
broader view of things than Señor Yrigoyen, and his attitude
towards the railways should be more sympathetic than they have
been accustomed to during recent years."[23]

Though not a xenophobe, Alvear never became a British flat-
terer. He often criticized the British and at times lost patience with
British railway interests. Shortly after assuming office, he learned
that a British loan arranged under the new Trade Facilities Act included a condition that, "if the construction of railways is concerned, lines must not be laid in a zone in which they could compete with established British companies." Alvear considered the
clause an effrontery."We are not a British Colony!" he emphasized
and he threatened to drop negotiations for the loan. He acted
quickly by striking from a proposed bill to expand the state railway
system a clause that had specifically authorized a loan under the
Trade Facilities Act. He replaced the clause with an authorization
to seek foreign loans in general.[24] Red-faced British officials acted
promptly to change the offensive provision, of which they had not
known. Apparently the Department of Overseas Trade had acted

[23] Ibid., April 22, 1922, p. 316.
[24] Alston to Tyrell, September 4, 1923; telegram from Alston to FO. September 18,
1923, PRO, FO 371/8419. Also see Alston, "Argentine Republic: Annual Report, 1924,"
January 25, 1925, PRO, FO 371/10604.

without consulting the Foreign Office. Actually, the proposed state lines would not have had an adverse effect upon the British-owned railways, and some of the new construction would have benefited the Great Southern. Alvear did not raise these issues. Rather, he wanted the British to realize that foreigners could not dictate economic policies to him.

Broadly speaking, the attack on foreign capital did not go much beyond Alvear's rebuke of the British. The new Argentine elite did not manifest the xenophobia of the Yrigoyen regime. Alvear encouraged prosperity between 1922 and 1928 by maintaining the status quo. He encouraged cooperation with the British railway companies. Yrigoyen had believed that Argentina had a mission in the world, and he saw the country as the leader of all America. He wanted to rid the nation of all "foreign" elements. In contrast, Alvear considered himself a realist and accepted the fact that Argentina depended upon Europe. According to him, "Like it or not we are dependent upon England, we perpetuate France, we are able to trade with the United States, and it is not worth the consequences to change the prosperity of the country through lyrical words . . . that do not have any juridical effect, and that would only earn us the bad will of the countries that have been victorious in a tremendous war."[25]

Obviously, Alvear did not speak for all Argentines on the subject, but he did reflect the attitude of the elite. Argentina faced difficult commercial years in the 1920's. The government wanted to resuscitate the pastoral-agricultural industries. Attempts to open markets in the United States for agricultural and pastoral produce failed. Fear of hoof-and-mouth disease and a policy of protectionism led the United States to restrict the importation of Argentine beef. Competition with U.S. farmers led to limitations upon the importation of Argentine grains, flaxseed, and corn. Alvear realized the dilemma. He also knew, by mid-term, that he faced trade difficulties with Britain. Sir Malcolm Robertson announced in Buenos Aires in 1926 his government's intentions to apply "Buy from those who buy from us" in future dealings with

[25] Félix Luna, *Alvear*, p. 54.

the Argentine Republic.[26] By necessity Alvear followed a cautious trade policy.

Attacks upon foreign capital came from opposition sectors. The Socialists continued to follow the antiforeign line begun by Justo in the 1890's. They still represented an urban-based middle class. Basically their charge remained that the foreign-owned utilities "did not have any other object than the conquest of the dividend, and their own growth, and . . . those that exploit the great national public services almost constitute a state within a state."[27] In spite of their attacks and those of other nationalists, the administration continued to encourage foreign capital and foreign companies to participate in Argentine undertakings. Perhaps Woodbine Parish, an Anglo-Argentine descendant of the first British representative to Buenos Aires, best described the attitude of most Argentine leaders between 1922 and 1928. "Is it not an axiom that the British-owned railways have been the predominating factor of this country? This has always been acknowledged by the governing bodies, who, while naturally protecting the interests of their people, have recognized that the prosperity of the railways and the country are identical. We must always remember that the railway is a permanent institution, linked in the closest association with the welfare and fortunes of the country where it exists—in other words, we stand or fall together."[28]

The friendly political climate and an improved labor situation helped the British-owned railways recover from the postwar depression. Few railway strikes took place during the decade as wages and the cost of living remained fairly constant. In contrast to the preceding five years, the companies averaged profits of 5 percent per annum between 1921 and 1928. The bigger lines managed to pay stock dividends of 7 to 9 percent after 1924, but their recov-

[26] *Review of the River Plate*, November 5, 1926, p. 21; November 26, 1926, p. 7; and *Buenos Aires Standard*, November 19, 1926. I am indebted to Mr. Dana Sweet for much of the information in the paragraph. For a recent study of Alvear's and Yrigoyen's trade policies published after this chapter had been written, see Carl Solberg, "The Tariff and Politics in Argentina, 1916-1930," *Hispanic American Historical Review* 53, no. 2 (May 1973): 260-284.

[27] Diputados, *Daily Issue*, July 23, 1924, p. 1007.

[28] *Railway Gazette*, November 22, 1926, p. 4.

ery did not lead to a new boom. The day of large British investments in Argentina had ended. Britain had lost its favorable trading
position with the United States. Foreign investors, in general, now
put their capital to work in industrial and manufacturing ventures,
not public services.[29] The companies did complete feeder routes to
the trunk lines in some parts of the country, but no major construction took place. The companies followed a policy of modest
operation. Most management representatives felt optimistic about
railway development in Argentina as the freight-carrying trade and
passenger service of the British-owned railways increased steadily
during the mid-1920's.

Management also had reason to doubt the railways' progress.
Operating costs rose sharply after 1919. Furthermore, a series of
droughts and a constant decline in grain production in the early
1920's threatened the companies with smaller margins of profits.
"It is sad," reported Viscount St. Davids, "to go up the main line
of the 'Pacific' where you travel over most beautiful soil—there is
no better soil in the world—and to pass stations that in my
recollection were grain stations for us, with piles of grain standing
like haystacks along the line, and to see that now there is
nothing."[30] It was sad not only in a romantic sense, but in a commercial sense as well, since railway men estimated that for every
pound sterling they received for carrying grain to a port they received another pound sterling in return freight on articles needed
to sustain the grain producers. It took few men to raise cattle, and
the men who tended the *estancias* had few wants and little capital,
thus reducing the amount of important return trade.

To satisfy mutual needs, the British-owned railways and the
Argentine government cooperated on a broad scale during the
mid-1920's. The era of large foreign investment in the railways had
ended.[31] Out of necessity the national government began a program of extending the state-owned railway system. This expansion
did not result from any particular ideological position. The Alvear

[29] Guido Di Tella and Manuel Zymelman, *Las etapas del desarrollo económico argentino*, p. 358.
[30] *The Financier*, October 25, 1921.
[31] Di Tella and Zymelman, *Etapas del desarrollo*, p. 370.

Radicals supported neither socialism nor xenophobia. They tried to meet the need for adequate transportation for the pastoral-agricultural groups. Yrigoyen embarked on the expansion program of the state lines without authority from Congress and with no provisions for financing their construction. Alvear continued his predecessor's program in order to help cattle interests. Until a congressional investigating committee discovered a major scandal in 1925, in connection with running the state lines, expansion went smoothly. Alvear ended the expansion program at the time of the scandal, which led to the resignation of several administrators, including the minister of public works, a former Yrigoyen man. He then began his own program of expanding the state-owned railway system.

Though they no longer had visions of expanding their lines, the British railways did cooperate with the national government in encouraging agricultural development. Agriculture had not disappeared. However, landowners continued to turn over large amounts of land to cattle production. In an effort to reverse this trend, the British-owned railways undertook two basic programs. They aimed the first at increasing the production of existing grain areas. The second program involved attempts to populate areas that could become major grain-producing sections. Struck by the relatively primitive farming methods employed along rail lines, railway managers finally instituted educational and agricultural extension services after years of neglect. They hoped to encourage farmers to use modern farming techniques and better seeds. Several large British lines even provided free seed-sorting services for farmers and taught farmers the importance of using clean graded seed. The companies also established experimental farms of their own. There they tried to develop proper soil cultivation methods and to create seeds genetically suited to their zones. These programs proved heartening but were instituted too late; the returns were small. The international economic crisis that began in 1929 aborted these belated efforts.[32]

[32] Based on information found in Tornquist, *Business Conditions in Argentina*, and in British economic periodicals and newspapers. Also see Buenos Ayres Western Railway Company, *Report of the Directors*.

The second program undertaken by the railways involved establishing a land-colonization consortium. Coordinated with the
national government, the consortium attempted to populate arable
sections of the nation with small farmers. Unfortunately, this program did not get a chance to prove itself. Although individual railways had encouraged immigration to Argentina and colonization
schemes since 1921, the consortium did not appear until 1927. The
depression soon made it ineffective. If the new consortium had
limited success in achieving its primary goal of bringing large areas
of Argentina under cultivation, it did have the immediate effect of
ameliorating relations between the British-owned railways and the
Argentine public. As one British diplomat observed, with noted
relief, "The colonization scheme has met with a unanimously
favorable reception in the press."[33] Two former Argentine ministers, Dr. Manuel A. Montes de Oca and José María Ramos Mexía,
supported the creation of the consortium. Argentine immigration
authorities pledged their support. "On the other hand, the British
railway companies stand to gain in popular esteem by their readiness to invest considerable capital in a scheme for increasing the
country's wealth and for fostering the increase of population,
which is one of the country's great needs."[34]

The tense railway situation of the immediate postwar years no
longer existed when Yrigoyen returned to office in 1928. To all intents and purposes, the railways and the government had resolved
their major differences. A great deal of the public hostility toward
the railways had subsided as well. In keeping with the peaceful climate of opinion, Yrigoyen made no effort to present himself as a
frenetic, anti-British nationalist. At times he even appeared to be
an Anglophile.

Several factors explain the change in Yrigoyen's behavior

[33] Robertson to Chamberlain, March 23, 1927, PRO, FO 371/11960. See also Robertson
to Chamberlain, April 2, 1927, PRO, FO 371/11960, for a list of members of the board of
consortium. For a U.S. point of view see Messersmith to SecState, February 23, 1929, DS,
NA, RG 59, 835.55/72. Messersmith reported that, "in spite . . . of the interest which has
been generally shown in the scheme and of the encouragement which it received, no
definite action appears to have been taken although such colonization projects would undoubtedly be eventually to the great advantage of the railways."

[34] Robertson to Chamberlain, March 23, 1927, PRO, FO 371/11960.

toward the British-owned railways. Corrupt and inefficient running of the large state lines had placed them in acute financial difficulties. The public knew the situation well and did not favor more state construction. Upon his return to office, Yrigoyen could not arouse widespread public support of the issue of expanding the state-owned railways. At the same time, he reacted to another threat to the British-owned railways. Rumors circulating through Buenos Aires in early 1929 that U.S. interests considered purchasing the British railway companies. U.S. manufacturers had been the largest suppliers of railway equipment to the state-owned railways since the turn of the century, but they had never gained the lucrative business of supplying the British-owned railways due to the latter's exclusive use of British goods. Now it seemed that businesses in the United States had their eye on a broader market, even if it meant buying out their British competitors in order to establish their economic hegemony in Argentina.[35]

As it turned out, no such plot existed. No U.S. investors planned to buy the British-owned railways of Argentina. The rumors seem to have originated in London, where the governing boards of the railways wanted to take measures to prevent any possible attempts to buy such control. Within three months after the rumors gained wide circulation, the major British-owned railways amended their statutes to limit the ownership of voting stock in their companies to British and Argentine citizens.[36] In taking this measure the British averted any threat of purchase by North Americans.

---

[35] White to SecState, and enclosures, May 13, 1929, DS, NA, RG 59, 835.77/100. Millington-Drake, "Argentine Republic: Annual Report, 1929," May 24, 1930, pp. 3-4, 8-10, PRO, FO 371/14196. P. M. Roberts, "British War Debt to the United States," January 6, 1933, PRO, FO 371/16664, suggests that certain U.S. groups advocated the acquisition of British investments in Argentina as payment of the British war debt.

[36] State Department Division of Latin American Affairs, "Report on British Railway Companies," October 12, 1928, DS, NA, RG 59, 835.77/180, which concludes: ". . . among the well informed Americans in the Argentine it is now generally accepted that there was no attempt by American capital to acquire holdings in the Buenos Ayres and Pacific Company. The American banking institutions in the Argentine were unusually interested in the press reports when they first appeared and asked their home offices to keep in touch with the situation. These institutions in the United States, which were in a position to know fairly well what was going on in New York, replied that no efforts to secure control were known

The British action received wide applause in Argentina, where widespread anti-United States propaganda had preceded the companies' decision. Overwhelming opposition to the transfer of the railways from British to North American ownership appeared in the nation's press. Articles in the Spanish and English presses of Argentina criticized U.S. capitalists as being inefficient, inexperienced, and selfish as compared with the British. Once again, Argentines spoke of their traditional ties with England and cited beneficial aspects of the century-old Anglo-Argentine economic relationship. Fear of the United States provided a common cause for both Britons and Argentines. As pointed out by *La Prensa*, although Argentines often mistrusted the British capitalists, they did feel that the British had always respected Argentine institutions. The record of U.S. capitalists in the Caribbean led the Argentine public to react differently, for "when North American capital arrives, it is said, with distrust, that the country is being invaded."[37]

President Yrigoyen joined the Argentine press in protesting the "invasion" of Argentina by North American capitalists, and he expressed alarm that ruthless Yankee businessmen might force the British out of Argentina. The rapidly increasing hold that U.S. financial and industrial interests had over South America concerned him. Accordingly, he promised to maintain the independence of Argentina as far as he could. One of his aides assured the British-owned railways that Yrigoyen would offer the companies any help he could to keep them in British hands.[38] In fact,

of in that market. As inquiries in London led to the same result it now appears that the opinion already set forth in this report may now be accepted as a fact, that the fable of the attempt of American interests to buy into the British railways in the Argentine was concocted by the powerful interests in London in the governing boards of these railways for the purpose of doing what they could to prevent possible attempts of purchase of such control."

[37] Ibid. See also Buenos Ayres and Pacific Railway Company, Minute Book of General Meetings, no. 1, May 17, 1929, pp. 169-170. See enclosures in White to SecState, May 13, 1929, DS, NA, RG 59, 835.77/170, for details; Atherton to SecState, June 20, 1929, DS, NA, RG 59, 835.77/171; Messersmith to SecState, August 22, 1929, DS, NA, RG 59, 835.77/178; Robertson to Chamberlain, June 4, 1929, PRO, FO 371/13460.

[38] Robertson to Craigie, May 10, 1929, and telegram, Robertson to FO, May 11, 1929, PRO, FO 371/13460.

Yrigoyen personally told one British railway director that he would protect their interests:

For thirty years before my former Presidency I had struggled to remedy the injustices from which the working class of this rich country suffered, and when at last I came into office it was my duty to keep my promises and satisfy the hopes and aspirations of those who trusted me. You know that wages were low and working conditions were bad, and that they were remedied during my first Presidency. You also know, however, that just before leaving office I gave the increase in tariffs which have continued untouched for six years and have brought you to your present prosperous situation.[39]

This, he stated, demonstrated his support of the British enterprises. In most other countries. Yrigoyen added, "there would have been such an outcry from industry and commerce as would have forced a new Government to reduce them." Yrigoyen appreciated the advantages which the British-owned railways had conferred upon Argentina. In stark contrast to the antiforeign stand he took before 1922, he now went so far as to say that Argentina owed everything to the British-owned railways. Without neglecting labor, he would protect the British railway investment because "that capital is sacred."

Yrigoyen promised to do all that he could to maintain the prosperity of the British-owned railways. But he felt that that prosperity placed obligations upon the British: ". . . obligations to march with the development of the country, to open up distant regions, to bring them into rail communication with the coast. Go north, south, east and west with your lines. Do not take the State Railways into account; their interests will not be allowed to conflict with your expansion."[40] In conclusion, the Argentine president noted: "Offers of capital, of vast sums, have been showered on me, but I see no necessity of accepting them from new quarters. We have worked with the English and with English capital for fifty years. We know them and what they are. I see no need of exchanging old friends for new."[41]

As a result of Yrigoyen's change of heart concerning British capital, Sir Malcolm Robertson, British ambassador to Argentina,

[39] Enclosure, Robertson to Craigie, March 14, 1929, PRO, FO 371/13460.
[40] Ibid.   [41] Ibid.

cabled his superiors in mid-May, 1929: "President confirmed in a surprisingly emphatic manner all that Molinari told me on the subject of possible sale of the British railways to American interests. 'I know I am speaking in the name of my country as well as in my own when I say we have confidence in British capital and British railways which we know. I do not want to see the railways sold to anyone whoever they may be. I tell you with all my soul. The matter rests, however, with your people.' "[42]

On the eve of his downfall, Yrigoyen held an attitude toward British capitalists much like that of his oligarchical predecessors. The Radicals had done little to alter the economic life of Argentina. Cattlemen and farmers still prevailed, and Alvear had encouraged their recovery. Alvear's government assisted supportive industries to the pastoral-agricultural sector. Argentina did not control its own economic destiny, as Yrigoyen had once promised it would. Still popular with the masses when he came to office in 1928, Yrigoyen was a senile old man by 1929, too sick to administer the nation at a time when vigorous action was most needed.

The opening statement of Mr. E. Millington-Drake's annual report on the Argentine Republic for 1929 contains a grain of truth when it reads: " 'Argentina can claim Dominion status.' This was said by the Argentine Minister for Foreign Affairs, privately and only half in jest, meaning that Argentina had always offered such a good field for British enterprise and capital that she was to some extent an economic dependency of Great Britain, and could, therefore, claim the same preferential treatment as the Dominions."[43] The minister may have made the comment in jest, but Argentines began to feel pressures from Britain in favor of giving preference to members of the British Commonwealth. Such a policy would have had disastrous results in Argentina, a fact well appreciated by Argentine public authorities. Thus, the Yrigoyen government adjusted its previous nationalism. It began to buy

[42] Robertson to FO, May 16, 1929, PRO, FO 371/13460; Kreek to SecState, July 29, 1929, DS, NA, RG 59, 834.77/52.
[43] Millington-Drake to Henderson, May 24, 1930, PRO, FO 371/14196. See also Solberg, "Tariff and Politics in Argentina."

more from the British, who bought a greater quantity of Argentine produce than anybody else. In order to disarm critics in Britain, Yrigoyen increasingly followed a program geared to maintain the existing Anglo-Argentine economic entente. Through the carefully planned visit of Lord D'Abernon's trade mission to Buenos Aires in 1929, the British made Yrigoyen aware of the minimum requirements they would impose to keep the British market open to Argentine meats and cereals. The agreement reached between the D'Abernon mission and Yrigoyen established, among other things, a reciprocal credit system by which administrators of the state-owned railways could arrange to buy equipment from British manufacturers without calling for open bids on the contracts as stipulated by law. The agreement accorded a near monopoly to British manufacturers of railway equipment, even though they charged admittedly higher prices than Belgian, U.S., and German competitors.

In the final analysis, the arrangement reached between Yrigoyen and D'Abernon fit into the traditional British economic philosophy toward Argentina. As so clearly voiced by Ambassador Sir Malcolm Robertson shortly before leaving Argentina in 1929: "My gospel out here has been: 'give the British workman work, and he will have money with which to buy more of your meat.' 'Buy from us that we may buy from you.' This has caught on in the widest circles and with the Government, for we are buying something in the neighborhood of £ 76,000,000 of produce a year. . . . Without saying so in as many words, which would be tactless, what I really mean is that Argentina must be regarded as an essential part of the British empire. We cannot get on without her, nor she without us."[44]

[44] Robertson to Henderson, June 17, 1929, PRO, FO 371/13460.

7. The Concordancia's New Direction

Modern Argentine historians treat the 1930's opprobriously as the Conservative Restoration; they depict the 1930's as an epoch of *vendepatria*, a decade of shame. They charge the Argentine government with having reverted to the lies and outrages of the previous "liberal" governments of the pre-1916 oligarchs, whose dealings with the British had made Argentina little more than an economic colony of Britain.[1] A number of popular opposition politicians leveled the same charge against the government. Notably, members of the Socialist, Progressive Democrat, and Radical parties attacked the conservatives governing between 1930 and 1943. Since their parties were

[1] See for example Ezequiel Martínez Estrada, *Radiografía de la pampa*, I, 62, first published in 1933, for a moderate view: "Our railways are not a means for producing wealth [for Argentina] but are the equivalent, in steel, of pounds sterling that must produce more pounds sterling. These subsidiary lines are set in motion from London, where they begin, and die. It is static capital, inflexible, which does not follow the curves of our national economy but of a vast international economy."

not in power, they enjoyed the degree of political irresponsibility afforded to politicians out of office. They, like the historians, could assume hypercritical attitudes toward the elite who ran the nation. In so doing, they gave impetus to a popular nationalism that had been increasing since the turn of the century. Their arguments did not change the political situation of the 1930's, although their arguments created a solid basis for the popular nationalism later used by Perón when he convinced large numbers of Argentines that the entire system was corrupted under the oligarchs. Perhaps unintentionally, many middle-class politicians and intellectuals convinced themselves and the public that the only salvation to Argentina's many ills lay in turning to *criollo* nationalism.

A close look at the decade reveals that there is no simple interpretation of Argentina's depression. The government of the Conservatives held basically pro-British sentiments. At the same time that it jealously guarded certain Argentine economic interests, namely, cattle producers, the government assisted a rising industrial group. The leaders of the nation attempted to follow an economic policy which fit into a narrow concept of a new Argentina. As a result, Argentina and Britain had several confrontations. Neither government chose to maintain the status quo. Friction resulted because leaders in both countries sought change. Internal and external reforms in Britain and Argentina upset the balance of the traditional economic relationship between the two nations.

Perhaps no other Americans have pitied themselves during the depression as much as the Argentines. Frustrated by the international economic crisis that seemed to leave Argentina an economic appendage of a dying British economic empire, and disillusioned by the collapse of middle-class democracy caused by irresponsible Radicals under Yrigoyen, large numbers of Argentines began to study the nation's past. They wanted to know what went wrong. Most notable, a new school of Argentine revisionist historians tried to explain Argentina's failure to achieve its destiny by attacking the precepts of traditional liberal historians. Liberal historians of the second half of the nineteenth century had written Argentine history from an anti-Rosas point of view. They began a tradition of measuring progress along European lines and saw the work of Rosas and his interior supporters as backward. Revisionists believed that the liberal historians had purposefully written inaccurate history. A complex movement, involving writers from both the right and the left, revisionism led to a thorough reevaluation of Argentina's past, including a revision of the Rosas epoch and the subsequent liberal era. Biased in their view, the revisionists tried to prove that previous governments had failed to make Argentina a strong and independent nation. They wrote emotional indictments of the existing Anglo-Argentine economic relationship, which they considered the basic cause of the Argentine dilemma. Their studies reflect the climate of opinion of a people who believed that foreigners had cheated them out of their rightful destiny. They did not consider Argentina a great nation, though they thought that it deserved to be one. In searching for a scapegoat, these scholars blamed foreign economic preeminence, especially Britain's, for Argentina's economic failure. As a corollary, they judged Britain's Argentine lackeys, the conservative oligarchs, guilty of perverting the Argentine dream.[2]

The shock of the economic depression produced a profound psychological reaction in Argentina. Its impact touched more than the intelligentsia and politicians. Workers, especially the growing urban labor class, discovered that political and economic reforms promised by middle-class politicians had gained them nothing. The workers' lot had not improved. They clearly saw the apathy of the Argentine middle class to the workers' plight. The labor movement caused few changes during the 1930's, and labor groups became increasingly disenchanted with democratic political solutions to their economic problems. Ignored during the 1930's, and

[2] For leading examples of two revisionist schools see Julio and Rodolfo Irazusta, *La Argentina y el imperialismo británico*, and Raúl Scalabrini Ortiz, *Política británica en el Río de la Plata*. For additional information concerning Argentine revisionists see Joseph R. Barager, "The Historiography of the Río de la Plata Area," *Hispanic American Historical Review* 39, no. 4 (November 1959): 588-642; Edberto Oscar Acevedo, "Situación actual de la historia argentina," *Estudios Americanos* 60, no. 43 (May 1955): 353-396; Samuel L. Baily, "Argentina,Twentieth Century,"in *Latin America: A Guide to the Historical Literature*, ed. Charles C. Griffen and J. Benedict Warren, pp. 556-570. For a recent study of Raúl Scalabrini Ortiz, published after this chapter had been written, see Mark Falcoff, "Raúl Scalabrini Ortiz: The Making of an Argentine Nationalist," *Hispanic American Historical Review* 52, no. 1 (February 1972): 74-101.

hardly a formidable political force, the workers' political education had just begun. The workers' attitudes became tinged with anti-foreign nationalism of the Rosas type.[3] This development provided Perón an inroad into the labor camp.

An unsettled atmosphere accompanied General Agustín P. Justo's assumption of the presidency. Justo, elected in November, 1931, assumed office a little more than a year after the popular revolution of September 6, 1930, swept Hipólito Yrigoyen and the Radical party from office. A military *caudillo*, Justo nonetheless shared part of the management of the government with civilians. In this sense he differed from his immediate predecessor, General José F. Uriburu. Uriburu had called for establishment of a corporate elite which would have kept the civilian population in its place. Justo, a former antipersonalist Radical, had a broader approach to governing. He had dealt with civilian governments before; under Alvear he served as minister of war. In that capacity he built up a substantial military following. He also won civilian support for his honest handling of the position. By 1932 he had become a nonparty man. Indeed, he surprised many of his supporters by including a dissident Socialist and only one Conservative in his cabinet. In his speeches he often appealed for the support of minorities and promised to hear them on all matters. His rule between 1932 and 1938 was half democratic. Though he acted at times as a nominal dictator and used fraud to engineer victories for his coalition, his administration permitted opponents ample opportunity to express their discontent in the halls of Congress and in the press.[4]

The Concordancia led by Justo, which comprised some anti-personalist Radicals, Conservatives (now known as National Democrats), and Independent Socialists, appeared at times to be the

---

[3] See Samuel L. Baily, *Labor, Nationalism, and Politics in Argentina*, pp. 51-70.

[4] This brief account of Justo's rise to power and his political ideas is drawn from accounts in Arthur P. Whitaker, *The United States and Argentina*, pp. 64-65; Ysabel F. Rennie, *The Argentine Republic*, pp. 226-228; José Luis Romero, *A History of Argentine Political Thought*, trans. Thomas F. McGann, pp. 227-238; Lisandro de la Torre, *Las dos campañas presidenciales, 1916-1931*; Carlos Ibarguren, *La historia que he vivido*; Federico Pinedo, *En tiempos de la república*, vol. 1. See also Henderson to Eden, January 27, 1937, "Report on Leading Personalities in Argentina," PRO, FO 371/20598.

party of cattle raisers, large landowners, and those benefiting from Argentina's economic relationship with Britain. Justo never served as a British lackey. Nor did he follow a program designed to suit all the needs of the Anglo-Argentine financial community. Rather, he followed an independent plan for domestic economic recovery aimed at diversification. In part Justo based his program upon ideas expressed by the Argentine economist Alejandro Bunge. During the previous decades Bunge had urged measures to diversify the nation's economy to end foreign domination.[5] Now some of his students had a chance to experiment with his theories.

In many ways Bunge represents a forefather of modern Argentine industrialization. Since 1918 he had strongly recommended the development of an industrial sector under Argentine control through government intervention. He opposed the laissez faire doctrine of the oligarchs. By developing a diversified economic base, he hoped to break away from the foreign-dominated agrarian economy. If Bunge did not fully work out a theory of change, he at least laid the groundwork for state-directed economic measures that the Justo administration used. He also suggested means by which a new Argentina could be created through centralized federal planning of all stages of Argentine economic activity. Though the Concordancia did not follow Bunge's concept of a diversified economy in detail, and the cattle industry remained the predominant economic sector, the Concordancia did shift from the laissez faire position of previous Conservative governments.

The restored conservatives could not force Justo to revert to the earlier economic liberalism. Military nationalists who supported the regime refused to do so. Also, the Concordancia reacted to a growing industrial group, which demanded protection. Both politicians and military men considered new industries an important part of the new Argentina they wanted to create. Justo tended to defend the basic interests of Argentine industry. Although he may not have given the industrialists the type of support they desired, he did protect them on occasion.[6]

[5] Alejandro Bunge, *La economía argentina*.
[6] For a sympathetic treatment of Justo see Robert A. Potash, *The Army and Politics in*

Shortly after assuming office in February, 1932, the Justo administration faced the necessity of redefining Argentina's economic relationship with Britain. At the Ottawa Conference of 1932, the British dispensed with the remaining free-trade system and adopted a protectionist policy which stated simply, "Buy from those who buy from us." Britain now favored the British Commonwealth nations over other nations in trade commitments. As a result of the Ottawa Agreement, relations between Argentina and Britain became strained. Since cereals, grains, and meat accounted for about 96 percent of their export trade, Argentines needed to preserve foreign markets for livestock and agricultural products. Most important, Britain bought over 90 percent of the chilled beef exported from Argentina.[7] Argentine cattle producers feared losing a major outlet for their meat export. Many Britons feared that the special position they had always enjoyed in Argentina would disappear. Others believed that the United States would reign in Britain's place, thus endangering Britain's vast stake in Argentina.[8]

By late 1932 the British protectionist policy had already dealt Argentina a severe blow. The British considered more restrictive measures regarding meat and wheat. Britons suffered as well. Argentine restrictions on remittance payments and unfavorable ex-

---

Argentina, 1928-1945, pp. 79-103. Also see Arthur P. Whitaker, *Nationalism in Latin America*, pp. 49-50.

[7] See table on inside of the back cover of Ernesto Tornquist, *Business Conditions in Argentina* (1933); also see Diputados, *Diario*, July 19, 1933, II, 349. Argentina's situation is best summed up in the following excerpt from the Department of Overseas Trade's publication, *Economic Conditions in the Argentine Republic*, published in 1933. According to its editor, Stanley G. Irving, "the war period not only created an extraordinary demand for the country's natural products, but also led to the development of a number of local manufacturing industries, and where formerly the only goods which the country made for itself on a considerable scale were such articles as boots and shoes and furniture, by the time the war ended factories of all kinds had sprung up and a large part of the people's needs for manufactured goods were being supplied locally.

"All her own manufactures being consumed in the country, the only means by which Argentina can purchase goods from abroad is by exporting her surplus grain and meat. It is therefore not to be wondered at that the increasing difficulty of finding markets for these products has created a general atmosphere of pessimism" (Great Britain, Board of Trade, p. 21). Hereafter cited as Overseas Trade, *Economic Conditions*.

[8] "White Paper," May 3, 1933, PRO, FO 371/16532.

change rates brought complaints from British investors. Especially upset were the widows, retired couples, and small investors who had placed much of their savings in Argentine rails. As a result of the Argentine policy they received no dividends and the value of their stocks fell to ruinous levels. With about 450 million pounds invested in Argentina the British had reason for concern.

In an effort to effect a temporary solution to this situation, an Argentine trade mission, under the direction of Vice-President Julio A. Roca, went to London in January, 1933. At this juncture the Concordancia, still dominated by the cattle barons, decided to protect the British meat market at all costs.[9] The British hoped that they could count on Argentine meat and wheat interests to aid the cause of British capital invested in Argentina, especially in the railways.[10] The British were eager to reach accord. The Prince of Wales set the tenor for the meetings during a welcoming banquet in honor of Roca. The prince, who had visited Argentina briefly during the Uriburu dictatorship, referred to himself as an old friend of the republic. He spoke optimistically of Argentina's future. But he told his Argentine guests, in no uncertain terms: ". . . there is a sense in which it would be true to say that the future of Argentina is a question of beef, and the future of Argentine beef depends, maybe entirely, upon the United Kingdom market. While Argentina requires this market I do not forget that there are things that we want from Argentina ourselves. We want security for our investments, and increasing markets for our goods, with facilities for obtaining remittances in payment."[11]

The British wanted assurance that the Argentine authorities would respect and protect their large investments in Argentina before they would promise to keep the British market open to Argentine beef.[12] As in subsequent Anglo-Argentine trade negotia-

---

[9] Peter H. Smith, *Politics and Beef in Argentina*, p. 143. See Roca's prenegotiation address in *The Times*, February 11, 1933, in which he informed the British that his government was prepared to give British capital the guarantees and protection to which it was entitled.

[10] Craigie on Parliamentary Question by Mr. Gritten, November 4, 1932, PRO, FO 371/15797/file 719.

[11] *The Times*, February 11, 1933.

[12] As one British businessman with much experience in Argentina, J. Montegue Eddy,

tions through 1948, British-owned railways formed an integral, though unofficial, part of any settlement of the meat issue. Railways provided an issue that demanded careful consideration by the negotiators, even if no specific provisions of the agreements mentioned them by name.

The British did not make guaranteeing benevolent treatment for British enterprises in Argentina a prerequisite to the London trade discussions of 1933. Before negotiations began, the Argentines indicated their willingness to protect British investments in their nation and offered to write such a provision into the preamble of the agreement. Thus the promise to protect British enterprises became a *fait accompli* before trade discussions began and did not become an important part of the negotiations. Since the British officials had been pressured by members of Parliament and the press to obtain such promises, they entered the trade meetings with optimistic relief. They had already achieved one of their major political goals. There remained the vexing matters of blocked sterling remittances owed to British shareholders and the rate of exchange for the conversion of pesos to pounds.[13]

Discussions between the Roca mission and a British delegation

---

pointed out in a speech to the Argentine Chamber of Commerce in London, "there is no country outside of those in the British Empire where Britain has had such vast financial and commercial interests at stake as in Argentina. . . . In defense of the interests of the investors in these undertakings and of the British manufacturers who supply them it is our bounden duty to point out to those in authority how great is the stake that Great Britain has in Argentina, a stake which cannot be ignored when considering any scheme for preferences . . ." (*South American Journal*, January 30, 1932, p. 140). The British aims are clearly spelled out in minutes to the negotiations found in PRO, FO 371/16532/file 48.

[13] Kelly in response to Parliamentary Question by Sir Bertram Falle, March 2, 1933, PRO, FO 371/16541. At no time preceding or during the Roca-Runciman negotiations did the British-owned railway companies petition the British government to include their condition in the trade agreement. At the time they still believed that they could solve their own dilemma by private negotiation and did not ask for help from the British government. Only the persistent duke of Atholl, director of the nearly bankrupt Anglo-Argentine Tramway Company, was in favor of government intervention. Atholl wanted a clause in the trade agreement that would specifically mention the Anglo-Argentine and promise assistance to that floundering corporation. Needless to say, government officials politely but firmly refused to consider Atholl's request, and the subject was not dealt with during the trade discussions.

headed by Walter Runciman, chairman of the British Board of Trade, finally ended in May, 1933. The joint commission proposed a three-year Anglo-Argentine trade agreement. As had been clear from the outset, Roca had had one goal in mind, preservation of the British market for chilled beef. In order to achieve his primary objective, he made a number of important concessions to the British. On paper, the treaty signed in May, known as the Roca-Runciman Pact, fulfilled the demands set by the British as prerequisites for maintaining the Argentine meat trade.

In return for guaranteeing Argentina a continuing, yet diminishing market for chilled beef, the British received several important privileges. Among these privileges they got the rights to license the *frigoríficos* that prepared the meat and to reserve for the six large British and North American firms operating in Argentina the handling of 85 percent of the beef exported to Britain. Argentina also granted Britain favorable exchange benefits. The British would have the first call on the sterling proceeds of Argentine exports. As desired by British manufacturing interests, the Argentines agreed to reduce the tariffs on British goods to their 1930 levels—a reduction of nearly 50 percent in most cases—and they allowed coal to be imported free of duty.[14]

Two provisions of the trade agreement related to the British-owned railways. By the first, the Argentine government agreed not to reduce passenger and freight rates. The second appeared in

---

[14] *Convention between the Government of the United Kingdom and the Argentine Republic relating to Trade and Commerce, with Protocol, May 1, 1933.* Hereafter cited as *Convention.* A text of the supplementary agreement by which tariff rates were settled is found in British Board of Trade, *Board of Trade Journal,* October 19, 1933, pp. 559-571, and Chamber of Commerce of the United States of America in the Argentine Republic, *Comments on Argentine Trade* 12, no. 8 (March 1933): 21. See also Virgil Salera, *Exchange Control and the Argentine Market,* pp. 77, 91. In a plan announced by Minister of Finance Federico Pinedo on November 28, 1933, an Exchange Rate Commission was set up to control the rate of exchange. Importers needed licenses, and under Pinedo's plan a lucrative margin between the government's buying and selling rates was established. The railways were permitted to buy pesos at the rate of sixteen pesos per pound sterling, as compared to the average rate of seventeen. Even so, the British-owned railways complained that they were being unjustly taxed whenever they converted pesos to pounds to pay remittances to Britain; they pressed for a more favorable rate throughout the 1930's until they received an exchange rate of fifteen pesos per pound in 1936.

a clause in the protocol to the treaty, which made a vague promise to accord British-owned public services and enterprises "such benevolent treatment as may conduce to the further economic development of the country, and to the due and legitimate protection of the interests concerned in their operation."[15] The second provision met with a hostile reaction from Argentine nationalists.

Heated debates preceded the ratification of the treaty by the Argentine Congress. Opponents of the Roca-Runciman Pact reflected a growing antiforeign nationalism that verged on anticolonialism at times. In Congress, conservative defenders of the trade agreement found themselves hard-pressed to defend their antiquated liberal doctrines. Popular politicians tried to upset the elitist Concordancia by expounding xenophobia. The nationalists lost the debate but severely damaged the conservatives' rhetorical defenses. They also popularized anti-British attitudes on a broad scale. In so doing they made the treaty an important political issue.

Most spokesmen for the Concordancia showed an appalling lack of understanding of their nation's economic potential. They defended their own interests by exhorting their colleagues to conserve a traditional concept of Argentina as a pastoral nation. They defended the Roca-Runciman Pact as beneficial to an agrarian nation whose economy depended upon the export of meat and cereals. They showed no concern for the future of domestic industries. Many argued that Argentina would remain solely a producer of foodstuffs. Extremists in their ranks even went so far as to oppose any industrialization. Others argued that it would be inexpedient to attempt to alter the nation's economic policy, based on the economic alliance with Britain. They believed that Argentina and Britain should continue to work together, as in the past, to solve their mutual problems. In this conviction Concordancia spokesmen backed Carlos Saavedra Lamas, minister of foreign affairs, who

---

[15] Article 1, Protocol, *Convention*, p. 10. The full effect of the clause can be seen in the opening sentences: "That the Argentine Government, fully appreciating the benefits rendered by the collaboration of British capital in public utility and other undertakings, whether state, municipal or private, carrying on business in Argentina, and following the traditional policy of friendship, hereby declare their intention to accord to these undertakings, as far as lies within their constitutional sphere of action, such benevolent . . ."

supported the treaty by noting that the government had done what it thought best for the nation by making certain that the British would not suddenly close their market.[16]

The Roca-Runciman Pact represents a key stage in the evolution of Argentine economic nationalism. In many ways the pact proved far more important as an emotional issue than as an economic measure. Antiforeign nationalists found it a natural issue for arousing the public. It provoked a highly charged political atmosphere as politicians and intellectuals attacked British "monopolies" operating in Argentina. After 1933 the Argentine public looked with increasing suspicion upon any effort to aid British firms. Revisionist historians pointed to the treaty as a sign of British avarice. Demogogic politicians easily convinced their followers of the worst about the foreign companies. Socialists and Progressive Democrats used anti-British nationalism as a major weapon in attacking the rule of the Concordancia. Radicals, returning to the political scene in the mid-1930's, further used anti-British nationalism as a political tool. Representatives of Argentine industrial interests also joined the critics of the Roca-Runciman Pact, for they strenuously opposed the tariff reductions it allowed.[17]

Among the most outspoken critics of the trade agreement were Lisandro de la Torre and Nicolás Repetto. They had recently run for the presidency and vice-presidency on a joint ticket against Justo, and their platform had combined populism with antiforeign nationalism. They had pitched their campaign to middle-class and laboring groups that opposed domination by the agrarian elite. In opposing the Roca-Runciman Pact de la Torre and Repetto followed an approach similar to that of their unsuccessful campaign. They wanted to embarrass Justo. For that reason they paid special attention to the clause that granted benevolent treatment to British-owned enterprises, which they interpreted as *vendepatria*. To de la Torre and Repetto these British businesses, especially the

---

[16] Ibid.; and Diputados, *Diario*, July 18, 1933, II, 270-285.

[17] Diputados, *Diario*, July 18, 1933, II, 299. Also see "Amplificación de la nómina de materiales que los ferrocarriles pueden introducir libre de derechos," *Anales de la Unión Industrial Argentina* 49, no. 808 (April 1936): 9-24.

railways, were pernicious agents of British imperialism, concerned only with their own salvation.

During the debates preceding the agreement's ratification in the House of Deputies, the Repetto-led Socialists protested loudest. Using the familiar argument that the railways made excessive profits in Argentina through unjustifiably high rates, Repetto launched a general attack on the government. He warned against British imperialism and defended Argentine pride. It was humiliating, he protested, to promise benevolent treatment to enterprises whose major purpose was to make profits. Repetto combined antiimperialism, Argentine socialism, and protectionism as he opposed the bilateral nature of the treaty. Basically, he argued that only free trade would solve the nation's troubles because governments protected vested interests. Yet, he urged the deputies to consider the importance of protecting Argentine industries. In his words: ". . . national industry is a reality, and we cannot use the politics of an ostrich in dealing with it; closing our eyes and putting our heads in the sand. Don't be alarmed, I am not becoming a protectionist, . . . but I do intend to defend interests that are defensible and respectable."[18]

Repetto's reasoning reflected his political identification with the workers. Industry provided jobs; therefore, its well-being benefited the nation and its laborers. Argentine industry would not survive treaties which imposed restrictions of the sort found in the Roca-Runciman Pact. For that reason Repetto doubted the sincerity of President Justo's promise to support industry. He felt that Justo would not live up to his statements to protect Argentine industry. Mistrust of Justo and the Concordancia provided a common theme for opponents of the treaty. Julio A. Noble, from Santa Fe, reiterated Repetto's words when he argued that the government promised one thing while it delivered another. He pointed out that the government had not tried to find new markets for

---

[18] Diputados, *Diario*, July 18, 1933, II, 285-299. In his *Mi paso por la política*, II, 50, Nicolás Repetto records with pride that his speech against the treaty was motivated by nationalism, especially his denunciation of the benevolent-treatment clause. He was also proud that revisionist historians Rodolfo and Julio Irazusta cited his speech as a leading example of Argentine nationalism in their *La Argentina y el imperialismo británico*, p. 82.

beef, but rather it had solved the problem by turning to Argentina's old trading partner, Britain. "What is this?" the deputy demanded. "We hang on to a 10 percent declining British market when there are others. For us Russia does not exist. We are voting for sentimental reasons."[19]

In the Senate, Lisandro de la Torre spoke for the interests of the small cattle producers and agrarian interests of the interior. His attack upon the Concordancia and the Roca-Runciman Pact has assured de la Torre a place among the most noted Argentine economic nationalists. He knew that he could not alter the vote, but he wanted to be heard. Heard he was. Blue eyes flashing between a shock of white hair and a white beard, using a vocabulary that interchanged erudite phrases with those of the gutter, he tore into the trade agreement. Undoubtedly he played partisan politics.[20] He also spoke for a larger Argentine cause, representing the growing anticolonial bloc. Sharp of tongue, quick of wit, he cut the agreement to shreds, made Roca out as a fool, and showed his contempt for a government that would sell the soul of the nation for a mess of pottage. As for the British-owned railways, he believed that the government had acted unpatriotically in promising benevolent treatment to companies which had always worked against the Argentine producer. He saw no reason to protect enterprises known to have watered stock and guilty of charging exorbitant rates.[21]

Most historians have interpreted the Roca-Runciman Pact as a victory for the British and for the large Argentine cattle interests. These cattlemen, representing only 18 percent of the gross national product, cared little for the industrialization of Argentina. They openly encouraged imports from Britain. They encouraged the agreement in an effort to keep the British market open for beef. As one writer has put it: "If economic independence meant upsetting the relationship with Britain which the beef barons had found so profitable, then the barons were against it. They made

---

[19] Diputados, *Diario*, July 18, 1933, II, 344.
[20] Smith, *Politics and Beef in Argentina*, pp. 148-149.
[21] Senadores, *Diario*, July 27, 1933, I, 568-581, and July 28, 1933, I, 605-611.

their position clear by supporting the Roca-Runciman Treaty . . ."[22]

Nationalists have exaggerated the long-range importance of the Roca-Runciman Pact. Since 1933, nationalists have treated the pact as a blatant example of British perfidy. Few critics have looked at Argentina's economic development since the signing of the first trade agreement. Actually, the agreement did not adversely affect Argentina's overall economic development. In the first place, the treaty was to last only three years. Neither British nor Argentine authorities considered it a permanent arrangement. Second, the pact did not radically alter the gradual industrial growth of the nation. Industrial growth continued during the 1930's as it had since the world war, probably at as rapid a pace as possible under the adverse conditions of the decade. Argentina lacked the infrastructure for large-scale industrialization. But it could support substitute industries which provided goods formerly imported but no longer available because of a lack of foreign exchange. Textiles, along with such new products as pharmaceuticals, developed rapidly. This process continued in spite of the Roca-Runciman Pact.[23]

The agreement had an adverse effect upon the British-owned railways. No immediate benefits resulted from the agreement. Public sentiment grew against assisting the British companies. The British-owned railways found themselves caught in a bind. On the one hand, the Concordancia had promised "benevolent treatment." On the other, Argentine authorities proved reluctant to appease the demands made by the directors of the larger British firms. In fact, the Concordancia soon launched into its own transportation program. The government began to compete with the private railway companies in an effort to lower the cost of transporting agricultural products and cattle. To make matters worse, British government officials did not give the railways' dilemma serious consideration. In their opinion, the railways

[22] Whitaker, *United States and Argentina*, p. 45.
[23] Guido Di Tella and Manuel Zymelman, *Las etapas del desarrollo económico argentino*, pp. 384, 424-425, 433-435, and 455.

operating in Argentina did better than any similar investment in South America and operated as well as any private railway system in the world.[24]

Shortly after the ratification of the Roca-Runciman Pact by the Argentine Congress, British railway directors discovered the vagueness of the promised benevolent treatment. In practice Justo and the Concordancia emphasized the second part of the benevolent-treatment clause, which stated that all measures taken by the Argentine authorities would be conducive to "the further economic development of the country." Argentina continued to maintain a guaranteed market in Britain for its chilled beef. British companies complained that Justo ignored their claims. British gains were nullified in the course of time. Several countries secured the release of frozen funds and gained access to Argentina's official exchange market. The reduction of import duties did not give Britain an advantage, since other nations gained the same benefits through most-favored nation clauses. British complaints increased during 1934 and 1935. Directors of the British-owned railways claimed that the Argentine government failed to observe either the terms or the spirit of the trade agreement. They charged that the Concordancia employed unfair competition against them through use of state-owned railways and federal highway projects. That competition, they suggested, hardly amounted to benevolent treatment.

Justo did not grant the British-owned railways the type of special treatment they desired. Instead, he made clear that he intended to organize a national transportation system that would operate for the benefit of Argentines, not foreigners. He made cheap rates, not high dividends, the order of the day. If this policy appeared antagonistic to the British, which it did, he could not help it. The times did not permit any other course of action. Argentina could not consider itself a British colony, no matter how

[24] Troutbeck, Foreign Office Minutes, October 24, 1935, PRO, FO 371/18633. As D. C. M. Platt ("British Bondholders in Nineteenth Century Latin America—Inquiry and Remedy," *Inter-American Economic Affairs* 14, no. 3 [Winter 1960] ; 3-43) points out, although the British government never denied its right to intervene on behalf of its nationals during the nineteenth century, it usually refused to do so as a matter of expediency.

great its dependence upon the British meat market. Furthermore, Justo felt that the railway companies should realize that the automotive age had reached Argentina. Available trucks and cars would naturally alter the traditional role of the railways. If the struggle between British rail interests and U.S. automobile manufacturers heated up in Argentina, the Argentines stood to gain nothing by siding with one particular group. Justo, like previous Argentine leaders, measured the success of any transportation system by its expense. He felt that the cheapest possible transportation—auto, train, or a combination—constituted the best transportation.

With the introduction of increased automotive competition, the Argentine transportation scene changed dramatically. In the past the railway companies had no reason to fear highway competition. Argentina lacked a good road system and existing roads were in poor condition. Only some 2,700 miles of paved highways existed in 1932. In the winter and after heavy rains, most roads became impassable. Over long distances railways remained the only reliable means of transportation. The railways had effectively resisted all attempts to initiate large-scale road building until then. Also, the scarcity of stone on the pampas made the cost of building concrete or macadam roads prohibitive.[25]

The automotive age essentially began in Argentina during the first year of the Uriburu regime. To finance road construction Congress levied a gasoline tax in February, 1931. Justo followed up the 1931 legislation by introducing a comprehensive road transport bill in August, 1932. His bill called for construction of a network of federal highways between major cities of Argentina.[26] The Justo government proposed that within a fifteen-year period Argentina would build about 55,000 kilometers of all-weather roads at the cost of nearly 60 million pesos. Although a minor un-

[25] Hartley to DS, December 4, 1930, DS, NA, RG 59, 835.77/187. See also Overseas Trade, *Economic Conditions* (1932), ed. Stanley G. Irving, p. 135.
[26] For text of the Road Transport Bill see *South American Journal*, September 17, 1932, p. 273. The bill was patterned after the Interstate Commerce Act of the United States. For Uriburu's highway program see Hartley to DS, December 4, 1930; Shillock to DS, November 7, 1931; and Shillock to DS, November 17, 1931, DS, NA, RG 59, 835.77/187, 835.77/193, 835.77/194.

dertaking by U.S. standards, the Justo proposal departed from the small-scale road-building projects sponsored by administrations since the passage of the Mitre Law in 1907. Previous governments had limited their highway projects to constructing feeder routes to railway stations or existing port facilities. No administration had attempted to build major arteries between large cities or to construct roads parallel to the railways.

In its original version, Justo's road transport bill called for gradual expansion of automotive transportation. It also recommended coordinating all the nation's transportation facilities under the direction of a central government agency.[27] The bill appeared to coincide with demands made by the directors of British-owned railways. The directors had pressed since 1930 for national transportation reforms, with the clear objective of limiting the rise of highway competition. Like railway men the world over, they wanted to relegate the truck and car to a supporting role.[28] The creation of a Dirección de Vialidad, under the regulation of the director general of railways, suggested that future road building would suit the needs of the railway companies. Article 10 of the new bill offered further evidence to the railway interests that the legislation would favor the railways. According to that article the government would give preference to the construction of roads "which converge toward the stations of railways or toward the ports."[29]

Because it seemed to have been designed for them, the British-owned railways supported the original road transportation bill. They advocated universal regulation of road building. As one British observer noted, the bill "will see that the huge amount of British capital invested in Argentine railways is to have its future safeguarded in a most thorough manner. . . . and there should in the next few years be much transport development in Argentina, beneficial alike to the railways and the commercial community,

---

[27] Overseas Trade, *Economic Conditions* (1932), p. 124.

[28] In late 1931 the railway directors petitioned the Argentine government to put a halt to unrestricted road competition. See *La vida de los ferrocarriles y la competencia en los transportes*, pp. 7-8. The issue is briefly discussed in Ricardo M. Ortiz, *Historia económica de la Argentina, 1850-1930*, II, 205.

[29] *South American Journal*, September 17, 1932, p. 273.

without any of the cut-throat competition which has been so wasteful and disastrous in other countries, especially Great Britain."[30] Apparently, the Concordancia had decided to determine what role highways would play in the development of the nation, whether to support railways or highways as the primary means of transportation. The United States had already turned to the highways, as had several European countries, including Britain. At first it looked as though Justo would subordinate all of Argentina's transportation facilities under one state agency in order to protect the railways. To many Britons and Argentines it seemed that he planned to limit the growth of a highway system to conform to the needs of the private railways.

Justo did not base his final decision upon the needs of the railway companies. More important domestic considerations determined his final road-building program. Reduction of the cost of transporting goods throughout Argentina, opening new regions of the nation, and creation of new jobs for large numbers of unemployed laborers ultimately decided the course of Justo's road-construction program. A pragmatic politician, he became an Argentine economic nationalist in his own right. Though more narrow than the popularists, he gave preference to Argentine interests. Clearly he attempted to protect the major users of the railways, especially the large cattle and cereal producers who would gain the most by reduced railway costs. To his way of thinking, this faction still was the most important to the immediate economic prosperity of the nation and to the continuation in power of the Concordancia. As events soon proved, Justo had little sympathy for public utilities which needed to make profits to survive. To survive, he felt, they had to serve the best interests of the Argentine public.

In short order, Justo made significant changes in his highway legislation which made it unacceptable to the struggling British-owned railways. When Justo appointed Federico Pinedo as minis-

[30] Ibid., p. 267. For the attitude of the British-owned railways toward road competition see ibid., September 10, 1932, p. 250. The Central Argentine and the Western railways were not bothered by highways, because construction was difficult and costly in their districts, and roads were therefore few and far between. This was also true in Entre Ríos and Corrientes, where highway competition was negligible. The Pacific, on the other hand, was definitely hurt by competition from the highways.

ter of finance in August, 1933, the road-building program soon took on a new emphasis. Under Pinedo, a bright young economist and Independent Socialist, the Concordancia moved farther from the Conservatives' traditional laissez faire attitude. The state intervened increasingly in directing the economy. Pinedo's Plan de Acción Económica Nacional called for state direction of various parts of the economy. Above all, it permitted the government to intervene in the operation of industry and commerce for the "welfare of the nation."[31] Ostensibly, at least, Pinedo designed the program in an attempt to diversify the economy. Among other things, the plan called for extending the state's control over existing transportation systems, including railways, highways, and water transport facilities, with the objective of reducing substantially the cost of operating these public utilities.[32] Directors of the British-owned railways had not advocated this type of coordination. Much to their chagrin they found that the government had decided to become their chief competitor of the field.

That the railways had failed to undertake any basic reforms of the industry during recent years hurt their cause. Although forward-looking railway men had often spoken of the need to modernize the Argentine enterprises, they did little to diversify their operations to meet the inevitable competition of highways. Plans to provide more efficient service by implementing interchangeable truck, trailer, and train units had been proposed long before the depression. No railway introduced in large number so-called piggy-back units before 1933. No company made a major effort to modernize equipment used on the lines. Changing over to diesel-electric locomotives would have cut costs and improved service, but high initial costs worked against such a change. The British showed a traditional reluctance to scrap the still serviceable but decrepit steam locomotives. Not gamblers by nature, the British directors decided to keep what they had. Electrification of the lines would undoubtedly have improved their service as well as their

[31] Salera, *Exchange Control and the Argentine Market*, pp. 97-104, 149.

[32] Lucio M. Moreno Quintana, "La recuperación de la economía nacional," *Revista de Ciencias Económicas* 25, no. 189 (April 1937): 259-268; and Argentine Republic, Obras Públicas e Industrias, *La crisis ferroviaria argentina*.

public image. But caution prevailed. In addition, any changeover from coal would have wrought considerable damage to the lucrative British coal trade. The railways consumed over one million tons of coal annually, the bulk of which came from economically depressed South Wales.[33]

The crisis faced by the British-owned railways stemmed not only from their inability to improve service, but also from the fact that they no longer had any political power in Argentina. Obviously they could still pay for special privileges, but, contrary to popular belief in Buenos Aires at the time, the companies had no political means by which they could restrict the growth of highways. They could not block the development of the state-financed road-building program initiated by the Concordancia. In spite of considerable effort, they could not coordinate national transportation to protect their investments. The national coordination established in January, 1937, showed little influence from the campaign that the British-owned railways had waged since 1930. The motor highway industry did not grow much during the 1930's in Argentina, and its slow growth did not result from the opposition of the British-owned railways. Rather, inaccessibility of trucks, cars, and buses explains the slow pace of automotive development. As elsewhere in the world, railways could not halt the progress of the motor car.

The directors of the British-owned railways had no reason for optimism about the future of their companies. Railway receipts had dropped by 31 percent between 1929 and 1933. Much of the decline resulted from increased highway competition.[34] Common shareholders had not received dividends since 1928, due in part to the blocking of remittance payments, but also to a drop in the volume of trade. Much bitterness resulted in Britain, where small shareholders—usually widows, pensioners, or members of Britain's humble middle class—suffered the most from the economic pinch of the depression. Larger shareholders, who controlled the bulk of the railways, became equally upset, though not so hard-pressed.

---

[33] [H. G. Chilton], "Argentine Republic: Annual Report, 1934" (January 22, 1935), pp. 34-35, PRO, FO 371/18639.

[34] *The Economist*, May 11, 1935, p. 1081.

Automotive competition scared the directors of the railways into action. Although lack of new trucks, autos, and auto parts slowed highway development, the day would come when nothing would deter growth of the highways.

Extension of the state-owned railways by the Concordancia added to the problems faced by the British-owned railways. Under previous governments the state-owned railways had served as *ferrocarriles de fomento*. Provincial governments had built them to remote areas of the nation that otherwise would not have attracted private enterprises. The state railway system mostly served to develop neglected regions. They also had strategic military purposes. Over the years a large, loosely organized network developed, without direct access to Buenos Aires. With some additions to its existing network, the Justo government hoped to achieve an integral state-owned system. For a number of related reasons, political and economic, the Justo administration departed from its predecessors' policies and began to build branch lines with the idea of competing directly with the private companies.[35]

Once cordial, relations between the British-owned railways and the president became strained. Representatives of the British-owned railways accused the state railways of openly competing with the private companies. Public statements by the British railway directors revealed a growing coolness toward Justo. Sir Eastman Bell, director of both the Great Southern and the Western, maintained that only a few shippers benefited from the "illicit" reductions and other "unfair" practices of the provincially owned railway of Buenos Aires. According to him, operations of that line alone cost the taxpayers of the province about seven million pesos annually.[36] All the British railway spokesmen echoed the complaints of Viscount St. Davids, director of the Buenos Ayres and Pacific Railway, who reported to his shareholders in 1933 that intensified competition from the state-owned railway between San Juan and Mendoza had forced his company to lower its rates, even though the Pacific had a shorter route to Buenos Aires. The state-

[35] Chilton to Simon, October 8, 1934, PRO, FO 371/17474.
[36] Bliss to SecState, December 28, 1932, DS, NA, RG 59, 835.77/210.

owned line had to transfer goods at Santa Fe, either to a private line or to barges.[37] Similar reports came from the chairman of the Central Argentine Railway, who complained that "intensified and illogical" rate cutting by state-owned railways, along with highway use, offered unfair and ruinous competition to his company.[38]

By the end of 1934, representatives of the British-owned railways began to wonder if they would ever receive the benevolent treatment promised under the Roca-Runciman Pact. Their profits did not rise, in spite of gradually increasing volume of trade. The companies again failed to pay dividends to holders of common stock. They could not keep their expenses down, and they needed capital to replace old rolling stock. To make matters worse, the Justo administration made it clear that, should its policy of offering the lowest freight rates possible come into conflict with the interests of the British-owned railways, the interests of the railways would be sacrificed to those of the Argentines.[39]

[37] *The Times*, November 11, 1933. The state-owned route to Buenos Aires was 1,500 kilometers and involved a transfer of goods to barges at Santa Fe, whereas the Pacific Railway was 1,220 kilometers from San Juan through Mendoza to Buenos Aires. The stretch between San Juan and Mendoza was part of the Andino Railway, which had been built by the Argentine government and sold to the British firm in 1909. Now the Argentine government was constructing a parallel line. See also Cox to SecState, November 13, 1933, DS, NA, RG 59, 841.00 P.R./310.

[38] Walter K. Whigham, chairman of the board of the Central Argentine Railway, as quoted by *The Times*, November 15, 1933. For the annual address to the shareholders of the Western Railway by its director, Sir Follet Holt, see *The Times*, November 8, 1933.

[39] Trimble to SecState, November 15, 1935, DS, NA, RG 59, 835.77/271.

8. The British Point of View

The British-owned railway companies considered that they demonstrated extreme patience until mid-1935. Despite many setbacks, including Justo's openly antagonistic use of state-controlled facilities to compete with private railways, they did not ask the British government for official assistance. They continued to believe they could settle matters through private negotiations and refused to request His Majesty's government to intervene on their behalf.[1] Perhaps they realized that to have asked for official intervention would only have resulted in even more unfavorable conditions. Justo had indicated as much in early 1935 when he told J. Montegue Eddy: "I and my Government are prepared to do everything possible to help the

[1] Only the Anglo-Argentine Tramway Company, whose director was the duke of Atholl, made any concerted effort prior to 1935 to urge the British government to intervene on behalf of British capital. This matter is thoroughly discussed in correspondence found in Atholl to Vansittart, March 1, 1933, and attachments; and Somerville to Treasurer, January 14, 1933, PRO, FO 371/16561.

railways. You may rest assured of that. But do not bring pressure to bear, because if you do I will do nothing. I perfectly realize that it is the Government's duty to help the Railway; but these things have to be done tactfully. Ever since, and indeed prior to, the 1933 Trade Agreement I have done my best to foster Anglo-Argentine trade, but the fact remains that it would appear that the British manufacturers do not understand their own position."[2]

When private negotiations proved futile by mid-1935, the British railway directors changed their approach. The directors discontinued their policy of direct dealing with the Argentine government and turned to the British government for assistance. Patience had paid no dividends. For a number of reasons the companies could not afford to wait indefinitely for Justo to demonstrate the benevolent treatment promised by the Roca-Runciman Pact. British railway men felt that they had a legitimate list of grievances. The government had failed to give any official assistance in settling their labor problems. In fact, a presidential award in 1934 had favored labor and worked against the railways. Nor had the government introduced legislation which would have enabled the railways to reduce working expenditures by pooling traffic and other redundant services. Rather, the government had built up the state-owned line from San Juan to Mendoza in direct competition with the Buenos Ayres and Pacific Railway and refused to allow the British line to charge special rates to combat the competition. As for the exchange rate, the Argentine government still refused to concede favorable rates for the remittance of funds to London. Finally, the Concordancia had remained indifferent toward the creation of national transportation coordination that the British companies had recommended in 1930 as a panacea for their many problems.[3]

The British-owned railways finally approached the British government for assistance in April, 1935. Sir Follet Holt, a leading spokesman for the London-based railways and member of the board of all major British-owned lines, requested help from the

[2] Holt to Troutbeck, May 16, 1935, PRO, FO 371/18633.
[3] Leguizamón to Chilton, April 3, 1935, ibid.

British government. Holt wanted what he called "moral support" from the government. "I have been able to consult my colleagues," he began, "and it is the opinion that it will be in the best interests of the railway industry if [Ambassador] Sir Henry Chilton is instructed to make the representation which you were good enough to suggest might be made informally to the Argentine Government, particularly in view of the Benevolent clause of the Roca convention."[4] In a letter sent to a friend in Parliament, Holt said that the railways did not want public reference made to their request for informal help from the government. "As we think it important that the question in the House at the present time on the treatment of the Railways by the Argentine Government should *not* be pressed I am venturing to ask you to use your influence as far as possible to help us in this direction."[5]

As requested, the British government pursued an informal policy regarding the British-owned railways. They had long recommended such an approach. Though government officials did not want to make the railways a major issue in dealing with Argentina, they wanted to resolve the problem of British investment in Argentina. But Chilton's overtures in late April proved the futility of a soft approach. His interview with Justo got nowhere. The Argentine president promised little action. "His Excellency, who is an ex-engineer officer, showed that he was well acquainted with the question and disposed to promote a solution," reported Chilton. He also added that Justo attributed the companies' plight to "an inevitable consequence of the rapid development of a new competitive means of transport, viz. the motor vehicle."[6] Justo offered no solution to the major problems faced by the railways.

British officials did not want to intervene on behalf of the railways. They had hoped that Justo might respond to informal talks. Purposefully, the British did not press the Concordancia for action. They believed that their bargaining position had diminished in proportion to the progressively decreasing market for Argentine beef.

[4] Holt to Troutbeck, April 16, 1935, ibid.
[5] Holt to Cobb, May 18, 1935, ibid.
[6] Chilton to Simon, April 30, 1935, ibid.

Dominion pressure, along with British economic nationalism, made it necessary for the British government to treat the question of Argentine beef carefully. Although the day approached when Britain might not need Argentine foodstuffs, that day had not arrived. It might not come for a number of years. The Dominion countries could not supply Britain's needs in 1935. Thus the British officials followed a cautious policy in dealing with Argentina. They preferred not to treat the sticky railway matter unless absolutely necessary.

In mid-October the British-owned railway companies attempted to force the British government to deal directly with the railway problem. Directors of the British-owned railways wanted the reluctant British government to intervene officially on their behalf. To achieve their goal, the companies threatened to undertake a protracted propaganda campaign in Britain. They considered the time right for a change. A new ambassador, Sir Neville Henderson, had just arrived in Buenos Aires; the Anglo-Argentine trade agreement soon came up for renegotiation; and the companies had reached the end of their patience.

Howard Williams, director of the Buenos Ayres and Pacific Railway, began the new offensive by giving one of the most inflammatory annual reports in the history of Anglo-Argentine railway enterprise. He felt it efficacious to "clear the air." In an address to the shareholders of his company, given in London on October 17, 1935, he voiced what many British observers had thought for several years. Calling the behavior of the Justo government scandalous, especially in regard to the state-supported railways, he accused the Argentine authorities of being "disloyal" to their British friends.[7] Argentines had not appreciated the sacrifices of Britons who had made Argentina such a great nation. This statement reflected the climate of opinion in London. The term *disloyal* appeared as *desleal* in the Spanish translation of the speech, which also meant "a cheat" to the Argentines. As a result, even some of Williams's oldest Argentine friends became indignant that a Briton should describe their countrymen in such terms. Justo

---

[7] *The Times*, October 18, 1935.

resented the accusation so much that afterward he refused to mention Williams's name when discussing the railway situation.[8]

Williams's statement achieved its desired effect. The Argentine reaction to his words made the British authorities take direct action, much against their better judgment. Argentine nationalists had taken the Englishman's chauvinism at its face value. His words proved what they already believed, that the railways served as instruments of British economic imperialists, who concerned themselves only with profits. To Justo and other Argentine friends, Williams had betrayed a trust by publicly embarrassing the Concordancia. The British government could not overlook the public reaction in Argentina. More to the point, it could not ignore the anger of Justo and his supporters.

A little over a week after his speech, Williams accompanied Sir Follet Holt on a visit to Lord Stanhope, secretary of state for foreign affairs. The two railway representatives wanted to explain their position to the British government. Six months before they had thought that they could continue with the moral support of the British government alone. They soon realized that they needed more tangible assistance. Since Chilton's interview with Justo in April, matters had grown worse. Now the companies felt that they needed the active assistance of the British government to save them from ruin. Both Williams and Holt stated that their interests could be saved only "at the point of the economic bayonet," an expression used by Holt throughout the conversation. To this Lord Stanhope expressed partial agreement. He felt that the government would have to apply stern economic sanctions to pressure the Argentine government into treating the British-owned railways fairly. But Lord Stanhope made no promise of specific action to Holt or Williams. British governments seldom interfered when other recourses lay open. Stanhope indicated that the British government could apply some pressure in connection with the upcoming meat negotiations. At least, he suggested that the government could persuade Argentines that unless they gave greater consideration to the requests of the railways they could not expect the

[8] Henderson to Eden, January 3, 1936; and Troutbeck, Foreign Office Minutes, January 24, 1936, PRO, FO 371/19760.

British government to show concern for the Argentine position once the Roca-Runciman Pact ended.[9]

Stanhope did not promise to pit Argentine meat against British investments in Argentina during the next round of trade negotiations between the two nations. He only suggested it as a possibility. Hard bargaining would govern both sides. He refused to commit himself to a hard line, because the British considered their export trade to Argentina as important as their investments. The British railways still provided a substantial market for British manufactured goods since they bought exclusively from British producers. Furthermore, although the railways represented the most important British investment in Argentina, they were by no means the sole investment.[10] The British government did not want to risk future trade agreements for the sake of the railways. Railways did not make substantial profits anywhere in the world at the time. It seemed unlikely that their recovery in Argentina would be great, even under more prosperous conditions. Finally, from a practical standpoint, many of the companies made secret profits as a result of involved interlocking companies they had organized with manufacturers in Britain. A complex system of keeping the books of the conglomerates hid these profits.[11] Thus the British position was uncertain and was made all the more so because the government did not know how much beef and wheat the Dominions would provide in the near future. At the present the Dominion countries could not supply enough of either commodity for the British demands. In considering these factors the British officials decided that they did not have a strong bargaining position. They could not afford to attack the Argentine government. One British official summarized the situation as follows:

My own impression is that we shall find ourselves inevitably forced to take all that the Dominions can send us, and that the Argentines will have to accept little better than the residue after our own producers and the

[9] Minutes of Conversation between Holt, Williams, and Stanhope, on October 24, 1935, in Foreign Office Minutes (Troutbeck), October 24, 1935, PRO, FO 371/18633.
[10] Troutbeck to Gwatkin, October 25, 1935, ibid.
[11] J. S. Duncan, "British Railways in Argentina," *Political Science Quarterly* 52, no. 4 (December 1937): 574.

Dominions have been satisfied. That is what the Argentines fear, and it goes some way (though not all) to account for their malevolent attitude towards the railways. In fact, their fears may go further, viz. that our demand for meat from any source is also contracting.

If I am right then, we do not possess any great inducement to offer to the Argentines either to take more of our exports or to treat our vested interests with greater consideration. I cannot, therefore, feel enormously optimistic as to the future because it seems to me that our takings of Argentine meat are likely to decrease progressively and, if so, we shall be lucky if we do not lose something either of our export trade or of our already shrunken investments in Argentina; and if it comes to a struggle between those two interests, the investors are hardly likely to come off best.[12]

British authorities feared bargaining from a weak position rather than with the traditional strength of Albion. Nonetheless, they saw no harm in having their ambassador call Justo's attention to the speeches of Williams and Holt "as evidence of increasing disappointment of the British public opinion at the losses we are suffering in our investments . . ."[13] They thought it wise to give positive evidence that the British government would "find it hard to treat Argentina in anything but a spirit of stern bargaining when the Roca Agreement comes to an end," unless the Argentines demonstrated a "more benevolent spirit" before that date. Such representation could not weaken the British position. From a psychological point of view British officials might do some good. The railways had just expressed their grievances publicly and discussions had begun to give the railways a better remittance rate.[14]

British officials proceeded with caution. They instructed Ambassador Henderson to give President Justo the British government's opinion on the railway situation. To accomplish their immediate objective—better treatment of the railways—they suggested that Henderson tie the issue to approaching trade negotiations. Henderson should inform the Argentines that the way the

---

[12] Troutbeck to Gwatkin, October 25, 1935, PRO, FO 371/18633.
[13] Ibid.
[14] Ibid.

Argentine government had fulfilled its obligations under the "benevolent" clause would influence the attitude of the British government when negotiations of the trade agreement took place. Accordingly, "His Majesty's Government are bound to take into consideration the increasingly unfavorable position of the railway companies as depicted in the Chairman's recent speeches . . ." Specifically, Henderson should point out that, when considering the revision of the Roca-Runciman Pact, "the unfortunate situation of the railway companies (if it still persist) and the fact that they owe their plight in large measure to what is regarded in this country as unfair treatment, will necessarily give weight to the criticisms which are already voiced against the agreement, and to make it difficult for His Majesty's Government to maintain their share of that mutual consideration on which the agreement was founded."[15] The British hoped to win by bluffing; they could not afford to wield a big stick.

Independently, the British-owned railway companies prepared to launch an extensive propaganda campaign in Britain aimed at gaining wide public support for their cause. Railway officials felt that they had nothing to lose by undertaking a full-scale offensive against the Argentines. They hoped to coerce the Argentines into assisting the railways. The timing seemed right. As Stanley G. Irving, commercial counselor at the British Embassy in Buenos Aires and an astute observer of the Argentine economic scene, noted, "I fear that if the opportunity offered by the present negotiations is not used to extract definite guarantees on behalf of the British Railway (and other public utilities) Companies' interests, they will be left without adequate means to defend themselves against political intrigue, and in danger of being reduced to a condition of complete collapse—especially in view of the approaching determination of their concessions." He supported more drastic action, but he did not take an optimistic stance. The British government would have to defend the railways. "Experience has abundantly proved," he continued, "that diplomatic representation unbased on any specific undertaking by the Argen-

[15] Troutbeck to Henderson, November 20, 1935, PRO, FO 371/18633.

tine Government offers no real security that foreign interests will receive even fair—not to say benevolent—treatment."[16]

No one understood the situation better than Ambassador Neville Henderson in Buenos Aires. Respected by British and Argentine authorities alike, Henderson worked assiduously to settle the vexing railway problem. He presented the British position in forceful terms, but he understood the Argentine point of view. Thanks to his efforts, Argentine and British officials worked out a compromise in early 1936. At least he opened new channels for discussion between his government and the Concordancia. Disgruntled railway officials did not like the compromise at first, but it suited the needs of both the Concordancia and the British government. By agreeing to discuss the matter, Justo opened a new phase in Argentine railway development. In seeking a mutually satisfactory solution, Henderson suggested that the Argentine authorities and the British railway companies seriously consider the possibility of nationalizing the British-owned railways. Justo first took this step in December, 1936.

Henderson also dissuaded the directors of the British-owned railways from organizing a vigorous publicity campaign in Parliament and the British press. Such a campaign, he felt, would have increased the hostility of the Argentine authorities. The campaign would have been more dangerous than beneficial in its probable effect on Argentine public opinion. Throughout December, Henderson met with directors of the British-owned railways, who had congregated in Buenos Aires. Although Howard Williams and his codirector Lord Forres did not agree with Henderson at first, they eventually concurred. Williams and Forres, with the other directors, unanimously decided to postpone any concerted propaganda campaigns until a later date, if necessary.[17] With calm thus assured, Henderson then tackled the question of confronting Justo with the British claims.

In order to impress upon the Argentine authorities the urgency of the matter, Henderson sought an audience with Vice-Presi-

[16] Irving to FO, January 16, 1936, PRO, FO 371/19758.
[17] Henderson to Eden, January 3, 1936, PRO, FO 371/19760.

dent Julio A. Roca. He knew that Roca, an Anglophile and a gentleman, would listen to the British case. Hopefully, Roca would convey the seriousness of the railway issue to Justo. On the evening of December 18, 1935, Henderson and Roca began a series of discussions directed toward solving the immediate problems related to the British-owned railways. At the outset, Henderson informed Roca of the publicity campaign planned by the companies in Britain. He impressed upon the Argentine statesman that he felt the campaign ill-timed and unnecessary and that he had worked to halt it. He also made it clear that the Argentine government needed to do something to help the railways. It would not suffice to argue that railways throughout the world found themselves in similar perilous conditions.

Henderson emphasized the time-worn theme of traditional Anglo-Argentine relations. Without endorsing Williams's October speech, which had been directed against Justo, the British diplomat argued that Argentina had been fortunate to have had British assistance in building its railways. British savings had built the Argentine lines, he stated, not vast loans. In effect, the railways constituted a loan. At least Henderson regarded the capital expended on them as a "debt of honour" in view of the benefits that Argentina had received from railway construction. Henderson told Roca that Argentina owed a debt to the British public. Improvement of the conditions for the British-owned railways would assure continued harmonious relations between the two nations. Realizing that the Argentine government could do very little until Congress reconvened in May, 1936, Henderson stressed the necessity for the Justo administration to do something concrete to prove its good faith. The approaching renewal of the Roca-Runciman Pact made it essential for the Argentines to act, since the way in which the Argentine government executed its obligations under the 1933 agreement would influence future negotiations.[18]

During his talks with Roca, Henderson emphasized the importance of railways to the prosperity of Argentina. The nation could not do without such public utilities. Argentina needed a

---

[18] Ibid.

modern rail system. It could not afford to maintain the railways on a nonprofit basis indefinitely. Unless the British-owned railways received better treatment than in the immediate past, Britons would not invest new capital in modernization projects. As Henderson recalled his conversation with Roca, he had told the Argentine: "It might well be that prosperity was round the next corner in Argentina, but, if full advantage were to be taken of that prosperity, considerable and expensive work on the railways was essential. The improvement of their situation was at least as much an Argentine as a British shareholder interest. . . . Reorganization on a long term basis was a necessity if confidence was to be restored and fresh money found for a modernization scheme which was already overdue."[19]

As a result of his meetings with Roca, Henderson finally received a "private audience" with President Justo on December 30, 1935. Henderson had little more luck than Chilton had had in April. The British ambassador did not succeed, partly because of a communication problem stemming from the language barrier and partly because of Justo's intransigence. Henderson modestly commented "As . . . General Justo has little knowledge of French and my own knowledge of Spanish is even less, I fear that our understanding of each other, in spite of the presence of the President's secretary as interpreter, was possibly less good than it might have been." More than the language problem hampered their conversation; their attitudes were at blame. Henderson repeatedly stated that the responsibility for the railways' plight rested with the Argentine government. Only steps by the latter would save the hard-pressed companies from financial ruin. Justo took a contrary position. He stated that his government had studied the whole matter and would do what it felt best to meet the British requests.[20]

Throughout the course of their hour-long conversation, Justo repeated his conviction that the present difficulties of the railways stemmed from their own mistaken policy. The British-owned rail-

[19] Ibid.
[20] Ibid.

ways no longer had administrations and managers of the caliber of previous generations. Also, the companies acted too much as monopolies and had done nothing to modernize their service. They had taken advantage of the provisions of the Mitre Law. Now they had to face the consequences of their previous actions. "He assured me in this connection," reported Henderson, "that he was not arguing but merely stating facts in order to make it clear that his Government was not solely, if at all, to blame for their position."[21] Justo did not commit himself, other than to promise to see what he could do to remedy the situation. As Henderson correctly assumed, in the mind of the Argentine president the railway question could not be divorced from the meat question. To the Argentine a "really favorable long term solution of the former depends on the generosity and farsightedness of His Majesty's Government in respect of the latter."[22]

A stalemate followed Henderson's audience with Justo. Neither side appeared to have a definite edge. The British did not feel they could exclude Argentine beef from their markets, largely because they believed that to have done so would have resulted in disastrous consequences for the railways. Also, they had no assurance that the Dominion countries would fill their needs for foodstuffs. The Argentines remained noncommittal primarily because of their uncertainties about the British market for meat. They did not want to favor the British-owned railways without preserving a market for their meat. As a result of the stalemate, the British government relaxed its position in February, 1936, and assumed an informal attitude on the railway issue. The British made it clear that they would not use their full powers to protect the railway companies. Above all, the British government decided not to treat the railway issue during the treaty negotiations of 1936.

This decision went against what the railway directors felt Sir Neville Henderson had promised them in December. They thought he had agreed that His Majesty's government would not

[21] Ibid.
[22] Ibid.

conclude a new trade pact with Argentina unless the Concordancia guaranteed to safeguard the railways. But the British government had never intended to take such a strong stand. Lord Stanhope moved quickly to clear up the misunderstanding. Some government officials charged that the British-owned railway companies had tried to maneuver them into undertaking much more than they planned to protect the British investments. To dispel this misconception, the Foreign Office informed Howard Williams, the leading proponent of government intervention, that it would continue to consider the railway situation in forthcoming negotiations. The British government, however, would not refrain from concluding a trade convention for want of assurances that the Argentine government would satisfy the outstanding grievances of the companies. Britain would not feel justified in giving the companies such a promise, "especially since many of those grievances are matters which it would hardly be possible to include specifically in a commercial convention."[23]

The Foreign Office decided to treat the railway matter as an Argentine internal affair. In keeping with this decision, Lord Stanhope gave Henderson new instructions. He informed Henderson of pressures upon the government to use the treaty to settle the railway's grievances. The companies had an understandable point; unless definite guarantees were extracted during the negotiations they faced inadequate means of defending themselves in the future. Stanhope, however, in reviewing the history of the previous agreement, argued against using the negotiations on behalf of the railways. Two difficulties appeared which made it impractical to work for obtaining safeguards for the British-owned railways. First, as a result of domestic and imperial policy, Britain now had less to offer Argentina in respect to meat. Stanhope expressed the conviction of the Foreign Office that "our bargaining position, even for retaining concessions already won, is less strong than in 1933." Second, the Foreign Office considered that "the majority of the companies' demands are matters within the purview of the Argentine Government's internal administration and en-

[23] Troutbeck to Overton, February 4, 1936; and Troutbeck to Williams, February 4, 1936, PRO, FO 371/19760.

tirely unsuitable for insertion in a commercial treaty."[24] Stanhope concluded that, with the exception of the question of exchange, the remaining grievances were not appropriate for inclusion in the trade negotiations.

Stanhope did promise that "every possible consideration will be given to the railway shareholders' interests in the forthcoming negotiations, apart from anything which it may be found possible to do officially in the meantime." He wanted Henderson to understand that Britain would not do more than raise the issue of the grievances. He urged Henderson to make the government's position clear to the railway companies. When the negotiations started, the British delegates might make fair treatment of British investments an important point in the preliminary discussions, but they would not make the conclusion of an agreement dependent upon that point.

The companies did not know what to do or to expect. Their own government refused to back them, except by following an informal and cautious policy. The British government favored the interests of Britain and the British Commonwealth nations at the expense of other economic interests. In Argentina they found a similar situation. Justo remained antagonistic to the British-owned railways' dilemma. He pursued a nationalistic program of economic recovery for Argentina. Argentine public opinion became increasingly hostile toward the British railways. Nothing, it seemed, alleviated their situation. Their government would not risk full involvement on their behalf; their grievances fell upon deaf ears in Argentina, where Justo argued stubbornly that he had done as much as he could to assist them; and they had to meet their obligations to Argentina.

[24] Stanhope to Henderson, February 18, 1936, PRO, FO 371/19758.

9. Transportation Coordination

Since the late nineteenth century, railways have been subjected to increasing public control. The very nature of railways as monopolistic public utilities necessitated some regulation of their activities. In England and the United States the problem received considerable attention during the early stages of railway development. Unlike France and Italy, leaders of these nations avoided strict governmental regulation of the railway industry. In the United States the influence of laissez faire economics proved strong enough to delay broad public control of railways until the last decades of the century. At that time the federal government finally acted, somewhat reluctantly, to regulate the railways. The creation of the Interstate Commerce Commission finally gave the national government a means by which it could control the larger railways. England, too, had faced the same problem. Since the beginning of its railway age, Parliament had played a direct role in railway expansion.

During the nineteenth century Argentines had patterned

their railway legislation after that in England and the United States. As a result the Argentine government had tight powers over some activities of the railways, but little attention had been given to the need to coordinate the nation's entire transportation system. Not until the widespread appearance of cheap automotive transportation did Argentine officials consider the need to coordinate a diversified transportation network. Suddenly they joined the United States and Western Europe in facing a transportation crisis. Should the government favor the existing railway enterprises, or should it encourage the new automotive industry through highway construction? As in the past, the Argentines tried to learn from the experiences of the United States and Great Britain. As a result the government decided to compromise. Studies showed that for short hauls trucks provided cheap transportation, but that railways cost considerably less for transporting goods over fifty miles.[1] Rather than sacrifice one transportation system for the other, the Concordancia attempted to devise a coordinated transportation network, uniting services of the highways and the railways.

British railway companies had begun to advocate coordination of Argentine rail and highway traffic since the mid-1920's. However, their concept of coordination remained narrow and traditional. They wanted highways to bolster the existing rail network. They feared the construction of public highways that allowed motor vehicles to compete directly with their enterprises. The companies knew such competition had dramatically altered the position of railways in both the United States and England. With the advent of the Justo government the British-owned railways began a campaign to tailor the coordination of Argentina's transportation system to suit their needs. Between 1930 and 1937 their efforts proved futile. In the end the Justo administration showed its unwillingness to favor the British-owned railways.

Failure to obtain favorable transportation laws proved bitter for the British-owned railways. Coordination of the national transportation systems had long been one of their goals. As their spokesmen pointed out in a petition sent to General Uriburu in

[1] Manuel María Díez, *Régimen jurídico de las comunicaciones,* I, 125.

1931, "competition has no reason for being and is absurd in the case of companies or persons dedicated to public service."[2] The British railway interests did not want a protracted struggle with the automobile industry. They hoped to eliminate competition through legislation by limiting the growth of highways. Justo approached the coordination of the nation's transportation system differently. He emphasized inexpensive service, increased traffic, and higher profits for producers through greater volume of trade. His effort to coordinate transportation did not come from an attempt to save the private railway industry. Instead he worked against their interests. The result, however, was to emphasize the increasing antiforeign economic nationalism in Argentina.

The Congress debated the National Transportation Coordination Act between 1932 and 1937. The struggle to establish a new coordinating body highlighted the conflict between the British-owned railways and the Justo regime. Socialists, dissident Radicals, and a growing number of independent politicians, who made the bill a focus for extended attacks on "avaricious" Britons, were not concerned with the actual intent of the law. Nor did they try to understand the position of either the railways or the Concordancia. The former they criticized on general principle as "foreigners," the latter because they represented a *vendepatria*, reactionary administration.

The National Transportation Coordination Act, called the "Law of Judas" by an irate Benjamín Villafañe, grew out of Justo's early highway construction program.[3] The original version of the coordination law went to the Chamber of Deputies on August 17, 1932, shortly after Justo introduced his highway bill. Its sponsor, the minister of public works, acted at the urging of the British-owned railways to introduce a bill aimed at avoiding unfair highway competition. In its original form the coordination bill clearly meant to establish the hegemony of the British railway companies over all future transportation development in Argentina. The British-backed bill met with little success. For a number of related

---

[2] *La vida de los ferrocarriles y la competencia en los transportes*, p. 11.
[3] Benjamín Villafañe, *La tragedia argentina*, p. 403.

reasons, Congress did not consider the measure until November, 1934. Then it acted only at the request of President Justo, who probably reacted to pressure from the British railway companies. Despite the president's request to include the bill on the agenda of an extraordinary session in 1934, the House of Deputies never reported it out of committee. Justo did not force the issue. He had only acted to placate British accusations of disinterest. Members of Congress, especially Socialists, made no effort to push for rapid passage of the bill. Thus the repeated efforts by the British to have the legislation introduced on the floor of the Chamber of Deputies proved futile. The Chamber of Deputies did not begin formal discussion of the bill until June 28, 1935. The bill they then treated appeared in a form much modified from the original.[4]

In its original version the bill called for the creation of a national transportation coordination system under the control of a director general of railways. The bill proposed to give both state and private interests representation on the coordination commission. That body looked similar to institutions in the United States and Europe. Essentially the bill would have ended possible anarchy of the highways. It also promised to halt unfair competition from the state-owned railways. Theoretically, the railways, which worked under rigid fixed costs, would concentrate upon efficient and rapid long-distance transportation. Highways would serve a supporting role. For some time Argentines had hoped to coordinate their transportation systems to accommodate export trade. National regulation of the various means of transportation appeared to achieve this objective. Argentina would have a more socially and economically useful transportation system.[5] At the same time, the private railways would receive the protection they desired.

[4] A brief history of the project is found in Trimble to SecState, September 20, 1935, DS, NA, RG 59, 835.77/265. See also Villafañe, *Tragedia argentina*, pp. 403-414. Also useful are "La coordinación nacional de los transportes," *Hechos e Ideas* 5, no. 18 (January-February 1937): 84-94; Juan José Guaresti, "La coordinación de los transportes," *Revista de Ciencias Económicas* 23, no. 165 (May 1935): 525-538; and Teodoro Sánchez de Bustamente, "La vialidad en la República Argentina: Su evolución y estado actual," *Revista de Ciencias Económicas* 22, no. 150 (January 1934): 35-68.
[5] *South American Journal*, October 7, 1933, p. 346; and *Financial Times*, March 16, 1934,

A radically different bill finally reached the floor of the Chamber of Deputies. It did not favor the British-owned railways, and the railways considered it useless except as a possible first step toward more important reforms. The original bill would have placed coordination under the direction of an existing railway commission. The final draft of the bill, however, established a separate seven-man commission to issue permits to concerns for interstate commerce. The commission served public interests and the national economy by coordinating land, water, and air transportation. Both public and private interests were represented on the commission. The Senate appointed an Argentine citizen as the commission's president. The chairman of the National Highway Commission and a representative of the independent automotive transport companies spoke for the automotive industry. Railways sent the administrator general of the state railways, the director general of railways, and a delegate of the private railway companies. The prefect general of ports served as the seventh member of the commission.[6]

In theory the commission included spokesmen for all the nation's transportation interests. Actually, the government gained a decided advantage. The administration and the Senate appointed four of the members. The president appointed the chairman of the commission, subject to approval by the Senate. Government agents obviously dominated the new organization. Contrary to charges made by nationalists, Justo did not propose to defend the British-owned railways through the Transportation Coordination Act. He tried to establish legislation that would balance the growth of highways and railways. At no time did he bend to British demands, nor did he attempt to establish a commission dominated by Britons. The companies did not consider Justo an ally. They thought he wanted to sabotage any chance they had for recovery by creating an Argentine-dominated commission. The private rail-

---

which states that the British interests regarded the proposed bill "as a movement towards the coordination of transport and the elimination of the intense and uneconomic competition which has prevailed for some years."

[6] Guaresti, "La coordinación de los transportes," pp. 525-538.

ways may have held a slight edge over the heterogeneous group of independent bus and trucking firms represented on the commission because of their closely knit relationship and interlocking directorates. All this meant little, though, for the overwhelming presence of Argentine government authorities reduced the role of the private railway representative to a minor one.

Congress might have passed the National Transportation Coordination Act much sooner, and with less anguish, had it not been associated with a second transportation law, the Buenos Aires Transportation Corporation Act. The latter act attempted to establish a British monopoly over public transportation in the capital city. Perhaps one of the most unpopular pieces of legislation ever considered by the Argentine Congress, the municipal transportation bill became a rallying point for dissident political factions and an object of public scorn. Few bills have ever sparked more dramatic public demonstrations against a government or against foreign capitalists than this one.

The Buenos Aires Transportation Corporation Act amounted to the creation of a British-dominated monopoly over Buenos Aires's transit system in order to save the floundering Anglo-Argentine Tramway Company. The Anglo-Argentine faced bankruptcy. Since the mid-1920's, the company had tried unsuccessfully to get the municipal government of Buenos Aires to pass legislation that would protect it from automotive competitors.[7] The company regained hope in 1933 when the *intendente* of Buenos Aires, Dr. Mariano de Vedia y Mitre, ordered a survey of the city's transportation problems. Dr. Vedia y Mitre appointed a special commission, headed by former Minister of Public Works Roberto Ortiz, to investigate.[8] When filed a year later, the commission's re-

---

[7] Atholl to Roca, March 1, 1933, PRO, FO 371/16561.

[8] Ibid. Also see *South American Journal*, November 18, 1933, p. 490; and John W. White, *Argentina*, p. 163. The committee appointed to investigate the Buenos Aires transportation situation included Roberto M. Ortiz as chairman, Manuel F. Castello, Pablo Nogués, Antonio Rebuelto, Alberto Schneidewind, Horacio J. Treslia, and Agustín Pestalardo. Ortiz had been minister of public works under Alvear, had served as a legal adviser to several of the British-owned railways, and had later been minister of finance under Justo. He was consistently sympathetic to the railways' plight.

port showed what was already common knowledge: the Anglo-Argentine Tramway and the British-owned subways of Buenos Aires faced imminent financial collapse. These companies had lost much of their passenger traffic to the independent drivers of over-sized taxis known as *colectivos*, who were not burdened by high operating fees or fixed routes. For a fee of one hundred pesos per year the chauffeur purchased a license which permitted him to compete directly with the inefficient tramways. The *colectivo* drivers operated at an obvious advantage. They did not have to pay high taxes, nor did they have the upkeep of numerous buildings, level crossings, or safety devices. They had the added advantage of flexibility in choosing routes. New suburban sections on the outskirts of Buenos Aires opened up for development as the *colectivos* went wherever business took them.[9] Because of their good service, they rapidly put the rail system out of business in the Argentine capital.

The duke of Atholl, chairman of the Anglo-Argentine, referred to *colectivos* as "pirate buses" and stated that they had "no responsibility to the community, and contribute nothing towards it excepting that they jam up the traffic and prevent the regularized service from paying either a dividend to their shareholders or an improved wage to their employees."[10] Some Argentines agreed. According to the pro-British members of the special Ortiz commission, the city had to save the rail companies from bankruptcy. To accomplish this the commission suggested that the national government limit the "disorderly" competition of the *colectivos*.[11]

A minority report, filed by Socialist members of the commis-

[9] Both Ysabel F. Rennie (*The Argentine Republic*, pp. 233-234) and Luis V. Sommi (*El monopolio inglés del transporte en Buenos Aires*, pp. 18-19) credit the *colectivos*, oversized taxicabs mounted on truck chassis, with having been responsible for creating a new suburban Buenos Aires by offering rapid transportation to the outskirts of the city, which previously had been isolated.

[10] *South American Journal*, June 25, 1932, p. 647.

[11] Leche to Simon, March 20, 1934; and [H. G. Chilton], "Argentine Republic Report, 1934," p. 12, PRO, FO 371/17466, 371/18636. *South American Journal*, April 21, 1934, p. 402; and April 28, 1934, p. 427. Teodoro Sánchez de Bustamente, "La coordinación de transportes de la ciudad de Buenos Aires," *Revista de Ciencias Económicas* 27, no. 218 (September 1939): 811-840. According to figures prepared by Alejandro Bunge for the

sion, argued that the municipal government of Buenos Aires should settle the matter. The majority report, however, contained a draft law authorizing the president to establish a national entity, the Buenos Aires Transportation Corporation, which would oversee all future developments of urban transit in Buenos Aires. In an effort to bypass the Socialist-dominated Municipal Council, the partisan majority recommended introducing legislation to the national Congress. They justified this action on the technical ground that the companies involved had received charters from the national government. For that reason they were subject to national legislation. President Justo followed the advice of the majority report. In so doing he removed the question from the hands of the Socialists, who would rather fight for the demise of the Anglo-Argentine than legislate its resurrection from the financial losses.[12]

Upon reaching the Chamber of Deputies, the bill first went to the Committee of Constitutional Affairs and Municipal Legislation. By a narrow vote of six to four, the four being Socialists, that committee decided that the question did lie within the jurisdiction of the Chamber.[13] Even so, tactics employed by the Socialists delayed the bill for nearly two years. Conservatives gave the measure only lukewarm support. Not until October, 1934, did a subcommittee of the Chamber of Deputies complete the first draft of the Buenos Aires Transportation Corporation Act. A final vote did not take place in the Chamber of Deputies until September, 1935, and in the Senate until September 30, 1936. Its approval followed several heated debates in both houses of Congress. The bill also caused a number of violent demonstrations against the British by outraged Argentines.

From the outset, the leading provisions of the proposal proved unpalatable to most Argentines. One provision that based

---

Revista de Economía Argentina 25, no. 221 (November 1936): 176, the *colectivos* carried over 45 percent of the passenger trade in 1934 and close to 49 percent in 1935.

[12] Leche to Simon, March 20, 1934, PRO, FO 371/17466; and *South American Journal,* April 17, 1934, p. 354.

[13] [H. G. Chilton], "Argentine Republic: Annual Report, 1934," pp. 12-13, PRO, FO 371/18636.

representation on the directorate of the new corporation upon the proportional capital value of each participating company especially disturbed the public. Under this arrangement, the Anglo-Argentine Tramway Company gained effective control of a monopoly since it represented nearly two-thirds of the total capital. The corporation also received generous financial assistance from the national and municipal governments in tax exemptions and a guaranteed 7 percent annual profit on its capital value.[14] To the public of Buenos Aires, the monopoly, which would last for fifty-six years, meant confiscation of the speedy and dependable *colectivos* to continue operation of the antiquated and unreliable trams. The law sacrificed an Argentine institution to save a British enterprise. The *porteño* commuters justifiably felt imposed upon by the British.

Many politicians expressed opposition to both transportation bills in Congress. Socialists and dissident Radicals attacked both measures. A U.S. company, General Motors, joined opponents of the laws. That automotive giant worked to defeat both consortiums in the belief that it could sell more chassis in Argentina if neither transportation coordination bill succeeded. Here was an unlikely union of Socialists with a leading representative of "foreign capitalism." The Socialists wanted to destroy the vestiges of British economic imperialism represented by the railways. General Motors intended to expand its Argentine market at the expense of the British-owned railways. While Socialists aroused the public through frenetic anti-British rhetoric in Congress and in the press, General Motors contributed to the *colectiveros'* funds, financed propaganda against the railways, and encouraged general strikes with the purpose of ruining the British-owned railways of Argentina. The Socialists and General Motors united for a common goal, the end of the Anglo-Argentine Tramway Company and

---

[14] Villafañe, *Tragedia argentina*, p. 258. The *7* percent guaranteed profit was not included in the text of the law as it was passed by the Chamber of Deputies on September 26, 1935. It did appear in the Senate version of the bill passed on September 30, 1936, however, and its mysterious addition was never fully explained, because Conservative members of Congress refused to investigate. For a translated text of the original bill see *South American Journal*, February 23, 1935, p. 210.

the British-owned railways. Both turned large numbers of Argentines against the British and their companies.[15]

Through partisan politics the Socialists obstructed the passage of both transportation bills in the Chamber of Deputies throughout most of 1935. At the same time, the unwieldy Concordancia failed to act in a coordinated manner. National Democrats could not raise a quorum in the Chamber of Deputies to vote on the bills until late September, 1935. Local politics preoccupied many Conservatives who sought reelection. Political involvement also explains Justo's reluctance to press the matter. He did not want to embarrass his followers as they faced reelection. Thus the two bills were delayed until too late to go to the Senate. Justo, sensing the political repercussions from the bills, wisely decided not to call an extra session of the Senate after the bills passed the Chamber of Deputies.

Shortly after midnight, September 26, 1935, the Chamber of Deputies approved the Buenos Aires Transportation Corporation Act and the National Transportation Coordination Act. The bills did not pass without a bitter fight. The retiring of the Socialist members as a bloc capped an exciting evening. Rather than vote on the bills, the Socialists walked out in protest. In the words of their leader, Américo Ghioldi: "It hurts us to take this stance. We retire en masse, and we want all the moral force of the Socialist party—recognized by friends and enemies alike—to bear on this project which will remain as a stain on this legislature."[16] In their absence both bills readily passed the Chamber and went on to the Senate. Radical representatives in the Chamber of Deputies did not take a firm or united stance against either bill. As their spokesman, Miguel A. Aguirrezabala of Entre Ríos, explained, the Radicals would not let party issues enter into the debates. Rather, they would accept what was best for the country. According to him, "This country depends upon the aid of foreign capital in order to realize its progress and in order to continue the grand evolution

[15] Fraser to Mason, May 31, 1934; Chilton to FO, telegram, December 12, 1934; Atholl to Troutbeck, July 18, 1935; Frank to Troutbeck, October 10, 1935, PRO, FO 371/17466, /17366, /18631, /18631.

[16] Diputados, *Diario*, September 25-26, 1935, IV, 349.

that ought to take place in its economic, political, and social life."[17]

Because Justo refused to call an extra session of Congress for October, the two bills did not reach the Senate until Congress reconvened in May of the following year. The Buenos Aires Transportation Corporation Act finally came up for a vote in September, 1936, receiving wide public attention. Senators debated the laws amid a general strike, led by *colectivo* drivers who wanted to dramatize the need for their services. They hoped that their strike would prove the inability of the subways and tramways to serve the public adequately. Symbolically, the strike began with the almost simultaneous explosion of bombs in front of the British Embassy and in the terminals of two British-owned railways. On September 25, 1936, the municipal government seized the *colectivos* of the striking drivers. The government then announced its intention to operate public transportation itself. An armed policeman accompanied each vehicle, but violence broke out again on the twenty-ninth. In spite of increased police protection, mobs overturned and burned tramway cars belonging to the unpopular Anglo-Argentine. An incendiary bomb exploded in a second-class coach of the morning train from La Plata to Buenos Aires, injuring several people. The passage of the municipal corporation bill early in the morning of September 30, 1936, after a stormy all-night session, signaled new demonstrations. *Porteños* burned more tramway cars. Some angry citizens even fired shots at passing British-owned passenger trains, while others vented their emotions by breaking the windows of cars standing at the stations.[18]

Popular politicians enraged the nationalists. By September nationalists realized they could not defeat either bill. Nonetheless, Alfredo Palacios, Socialist from Buenos Aires; Lisandro de la To-

[17] Ibid., pp. 365-366, 384. The Radical party began reentry into the political life of the nation in 1935, when it lifted its self-imposed abstention from voting and prepared for the elections of 1938. But the party was fragmented, and Aguirrezabala's opinion was not in tune with other factions of the party. It was in keeping with a view expressed by the party's nominal leader, Marcelo T. Alvear, as quoted by Daniel Cruz Machado, *Frondizi*, p. 55.

[18] From accounts in the *Buenos Aires Herald*, September 21-29, 1936; *Review of the River Plate*, October 2, 1936, p. 9; *Financial Times*, September 26, 1936; *South American Journal*, October 3, 1936; Henderson to Eden, October 9, 1936, PRO, FO 371/19761; and Rennie, *Argentine Republic*, pp. 239-244.

rre, leader of the Progressive Democrats of Santa Fe; and Atanasio Eguiguren, a Radical from Entre Ríos, spoke out against the municipal transportation legislation in the Senate. Using emotionally charged rhetoric and decidedly anti-British arguments, they lashed out against the pending transportation law. Of the three, Palacios took the most extreme position. He played heavy partisan politics and wanted to promote Argentine nationalism. He used the opportunity to create an awareness among the Argentine proletariat of their own need to liberate Argentina. He wanted to awaken in the masses a sense of national identity.[19] To do this he accused the British of perfidy, cynicism, and dominating self-seeking. Palacios linked the two transportation bills to the pending renewal of the unpopular Roca-Runciman Pact.[20] In a six-hour speech he harangued the assembly, stating his case against the British. He repudiated the intervention by British ambassadors who demanded sanction of the two laws. He considered both measures the consequence of Britain's will to dominate Argentina. "England's policy of penetration and domination is characterized by attacking small objectives, and by capitalizing upon petty rivalries and trivial differences between sectors of the community." In that way the British achieved their goals without seeming to act according to a plan. Finally, Palacios concluded by quoting Raúl Scalabrini Ortiz, the revisionist historian and xenophobe: "England would like the Argentine Republic to be an immense *estancia*, having only the population indispensable to work the land, herd the cattle, and run the trains which carry to her ships the raw material and food she needs. She wants Argentina to be a country without more intelligence than is necessary to serve her . . . in connivance with

---

[19] Leche to Troutbeck, March 10, 1937, PRO, FO 371/20597. On leaving Buenos Aires, John Leche wrote of a recent conversation he had had with Palacios. In discussing Palacios's anti-British attacks over the Falkland Islands, Leche reports that Palacios said he carried on his propaganda "partly as a protest against an injustice and partly to foster the spirit of nationalism." In conclusion Leche wrote that Palacios "expressed sincere regret that *such* a bone of contention between the two countries exist[ed], and the whole conversation showed that he is not moved by any spirit of enmity to Great Britain."

[20] Senadores, *Diario*, September 23, 1936, II, 467.

those who ought to be the leaders of our yet-not-apparent national will."[21]

Senator Eguiguren voiced similar sentiments. "How can we continue this situation," he lamented, "all the more incredible when England at this moment is treating us like an African country of the most inferior sort in the matter of the meat convention."[22] He, like Palacios and de la Torre, no longer accepted the myth of economic dependence upon Britain, fostered by such repeated phrases as "a century-old bond of union" and "traditional friendship." Rather, the frequent reminders of the debt of gratitude that Argentines owed to Britain provoked Eguiguren to retort: "I do not share, and it is far from my mentality to share the admiration displayed by the Senator from Buenos Aires [Matías G. Sánchez Sorondo], that foreign capitalism should come to the Argentine Republic to civilize us. That capital has not come for altruistic reasons. It has come seeking interest, profit; because capital is like water: it always seeks its own level. Capital always seeks a good interest return."[23]

Palacios's speech drew sharp responses from British interests. It infuriated Ambassador Henderson, who resented Palacios's accusation that he had taken improper action.[24] The British diplomat argued that he had always assumed that the transportation bills concerned the Argentine government as internal affairs. He had pointed out that the psychological effect of the passage of the bills would have a positive influence upon the British attitude concern-

[21] For full text of Palacios's speech see ibid., September 28, 1936, II, 467-492. Part of the discourse appeared in the *Review of the River Plate*, October 2, 1936, p. 7.

[22] Senadores, *Diario*, September 29-30, 1936, II, 587.

[23] Ibid. For Senator Sánchez Sorondo's defense of the Corporation Act see ibid., September 29-30, 1936, II, 544-563. See pages 530-542 for comments by Palacios and Lisandro de la Torre, similar to those of Eguiguren. De la Torre, in one of his last fights on the floor of the Senate, said little but made clear to his constituents that the law was only a means of salvation for the British-owned Anglo-Argentine.

[24] Henderson is quoted by the *Review of the River Plate* of October 23, 1936, p. 5, as having said, "Now I should be the last to claim that British capital came to this country for any other motive than profit, and indeed the idea of purely philanthropic business is sheer nonsense . . . people who should know better have put forward the monstrous and utterly unfair suggestion that British capitalists have exploited this country in the past and constitute a threat to its economic independence in the future."

ing treaty negotiations. This did not amount to intervention by his standards. Foreign Minister Ramón Castillo assured Henderson that Palacios did not represent the view of either the Argentine government or the Argentine people. Henderson did not feel mollified; he deplored the whole tone of the Palacios speech. Argentine xenophobes, he argued, had lost all sense of justice and fair play. "No impartial observer could fail to be struck by the many services which British money and enterprise had rendered to Argentina in the past," Henderson wrote to his superiors. In his opinion British capital had given Argentina a square deal. The attacks upon everything foreign troubled him. He saw a danger in allowing popular politicians to make sweeping charges against foreign capital. "Dr. Palacios`might not represent the Argentine people or government," he noted, "but as a Senator he gave an example which was unfortunate."[25] More important, "public declarations such as these merely encouraged rascals to throw more bombs at my Embassy."[26]

The *Review of the River Plate* of October 2, 1936, also criticized the nationalistic statements by Palacios and de la Torre. Palacios, they noted, had great influence with the masses. Statements by him in the popular press which "purveys pablum to an anti-foreign bias" would have wide circulation. "It would be wrong to assume that his anti-English vehemence is all or even partly mere rhetoric. In all probability he has convinced himself by now of the reality of the Frankenstein Monster he has created."

Despite the uproar, the Senate approved the Buenos Aires Transportation Act early on the morning of September 30, 1936. The accompanying act, the important National Transportation Coordination Act, did not come to a vote until January of the following year. Neither the Argentine nor the British government wanted to risk damaging their trade negotiations by pressing for the acceptance of the transportation coordination bill. Statesmen in both countries knew the second bill would pass. As Alfredo Palacios rightly assumed in opposing the Buenos Aires bill, "If we

[25] Henderson to Eden, October 9, 1936, PRO, FO 371/19761.
[26] Ibid.

are unable today to resist the project for urban coordination, we shall have no argument tomorrow wherewith to reject the project for national coordination . . ."[27] Nobody wanted repeated the public demonstrations that accompanied the approval of the Buenos Aires Transportation Corporation. Such violence had stirred up hard feelings on both sides of the Atlantic. Argentines felt betrayed by Congress's acceptance of the municipal monopoly. British railway interests felt neglected, both by their government and by the Justo administration. They still believed that Argentina owed them a debt of gratitude.

In an effort to clear the air the *Buenos Aires Herald* of September 30, 1936, cautioned its readers that Palacios's charges had some truth. "More than one peculiarity in past balance sheets and past expenditures calls for further explanation than has yet been vouchsafed." British transportation companies had disregarded the public in the past, primarily because they had dealt exclusively with "those eminent elected gentlemen who were in complete command of the destinies of the plain citizen." As a result, the companies often acted without regard for the rights of the individual who footed the bill. Now, the *Herald* explained, this "happy-go-lucky" policy had left its legacy. "Those who sought and obtained the spoils are dead; the transport companies remain; and the public is demanding a voice in the conduct of its own affairs." The *Herald* could find few kind words to say about the Anglo-Argentine Tramway Company. Its attitude toward the Argentine public had been "scarcely less censurable" than the public's present treatment of it. Previously the company had dealt solely with the politicians and had ignored the taxpayers. It forgot its shareholders. Argentine authorities paid too little attention to the British behavior and financial practices. Palacios had pointed out the truth, having had access to documents which the British could not discount. "Local managers or directors, and even lower subordinates, have engaged in manipulations which have not deceived Argentine onlookers, but which have provided centavos of profit today, and a wagon-load of mischief for tomorrow."

[27] *Review of the River Plate*, October 2, 1936, p. 9.

Despite its indictment of the Anglo-Argentine, the *Herald* joined other pro-British newspapers in a campaign to encourage the peaceful acceptance of the impending National Transportation Coordination Act. In its October 2, 1936, edition an editorial urged readers to forget the problems of the immediate past. Change would handicap interests on both sides of the Atlantic. Some automobile dealers would suffer, but coordination would help the car dealers and the railways find a happy medium. The editorial also thanked Conservative Senator Matías G. Sánchez Sorondo for his presentation of the British position: "... he was above petty prejudices, by speaking in calm defense of the British investor. He was just and even flattering on the subject. His gesture will not be easily forgotten by local Britons, who were naturally somewhat grieved at previous Senatorial outbursts."

Most supporters of the National Transportation Coordination Act emphasized the importance of foreign capital to Argentina's growth. They believed that British capital represented the keystone of Argentine development. Argentina still depended upon railways to maintain its export economy. The National Transportation Coordination Act would give tardy reassurance to the British investor that Argentina still recognized its financial obligations. The British, in particular, could not understand the xenophobia they encountered in Argentina. According to one British observer, Argentine nationalists had no reason to fear that foreign companies might take over control of the nation. Argentina had its own laws and courts, all of which protected the nation from domination by foreign capital. "As a sovereign state, holding undisputed sway over her vast domain, at peace with her neighbors and the whole world, upright in her commitments, whether political or financial, how is it possible that Argentina could—or would—tolerate for one moment the imposition of foreign capitalists? Yet such is the story bruited through the streets."[28]

Many diverse Argentine groups supported the National Transportation Coordination Act. The conservative cattle and agricultural sector gave important backing to the legislation. As

[28] Ibid., October 9, 1936.

gentlemen they considered it their duty to help foreign capitalists who had contributed to Argentina's prosperity. As businessmen they believed their support of the coordination law would win friends in England. They still believed that they had a weak bargaining position in Britain. Accordingly cattlemen and farmers linked the passage of the transportation law with the successful renewal of the trade pact.[29] They also depended upon efficient railway operation to ship their produce. Railway workers, about 131,-000 in number, also advocated approval of the transportation bill. As early as June 27, 1932, the large Unión Ferroviaria—railway workers not involved in the actual operation of locomotives—passed a resolution in favor of transportation coordination and petitioned the Chamber of Deputies to pass a coordination law.[30] Railway workers wanted to protect their jobs. By limiting the growth of the highways they felt they could achieve their major objective, future job security. Since highway transportation employed less than 12,000 at the time and involved a correspondingly smaller capital investment, the railway workers believed they had a strong bargaining point.[31] The Argentine government had a stake in the outcome of the transportation bill as well. The government had large railway holdings, which it desired to protect. The Concordancia had vested interests in placing railway operation on equal footing with highway transportation, especially in order to guarantee cheap but equitable transportation for agrarian products. For that reason the ruling party joined in urging acceptance of the bill.

The conservative newspaper *Bandera Argentina* expressed another view in its issue of October 2, 1936. It contrasted contributions of the British-owned railways to those of the North American automobile manufacturers to the economic development of Argentina. The British, it said, had helped create modern Argentina by building railways that united cities and people. The U.S. au-

---

[29] *La Res* as quoted by *South American Journal*, August 22, 1936, p. 180.

[30] For text of petition see Diputados, *Diario*, September 26, 1935, IV, 363-364.

[31] For examples of procoordination arguments in the Argentine press see Argentine Republic, Dirección Nacional de Vialidad, *La coordinación nacional de los transportes.*

tomobile industry arrived much later, at a time when the nation had already progressed. Auto manufacturers started a belated propaganda campaign in favor of highways. Since the government constructed roads with the aid of taxes paid by the railways, the editorial continued, "this state of affairs means that the agent who is dedicated to selling autos makes a fortune, while the capitalist who brings his money and constructs subways that increase the national wealth loses his capital." *Bandera Argentina* did not believe that campaigns against the Buenos Aires Corporation Act were based upon defending the nation from foreign capital, nor would it accept *colectivos* as symbols of an autonomous Argentine economy. *Colectiveros* hardly constituted defenders of the Argentine economy. The automobiles they drove came from foreign producers. Nationalists who defended the *colectivos* had forgotten the interests of Argentine railway and tramway workers. In effect, the editorial maintained, nationalists protected a North American institution. Once again defenders of the British-owned railways interjected fear of U.S. economic penetration into their defense. They suggested that the automobiles sold to Argentines by North American firms enriched only the latter, who concerned themselves solely with increased profits. Argentines now sent larger amounts of capital to the United States for autos and trucks than they had in dividends to British railway shareholders. *Bandera Argentina* warned its readers not to ignore the fact that British capital had made lasting contributions to Argentine development. Furthermore, Britain remained Argentina's best customer, while the United States posed the greatest barrier to Argentine commerce.[32]

When the coordination bill came up for final discussion in the

---

[32] Further justification for the bill was found in the report of a special commission appointed by Justo on April 12, 1934. Filed in mid-1935, the commission's findings argued, in brief, that the railways were essential to Argentina's internal commerce and to maintaining its external credit. The coordination would, it was stated, improve the situation. The commission, headed by Minister of Public Works Manuel R. Alvarado, also included Roberto M. Ortiz, who had headed the investigation of the Buenos Aires transportation problem. Other members were Juan B. Mignaguy of the Buenos Aires Stock Exchange; Pablo Nogués, director of the state railways; former Minister of Foreign Affairs Adolfo Bioy, who repre-

Senate in January, 1937, no one doubted that it would pass. The violent atmosphere of September had cleared. Argentines would not repeat the destructive acts, primarily because approval of the Buenos Aires Transportation Corporation Act had left the opposition depressed and disjointed. Both Socialists and Progressive Democrats lost impetus after the municipal bill became law. Alfredo Palacios had correctly predicted that nothing could block the national coordination bill. On the very day that the Senate approved the National Transportation Coordination Act its other great critic, Lisandro de la Torre, sent his letter of resignation to the Senate. In that document he spelled out his disillusionment and frustration. For years he had opposed the Concordancia without effective support from the Radicals or from the large newspapers. On more than one occasion he had risked his life to expose corrupt acts by the ruling elite. As he wrote to a friend, he had worked without success to thwart the government. "I have fought savagely, attacking all the serious abuses that come up, despite the conspiracy of silence of the important dailies and the absolute lack of solidarity of the opposition parties, the Radicals and the Socialists."[33]

As de la Torre claimed, the Radical party was not united on the question of the two transportation bills. On the one hand, the Radical senator from Entre Ríos, Atanasio Eguiguren, opposed the laws because they resulted from British pressure, would benefit only the British-owned railways, and illustrated the government's excessive generosity toward British capitalists. He considered the national coordination law "untouchable, inviable, intangible, and cursed."[34] On the other hand, in the Chamber of Deputies a member of the same party from the same province, Miguel A. Agui-

---

sented the Sociedad Rural Argentina; Ramón Videla of the local Board of the Buenos Ayres and Pacific Railway; and Luis Colombo, president of the Unión Industrial Argentina. See Gregorio Etcheguía, *Los ferrocarriles argentinos vistos por ojos argentinos*, pp. 217-226; also *South American Journal*, September 23, 1933, p. 298; April 21, 1934, p. 411; and May 12, 1934, p. 482.

[33] Rennie, *Argentine Republic*, p. 263; and Elvira Aldao de Díaz (ed.), *Cartas íntimas de Lisandro de la Torre*, pp. 67-68.

[34] Senadores, *Diario*, 1936, January 5, 1937, III, 862; and *Hechos e Ideas* 5, no. 18 (January-February 1937): 84-94.

rrezabala, spoke and voted in favor of the bills. As one observer dryly commented on the Radicals' behavior, "that is staying on good terms with God and the devil."[35]

God and the devil, meat and railways, Argentina and Britain—the transportation issue exaggerated tension and antagonism between the two nations. Throughout the mid-1930's the transportation coordination laws focused the attention of the Argentine public upon the traditional Anglo-Argentine economic relationship. As a result many Argentines began to make economic independence of the nation an increasingly popular goal. Unfortunately for the British railway interests and the Concordancia, the passage of the transportation laws coincided with the renewal of the Roca-Runciman Pact in late 1936. The Argentine public saw the two as inseparable. They believed a simple formula: the British kept their railways and the Argentine cattle barons their market for meat. Even Conservatives believed this interpretation. *La Res*, organ of the meat interests, accepted the popular notion that the British would not renew the trade agreement until the Argentines settled the fate of the British-owned railways. In August, 1936, it informed its readers that a solution to the railway issue was necessary in light of the discussions concerning the renewal of the Roca-Runciman Pact. "In a word, we mean that, as those two bills are now before the Senate who will discuss them during the present session, a date might be fixed for the debate, a simple matter which in Great Britain would redound greatly in favor of the new treaty. . . . The Senate cannot help but know the effect caused in British opinion, both in official and financial circles, by preserving silence on the outcome of those bills, and it will be easily understood that if something definite were done about them now, it would at once exert an influence in the negotiations."[36]

Contrary to popular belief, the British government did not make the transportation bills a *sine quo non* of a new trade agreement. To begin with, the British railway interests did not consider the national coordination laws significant. Directors of the major

---

[35] *Bandera Argentina*, October 2, 1936.
[36] *La Res* as translated and quoted by *South American Journal*, August 22, 1936, p. 180.

British-owned railways believed that the National Transportation Coordination Act served them only as a means to new and more meaningful reforms. Certainly the bill signed on January 16, 1937, had little in common with the type of legislation the companies had sponsored in 1932. The law did next to nothing to free the railways from the burdensome and antiquated legislation to which they were subjected. It did not give them a more favorable exchange rate, which by 1936 had become of primary importance to them. The British railway directors felt defeated by the laws. The Buenos Aires Transportation Corporation Act may have promised to save the Anglo-Argentine Tramway, but the National Transportation Coordination Act fell far short of the demands made by the British-owned railways. If anything, the laws stirred up hard feelings in Argentina and in Britain and made smooth operation of the railways more difficult.

Ambassador Henderson summarized the situation well. As he explained the problem, he did not anticipate "any more indiscreet, or rather impolitic" references in Britain to the transportation bill. He felt that the British should see the bill in its right perspective. The British had attached too much importance to the legislation. The British-owned railways will benefit, Henderson noted, but the Argentine government drew up the bill in the interests of Argentina, not British shareholders. "Nearly every country has been obliged to introduce legislation for the coordination of its transport and Argentina has merely been following the examples of other countries in this respect." Henderson still considered the matter one of Argentina's internal administration, not a subject for discussion during the treaty negotiations. He wanted someone in Britain to make clear that the transportation question had not arisen in the negotiations to renew the Roca-Runciman Pact. He wrote to the Foreign Office in early January, 1936, "While therefore, as I have said, it is calculated to give the shareholders in the British Railways in Argentina a better chance of seeing some return on their investments (though, even so, the Bill is far from being so favourable as it might have been) the real gainers by the Bill are the Argentines themselves, since it affords a juster and more equitable prospect for State and British Railways alike to develop on lines which can only be beneficial to the prosperity of both that potentially great country and of its people."[37]

For political purposes, leading Argentine economic nationalists refused to accept this position. For economic reasons, many Englishmen did not accept such an explanation. Yet the evidence clearly demonstrates that passage of the transportation bill did not entail renewing the Roca-Runciman Pact. Negotiators did seriously discuss British public utility companies operating in Argentina during the negotiations. The Argentine government only offered to extend the existing "benevolent clause." The Argentines would go no farther. In light of the embarrassment caused by the failure of the Argentine government to abide by the original provision, it seemed the height of irony to retain the benevolent-treatment clause. As much as British officials may have desired a clause that would have protected British investments, they acknowledged that a more likely chance of reaching satisfactory agreement between the railways and the Argentine government lay in negotiating outside the treaty.[38] As Neville Henderson cautioned in November, 1936, "Specific reference to exceptional favour for foreign companies would merely antagonize public opinion and make the task of the Government harder than it might otherwise be."[39]

Throughout the negotiations of the new trade pact, the Argentines refused to consider any proposal to include provisions securing more satisfactory conditions for the operation of the British-owned public utilities, including a preferential rate of exchange. The Argentine negotiators gave an informal promise that upon successful renegotiation of the treaty Argentina would grant the railway companies a continuation of the present exchange arrangement for a period of up to three years. The British understood that this meant that the railway companies could get a

[37] Henderson to Craigie, January 8, 1937, PRO, FO 371/20596.
[38] Henderson to Eden, January 20, 1937, PRO, FO 371/20598.
[39] Henderson to FO, telegram, November 5, 1936, PRO, FO 371/19760.

favorable rate of exchange by private negotiations. For a price the railways could obtain a special rate, but the other public utilities would have to do without it. None of the British companies involved appreciated this private approach. The railways did not want to pay the price again. Other companies could not afford to pay and could not survive under such terms. The British negotiators believed that they should not sacrifice the treaty for favorable exchange rates. Britain still needed Argentine meats and grains. The diplomats finally resolved the matter by covering the guaranteeing of favorable rates of exchange for the railways in agreed confidential minutes to the negotiations at the signature of the treaty. This arrangement seemingly made it possible for either government to denounce the treaty at any moment, but it offered the best solution. It permitted each party to gain its short-term goals without risking failure of the treaty at large.[40]

By late 1936 both Argentine and British authorities attempted information campaigns aimed at dissociating the renewal of the Roca-Runciman Pact with the imminent passage of the unpopular National Transportation Coordination Act. Neither party wanted to stir up the *porteños*, who had shown the nature of their fury in September. Both governments tried to divorce successful conclusion of the transportation act from final acceptance of the new trade agreement. For that reason the Argentine Senate postponed final action on the transportation bill until January, 1937, following the signing of the new trade pact. Though this delay would normally have provoked criticism from sensitive British investors, Henderson explained it as a purposeful decision of the Justo government. "Though the Minister for Foreign Affairs assured me that the Transport Bill would be passed," he reported, "it is fairly clear that the government is determined not to pass it until after the signature of the Treaty on the ground that prior passage would

---

[40] Troutbeck to FO, September 16, 1936; Minutes of a meeting held at Board of Trade, September 27, 1936; Henderson to FO, October 8, 1936; Henderson to FO, November 5, 1936; Minutes to communication from Board of Trade to FO, November 18, 1936, PRO, FO 371/19760. American Embassy Memorandum, December 4, 1935, DS, NA, RG 59, 635.4131/187.

be regarded as due pressure from His Majesty's Government in the Treaty negotiations themselves."[41]

The *Railway Gazette* explained the belated promotion of the transport bill on similar grounds. It emphasized the fact that the bill did not really benefit the British-owned companies.

There seems little doubt that the reason why the Senate delayed so long the passing of this, the second Transport Bill—as opposed to the Buenos Aires local transport measure—was its desire to await the renewal of the Roca-Runciman Pact, in order to avoid being accused of pandering to the people in Great Britain with that end in view. Even when introducing the Bill, the Minister of Public Works considered it necessary to refute the arguments put forward by the opposition that to pass the Bill was to pander to British capitalists. The composition of the National Commission of Transportation Coordination is now revealed, and it appears that only one of the seven members will represent all private railway interests of whatever nationality, and he will be nominated by the Government from a list of candidates selected by the respective entities. In view of the capital sum involved and the percentage of the total transport of the Republic carried by these railways, it can hardly be said that they are overrepresented on the commission.[42]

Although the renewal of the Roca-Runciman Pact did not depend upon the passage of the transportation bill, the Argentine public would not believe otherwise. Nothing dissuaded them from the conviction that the National Transportation Coordination Act was Argentina's price for renewal of the Anglo-Argentine trade agreement. To a public that believed the worst of the British-owned railways and that hated the Concordancia, it seemed a logical conclusion that the cattle barons had saved English investments to retain a market for beef in Britain. By 1937, disillusioned and defeated by a political system that did not serve their interests, most Argentines gave up on legitimate political activities.

[41] Henderson to FO, November 21, 1936, PRO, FO 371/19760. An observation that was borne out in part by such comments as the following, which appeared in *La Vanguardia*, January 27, 1937: "The recent Coordination Transport Law is a fresh submission to foreign capitalistic pressure, since it presents the handing over of a real monopoly in favour of the private interests of the British Companies . . ."

[42] *Railway Gazette*, February 12, 1937, p. 267.

An increasingly anticolonial climate spread in Argentina. Catch phrases, such as "economic independence," "national sovereignty," and "social justice," became a basic part of the lexicon of all classes, including popular politicians. These phrases incorporated economic nationalism into the ideology of several of the leading political parties. Political rhetoric of the late 1930's regularly included references to Argentina's colonial status. Public opinion reflected decidedly antiimperialist characteristics. Buenos Aires became rife with charges of corruption, bribery, and misuse of office by those dealing with the British-owned railways. Political opponents of the Concordancia upbraided the Justo administration for catering to foreign capitalists. Thus, at the same time, the British were targets for political attacks against a "traitorous" Concordancia and for a growing anticolonial wrath. The railways served as symbols of economic intervention by foreign imperialists. In simple terms, Argentines of all classes began to resent the fact that their nation did not control its own destiny. They felt cheated by foreign investors who appeared to have the protection of a *ven-depatria* government.

10. Nationalization: The First Steps

"Once more it may be said that Argentine relations with Great Britain have remained normal and friendly in spite of the railway question and of differences of opinion in connexion with the new commercial treaty, which could not be expected to satisfy everybody."[1] Thus Neville Henderson, the British ambassador to Argentina, commented upon Anglo-Argentine relations for 1936, a year highlighted by anti-British demonstrations in September and marked by a steady deterioration of the railway companies' public image. The economic year was disappointing for the British-owned railways. Receipts continued to decline and prospects for recovery appeared remote. Yet the British could enter some items on the credit side.

One important development of the year was the Concordancia's decision to nationalize the British railways. President Justo announced the plan for gradual acquisition of the railways to Con-

---

[1] Henderson to Eden, January 20, 1937, PRO, FO 371/20598.

gress on December 23, 1936. To begin, his government planned to purchase the British-owned Central Córdoba Railway and the associated Rafael Steam Tramway Company for 10 million pounds. In making that announcement Justo reflected what he, his opponents, a large segment of the Argentine public, and the majority of the British-owned railway companies had come to conclude; the ultimate solution to Argentina's railway problems lay in nationalizing the industry. Though each group arrived at this conclusion for entirely different economic and political reasons, they agreed in general that the government should acquire an increasing share of the private companies. All agreed that ultimately the government should nationalize the industry.

President Justo's announcement to Congress brought an end to over a decade of bargaining between the Central Córdoba and the Argentine government. The announcement also introduced a new phase of the nation's railway history: the government formally stated its commitment to nationalize the industry. Justo did not contemplate a sudden acquisition of the private railways. Rather, he called for a gradual purchase of foreign-owned railway companies whenever government financial resources permitted such purchases.[2] He advocated a program of the future, based upon sound economic principles. Purchase of the Central Córdoba represented the first step toward nationalizing all the foreign-owned railways operating in Argentina. Justo also stressed the short-term importance of the purchase in view of his own state-owned railway program. Prior to his announcement, one major shortcoming of the state railway system was that it lacked a direct rail route to Buenos Aires. The purchase of the Central Córdoba would give the state railway network access to Buenos Aires.

Lack of a direct route to Buenos Aires had long concerned proponents of the state-owned railway system. This received special attention during the first Yrigoyen administration, when many Radicals thought seriously about nationalizing the entire railway industry to make it conform to their development program.

[2] For a text of the order see Diputados, *Diario*, December 28-29, 1936, pp. 920-922. For details see Emilio Dickmann, *Nacionalización de los ferrocarriles*, pp. 54-55; and Ernesto Tornquist, *Business Conditions in Argentina*, no. 213 (January 1937), pp. 22-24.

Yrigoyen considered the domination of the railways and their extension by the state "fundamental for the social, political, and economic development of the nation." He added that, "in countries of constant growth and progress, such as ours, the public utilities have been considered principally as instruments of the government."[3] Several Argentine economists shared this view at the time. They gave the question of nationalizing the railways considerable attention. The prominent economist Alejandro Bunge presented a well-reasoned argument in favor of nationalizing the industry in his *Ferrocarriles argentinos: Contribución al estudio del patrimonio nacional*, published in 1918.

According to Bunge, Argentina needed to nationalize the railways to diversify its economy. The industry held the key to expanding manufacturing industries. Furthermore, the nation needed to replace foreigners in the dominant positions of the industry. Although Bunge did not present a politically satisfactory method for expropriating the railways, he did encourage further discussion of the problem. Other contemporary arguments followed much the same line. Two brief articles which appeared in the *Revista de Economía Argentina* in August, and September, 1918, succinctly distilled the pros and cons of state ownership of the railways. In the first article, Augusto J. Coelho discussed various proposals concerning state and private ownership of the industry. Although he favored state ownership, he concluded that the railways should remain in private hands, with a large part of the benefits reserved for the state. The second article, written by J. J. Díaz Arana, argued in favor of state ownership. Díaz suggested that the nationalization of railways take place gradually over a number of years, after the government educated the public on the matter.[4]

---

[3] Gabriel del Mazo, *El pensamiento escrito de Yrigoyen*, p. 95.

[4] Augusto J. Coelho, "El rescate de los ferrocarriles argentinos," *Revista de Economía Argentina* 1 (August 1918), pp. 199-204; and J. J. Díaz Arana, "El rescate de los ferrocarriles argentinos," *Revista de Economía Argentina* 1 (September 1918), pp. 275-279. A stronger statement was made by Rafael P. Emiliani in *Reorganización económica, política y social*, in which he argued that a conscript army of laborers should be used to build state railways, which would simply replace the private companies. In fact, conscripts were already at work on various state-owned railways. In his annual report for 1921, the director general of state railways reported: "I bring to attention the efficient cooperation of the Argentine Army in

In a somewhat different vein, Domingo Fernández Beschtedt, director general of state railways, dealt with the question of expanding the operation of the state railways. In his annual report for 1921 he addressed himself particularly to the need to obtain a direct route to Buenos Aires. Wanting to improve the services rendered by the existing state railway network, Fernández Beschtedt pointed out that without direct access to Buenos Aires the state system would never serve the broad interests of the nation. It would neither increase national unity by tying the provinces to the capital, nor stimulate economic development of the interior by giving producers there an opportunity to attach themselves commercially to Buenos Aires, the principal market for consumption and distribution. In discussing past developments of the state system, Fernández Beschtedt noted that "the gravest error committed—one that seems to be perpetuated with singular complacency, the most extraordinary and unjustifiable of all—is the failure of the state railways to have an outlet at the capital of the Republic." The state spent millions of pesos annually to pay private lines to transport goods into the capital from nearby terminals of the state network. The transfer of produce from state to private railways or onto barges at cities along the Paraná River offset the benefits of the low freight rates charged by the state railways to the transfer points.[5]

In spite of their professed interest in strengthening the state network, the Radicals did little to obtain a route to Buenos Aires. Even in 1924, when the financially weak Central Córdoba Railway first offered to sell its properties to the government, the Radical administration turned the proposition down on the ground that the company asked too high a price. The Alvear administration failed

---

this work . . . For the first time, the conscripts of the Railway Regiments have had practical work in a really positive way. The First Regiment, Col. Grosso Soto's, works enthusiastically on mountainous territory opening up cuts, blasting out embankments, removing stone, ballasting, constructing roads for trucks, and in short undertaking all sorts of railway construction. To me it is a matter of high pride in passing Tunal, some 2,000 meters high, to see the conscript camp with its large national flag flying, and a short distance away young and vigorous soldiers working away with ardor" (see White to SecState, December 17, 1921, DS, NA, RG 59, 835.77/73).

[5] Fernández Beschtedt's report was printed in *La Razón*, October 18, 1921. See enclosure, White to SecState, December 17, 1921, DS, NA, RG 59, 835.77/73.

to pursue the matter further. Actually, the Central Córdoba suited the needs of the state railway. Not only did its lines cross the state's right of way in several places, but also its entire system used track of the same gauge as that of the state railways.[6] Its acquisition would have provided a convenient link with Buenos Aires. After the Radicals dropped the subject in 1924, negotiations between the Argentine government and the Central Córdoba did not resume until 1934.

Justo's decision to buy the Central Córdoba in 1936 seems natural because of his open advocacy of extending the state railways. Since 1933 he had encouraged the state system to compete against the private companies. In 1934 he resumed discussions with the floundering Central Córdoba to open a route to Buenos Aires. Many groups had called for such a move in the past. Conservatives, Radicals, Socialists, and other political parties agreed in principle with the deal.

Because of the poor performance of the Central Córdoba, the purchase plan drew wide criticism. Few doubted the advisability of nationalizing the British-owned railways. Even British railway directors suggested transferring ownership of the entire British system to the Argentine government by 1936. But the price asked by the Central Córdoba seemed too high. Since Justo agreed to the company's terms, many Argentines suspected collusion. In an atmosphere charged with anti-British economic nationalism, critics attacked the purchase on an emotional basis. In the aftermath of the anti-British demonstrations against the establishment of the Buenos Aires Transportation Corporation Act and in the heat of the renegotiation of the Anglo-Argentine trade agreement, few trusted the Justo administration in dealing with the British. Many charged that the British had made the sale part of the price of renewing the Roca-Runciman Pact. A rumor circulated in well-informed Argentine circles that secret clauses of the trade agreement of December 1, 1936, imposed the purchase of the nearly bankrupt Central Córdoba upon the Argentine government. Even the usually objective *La Prensa* expressed this sentiment in a series

[6] *South American Journal*, November 17, 1935, p. 460.

of articles concerning the impending purchase. The January 20, 1937, issue of the newspaper warned that Congress should know "everything that went on behind the scenes in connection with the negotiations." The secret agreement explained the reduction from 3 million to 1.5 million pounds as the amount set aside for debt service outside the United Kingdom. According to *La Prensa* the treaty contained several secret clauses: "The purchase of the Central Córdoba Railway *may be another.*"[7]

Major objections to the proposed purchase of the Central Córdoba resulted from the cost of the project. As the *South American Journal* of January 2, 1937, remarked, "That the company will accept these terms if they are definitely offered goes without saying, for £10,000,000 for this property, which has never been successful, is a good price, notwithstanding the fact that its issued capital is more than twice this figure." To shareholders of the Central Córdoba the impending sale had a salubrious effect. First rumors of the sale in late 1934 caused the railway's debentures to rise rapidly on the London exchange. They rose so rapidly, in fact, that the Argentine minister of the interior denied an imminent purchase. After Justo's announcement in December, 1936, the company's first debentures, which had dipped as low as twenty-four and one-half points during 1936, reached fifty-nine and one-half on December 29, 1936.[8] When figuring the 4.5 percent interest into the cost, the railway's price actually amounted to 12 million pounds. Further costs resulted from repeated stoppages due to labor demands for better working conditions and higher wages during 1936. By rough estimates, the Central Córdoba operated at a deficit of nearly 3.5 million pesos and verged upon financial collapse. Before Congress enacted legislation for the purchase, it approved a wage increase of 1.5 million pesos and agreed to let the

[7] Italics added. *La Prensa* ran a series of articles on the purchase. For similar comments see Raúl Scalabrini Ortiz, *Historia de los ferrocarriles argentinos,* p. 210; and Virgil Salera, *Exchange Control and the Argentine Market,* p. 161. Ysabel F. Rennie's account of the purchase in *Argentine Republic,* p. 241, was in turn based upon Salera's book.

[8] Dillingham to SecState, December 31, 1936, DS, NA, RG 59, 835.77/293. According to the *South American Journal* of January 23, 1937, p. 75, "although the bill is one of some importance it would be wrong to assume that its importance is as great to Argentine interests as to those in London."

government lease the railway for one year while considering the purchase, with the guarantee that the company would receive a net return equal to that obtained during the last fiscal year.[9] Hence the government seemed to lose over 5 million pesos before it bought the railway.

The cost seemed ridiculously high. Radical Deputy Ernesto E. Sammartino may have exaggerated when he argued that the state could build a narrow-gauge railway between Santa Fe and Buenos Aires at a third of the cost of the purchase of the Central Córdoba. He correctly observed, however, that "the project to acquire the Central Córdoba offers only promising prospects to a bankrupt foreign company."[10] Even the Socialists, who had campaigned incessantly since their founding to nationalize the railways, balked at the high price offered to the British firm. Initially, their leader, Nicolás Repetto, reacted favorably to Justo's proposal to nationalize the railways. On first hearing the proposal he stated, ". . . it will be a successful undertaking which will give the country good benefits and the public administration an honorable note."[11] When the final terms of the transaction came up for discussion in the Chamber of Deputies in 1938, Enrique Dickmann, a Socialist who had served on the congressional subcommittee that drew up the final purchase terms, spoke against the bill. He still favored nationalization of the railways—gradual nationalization at that—but felt that the Central Córdoba asked a price twice as high as it should be. "This is," he emphasized, "a company in liquidation, in bankruptcy, and it is practically abandoned."[12] Partisan politics also entered into the Socialists' decision to oppose the purchase. The Conservative Concordancia had claimed credit for formulating a nationalization plan. Socialists refused to support the Conservative-sponsored bill, no matter how much they agreed with its basic objectives. Rather than cooperate with the Concordancia they

[9] Tornquist, *Business Conditions in Argentina*, no. 216 (October 1937); and *La Prensa*, June 26, 1937.

[10] Diputados, *Diario*, May 19, 1937, p. 37.

[11] Ibid., January 20, 1937, p. 457.

[12] Ibid., August 31, 1938, p. 334. See also Dickmann's book, *Nacionalización de los ferrocarriles*, for his nationalization scheme.

reverted to a nationalistic stance. They now maintained that any agreement made with an Englishman constituted a betrayal of national interests. In so doing they took an ambivalent position, supporting the concept of nationalizing all private railways but opposing the particular scheme put forth by the Concordancia. Ostensibly they opposed the deal on the ground that the payment of millions of pesos to the British for a run-down railway made little economic sense. They also wished to embarrass the Concordancia as they had in the past.

Local and international business observers also considered the purchase economically unsound. The undertaking placed a considerable burden upon the taxpayers, no matter how much the customers of the state railways benefited by having low rates to Buenos Aires. Not only did the railway need costly repairs, but it also seemed unlikely that it would operate profitably in the future. Moreover, there remained the question of an increased government debt, especially the issuing of new bonds which would bring bearers a substantial 4.5 percent interest whether the line made profits or not. As one experienced observer noted, "Over and above the dubious benefits of government administration of the railways, which is continually subject to changing political influence, an active policy of forcing foreign capital out of the country will, it is feared, have an ill effect on the nation as a whole since it is hardly to be expected that foreign enterprise now established here will improve their services when at any future date their investment may be absorbed by the government."[13]

In Rosario and Santa Fe, two important river terminals of the state railway network, doubts grew among business interests about the immediate and the long-term economic advantages of establishing direct rail service to Buenos Aires. The Rosario Chamber of Commerce had endorsed the incorporation of the Central Córdoba within the state railway system. But a study prepared by a group of prominent Santa Fe business and professional men revealed that the purchase would have adverse effects. North-south traffic would be diverted from Santa Fe and Rosario, seriously

[13] Dillingham to SecState, December 31, 1936, DS, NA, RG 59, 835.77/293.

damaging the business of those ports. The government's acquisition of the Central Córdoba would not make either city the key to the state railway system. Buenos Aires would assume that role. As traffic flowed directly to Buenos Aires the two upriver ports would lose important transshipment business. In many ways the cities had brought this situation upon themselves. Their prosperity and growth had depended upon services that their port facilities offered to the railways. For many years the ports had had deficient installations and expensive charges, factors which had led to the extension of the Central Córdoba from Rosario to Buenos Aires some twenty-five years before. Consequently, the expansion of the state-owned railway did not promise to stimulate the prosperity of either port city.[14]

In Britain the proposed purchase of the Central Córdoba raised few eyebrows. Although the major British-owned railway companies preferred to delay the transaction as long as possible to postpone detrimental competition from the state lines, they made no concerted effort to oppose it. The companies saw no reason for urgency. Discussions had dragged on since 1934 with little progress. It seemed unlikely that the Argentine Congress would act rapidly on the issue, especially since Justo refused to press for its quick passage during an election year. Most British railway directors wanted the sale completed. They considered the smaller British-owned lines major obstacles to smooth relations with the Argentine government. The Big Four broad-gauged railways—the Central Argentine, the Southern, the Pacific, and the Western—showed little concern for the continued operation of the other British-owned companies. Most British railway experts agreed with Sir Follet Holt when he wrote about the Central Córdoba, the Transandine, the Entre Ríos, and the Argentine North Eastern, "I have always hoped that these last four could be got out of the way, namely the Córdoba and the Transandine, leaving the Entre Ríos and the Argentine North Eastern to be dealt with."[15]

---

[14] Lightner to SecState, July 29, 1937; Lightner to SecState, August 26, 1937, DS, NA, RG 59, 835.77/300, 835.77/302.
[15] Holt to Ovey, November 26, 1937, PRO, FO 371/20596.

Although the idea of gradual nationalization of the foreign-owned railways surprised many Argentines in 1936, it had already received wide support in Britain. The British-owned railways had prepared for such a contingency throughout 1936. Directors of the leading railways played an instrumental role in encouraging Justo and the Concordancia to take such a step. The companies took action to coordinate their efforts by organizing a new British-Argentine Railway Committee in Buenos Aires in June, 1935. Headed by Dr. Guillermo E. Leguizamón, a lawyer and director of the local board of the Pacific Railway, the committee included the managers and principal local directors of all the British-owned railways. Their task was to represent the railways in Buenos Aires and to safeguard the interests of all British-owned railway companies. Shortly thereafter the companies established a similar committee in London, made up of the directors of the various companies. This body's powers could override its Buenos Aires counterpart.[16] In the past Justo could play one railway off against another in individual confrontations. Now the railways offered a united front with common objectives.

Opinions still varied among the British directors as to the best action in planning for the future. They hesitated to press for action during the last two years of the Justo administration. Under Justo the Concordancia had proved incapable of acting decisively and swiftly on railway matters before 1936. Few expected them to act any faster after 1936, especially during the election year of 1937. Furthermore, the British directors did not want to form long-term plans until after the renegotiation of the trade agreement in 1936. If the negotiations failed, the directors knew they faced an exceedingly dangerous situation. If, on the other hand, a new treaty were negotiated, the directors could hope for reasonable treatment by the Argentine government. For that reason they tried not to become involved in the treaty discussions. British railway directors advised the British Foreign Office to follow a hands-off policy regarding the impending purchase of the Central Córdoba. They

---

[16] *The Times*, June 6, 1936; and Foreign Office Minutes, July 20, 1936, PRO, FO 371/-19761.

did not want it made a part of the trade agreement. The Central Córdoba had no voice in the decision since it represented one of the smallest and poorest of the British-owned railways in Argentina.[17]

Most British railway directors remained reluctant to take any positive steps until after the 1937 presidential elections, at which time they anticipated a more friendly Radical administration. Sir Follet Holt did not believe that the Justo government would ever agree to any outright purchase plan, especially since negotiations concerning the Central Córdoba were delayed. In Buenos Aires, Guillermo Leguizamón expressed a similar conviction. He did not believe that the present Argentine government would enter into any scheme of purchase or partnership for two reasons. First, the present director of the state lines, the determined and ambitious Pablo Nogués, would not cooperate with the private companies. Nogués desired complete authority for himself and wanted to be rid of the British concerns. Second, political uncertainties and turmoil did not permit the passing of necessary legislation during the election year. Leguizamón, like Holt, suggested that the compa-

---

[17] The companies had good reason to feel this way, for continuation of the British market for Argentine meats and grains was a prerequisite for future benevolent treatment of the railways. On February 15, 1936, new Minister of Finance Roberto M. Ortiz reached an agreement with the British-owned railways by which the latter were accorded a more favorable exchange rate of 15.75 pesos per pound sterling as opposed to the previous rate of 17, and a promise that freight rates would not be lowered, except for a reduction for maize, which would total some 3.5 million pesos for the year. There were strings attached to the agreement, however, in the form of a commitment from the companies to represent the interests of the Argentine government in the forthcoming trade negotiations. If the negotiations did not go through, the railways were informed that they could expect immediate reprisals, almost certainly in the form of a cancellation of the special exchange rate, a reduction in freight rates, and an administrative squeeze from all sides. In conveying this information to the British government, J. Montegue Eddy noted that previously the Argentine government had refused to do anything to help the railways in order to maintain their bargaining power. "Subsequently they have been induced to modify this attitude and had now given the railway companies this satisfactory, if temporary, arrangement on exchange, the object of which was to bring His Majesty's Government into a mood in which they would be ready to deal gently with Argentine meat." Should the matter be settled in a manner unfavorable to the Argentines, however, the latter would proceed to ruin the companies. See Holt to Troutbeck, February 28, 1936; and Buenos Aires Chancery to FO, February 10, 1936, PRO, FO 371/19760. Also *The Times*, February 16, 1936.

nies make plans to treat the matter with the new government
which would come to power in early 1938.[18]

Justo's decision to purchase the Central Córdoba signalled
new developments. He had not proposed the purchase for economic considerations alone. His announcement of the proposed
purchase, made on December 23, 1936, reflects his awareness of
growing antiforeign nationalism in Argentina. Like other leaders of
his day, he placed national objectives ahead of efficiency and economy, which he sacrificed to gain public support for his administration. As Justo observed in urging the transaction: ". . . in the
frequent conflicts that have arisen with the employees of the privately owned railways there is a growing difficulty in finding reasonable solutions to the differences between the parties, because
the mass of workmen regard themselves as being exploited by
foreign capital, the profit-seeking ambitions of which they blame
for their economic situation; and owing to the hardships they have
had to suffer for years past they have no disposition to attempt to
overcome differences in a reasonable manner. It is felt amongst the
workers that shareholders have no right to any dividend, and there
is increasing resistance to contribute in any form at the expense of
wages to the companies' fixed charges."[19] Justo had learned the
rhetoric of nationalists, and the purchase of the Central Córdoba
gave him an opportunity to make a symbolic concession to the
rampant nationalistic spirit in Argentina.

British officials also recognized the effects of Argentine economic nationalism upon future operation of the British-owned railways. In particular, Neville Henderson showed sensitivity to the
phenomenon in Buenos Aires. He urged his government to consider the normal rise of economic nationalism in Argentina in dealing with railway questions. "For foreign capital invested here this
economic nationalism cannot but have certain disagreeable aspects
and must often appear exaggerated; but it is not an unjustifiable
phenomenon and it is, in any case, inescapable and a fact which British capital must take into account if it is to continue to carry on its

[18] Foreign Office Minutes, July 20, 1936, PRO, FO 371/19761.
[19] Overseas Trade, *Economic Conditions*, 1938, pp. 21-22.

traditional role of cooperation with this country."[20] Argentina had not reached the level of self-sufficiency that Argentines liked to imagine, Henderson noted, but the nation's economy had changed dramatically since World War I. "In a country as conscious as Argentina has become of her national dignity," he continued, "it is impossible much longer to conceive of such British railways directed in a watertight compartment 6,000 miles away in London on a sterling basis. So long as this is the case, or rather (since presumably transformation must be a lengthy business) until the railway board in London shows at least its complete readiness to modify a state of affairs so little in accordance with Argentine aspirations, the unfortunate shareholders are not likely to see any adequate or secure return on the money which they have invested."[21]

Henderson's comments reveal his awareness of the problems related to economic nationalism in Argentina, which he saw from an angry Buenos Aires. For that reason he remained apprehensive throughout 1936 about the fate of the railways. The growing hostility against the railways concerned him. He believed that the railways had done nothing to allay the anti-British sentiments attached to the railway problem. If the British government did nothing to improve the situation they ran the risk of hastening the deteriorating Anglo-Argentine relations in general. This Britain could not afford, not only because it needed the Argentine market for manufactured goods provided by the British-owned railways, but also because Britain still depended upon beef and grains from the interior to feed its working population.

Henderson did not make concrete proposals to remedy the situation, but he did suggest two steps to alleviate the strain caused by the railways. First, railways could improve their image through a public-relations campaign. The Argentines' aggressive frame of mind, he lamented, made it unlikely that hostility and future discrimination could be diverted. "For the fact is that the set of circumstances which held the field in the Argentine in the 19th cen-

[20] Henderson to Eden, January 20, 1937, PRO, FO 371/19760.
[21] Ibid.

tury is no longer applicable to the 20th and requires an entirely different treatment. Admittedly the British railways contributed greatly to securing the unity and prosperity of Argentina, but both these benefits, having now, for some time past, been achieved, it is useless to seek for gratitude, which is appreciably less common with nations than with individuals."[22] The Argentine public was not interested in what the British railways had done for Argentina in the past, but rather what they could do in the present. The railways had to change their propaganda. They had to improve their image before hostility became more dangerous than it was.

Henderson's second suggestion related to the prospects of nationalizing the railway industry. He thought that the Argentine government might be able to join private capital as a partner in the railway industry. This scheme, he maintained, would have an immediate effect. First, it would undoubtedly influence public opinion in the companies' favor. Second, such an undertaking would help stave off further encroachment of the state railways on the operations of the foreign-owned railways.[23]

British railway directors shared Henderson's belief that joint Anglo-Argentine railway operation offered a viable solution to most of their grievances. The directors, however, could not agree upon a satisfactory means of achieving a working relationship with the Argentine government. A wide divergence of views existed among railway officials, government agencies, and banking and financial interests that controlled substantial shares in the British companies involved. The differences resulted mainly from procedures and tactics. All these groups believed that the Argentine government had to increase its role in the operation of the private railways. In this sense they all reacted to rising Argentine economic nationalism, which by mid-1936 had made the economic running of the railways all but impossible. As one observer noted, no matter how much some thoughtful Argentines might recognize that their

---

[22] Henderson to Eden, April 30, 1936, PRO, FO 371/19760. For a survey of Argentine public opinion toward the British-owned railways during the 1930's see A. Vigil (pseud.), *Railway Propaganda and Publicity*, a study prepared for the Institute of Transport—Argentine and the River Plate Centre in 1939.

[23] Henderson to Eden, April 30, 1936, PRO, FO 371/19760.

country owed its present development to the courage and enterprise of British investors, there existed "deep-rooted feelings that the main arteries of Argentine commercial and agricultural life are exploited for the benefit of the foreign capitalists."[24] British railways had become the target for every political sharpshooter. Labor quickly realized that the situation might implement its demands. As for the Argentine government, many Britons felt that, although it may have wished to be fair to the railways, the government feared to counter public opinion. According to a Baring Brothers' representative in Buenos Aires, "If public opinion moved permanently in favor of the Railways, the Government would be encouraged to foster the development of the whole system, labour would gradually recognize that it must also contribute to the well-being of the Railways as the biggest employer of labour in the country, economies in exploitation would be welcomed, and the renewal of the Mitre Law would be greatly facilitated."[25]

In an independent action, aimed at gaining public support for the faltering railways, the Association of Investment Trusts and Insurance Companies, which controlled about 40 million of the total 270 million pounds invested in Argentine railways, requested Baring Brothers and Company to approach President Justo through their Buenos Aires agent. The association wanted to determine whether the Argentine government would consider some scheme for nationalizing the railways. It wanted to know whether the Argentines would accept gradual acquisition of a substantial interest in the British-owned companies. Baring Brothers thought this could be accomplished in a number of ways. The British companies could convert themselves into Argentine companies and express their share capital in pesos rather than pounds sterling. Or they could sell or lease their holdings and assets to an Argentine operating agency in exchange for stock in the new companies. Baring also suggested a scheme in which the Argentine government would buy outright 30 to 40 percent of the equity interests of the

---

[24] Baring to Irving, July 16, 1936, PRO, FO 371/19761.
[25] Ibid.

companies, paying for the purchase in 3 or 4 percent bonds. Baring Brothers wanted to encourage Justo and the British-owned railways to accept the latter plan. In such manner, the Argentine government would gain immediate representation on the boards of the private railways. The management, however, would remain under British control until the government acquired at least 60 percent of the equity. As an alternative, Baring Brothers proposed to Justo that the Argentine government consider a plan to buy the British railways on the open market. To do this the government could apply earnings over 2 percent on ordinary stocks toward the purchase price. The last suggestion had the advantage of guaranteeing the state a percentage of the companies' equity in return for a guarantee of a certain percentage of profit to shareholders. Furthermore, it would give incentive to the Argentine government to treat the railways fairly to facilitate the transfer from British to Argentine hands.[26]

The directors of the major British-owned railways opposed any radical scheme. They did not want to give up their vast holdings so rapidly. They felt it best to urge the Argentine government to extend the basic railway law, the Mitre Law, which expired in 1947. They proposed several modifications in that law, including a change in the percentage of profits they could make. By reducing that figure from 6.8 percent to a lower figure, they argued, the government and the companies could divide profits above that rate. The government would receive 75 percent of that share. The Argentine government could thus apply the sums accruing to it to gradually acquire a share of the railways by purchasing shares on the open market. By this process, it would take anywhere from twenty to forty years for the Argentines to acquire a substantial interest in the companies, let alone a controlling interest. This plan had a broad appeal in Britain. It suited the immediate needs of the railways. It also pleased the British manufacturers, since it meant that the market for British manufactured goods provided by the British-owned railways would continue.[27]

[26] Ibid.; Henderson to Eden, January 20, 1937, and Foreign Office Minutes, July 20, 1936, PRO. FO 371/20598. 371/19761.

[27] Foreign Office Minutes, July 20, 1936, Henderson to Eden, January 20, 1937, PRO, FO 371/19761, 371/20598.

Representatives of the British government did not want to become directly involved in transferring the ownership of the railways to Argentina. They did not want to bear the criticism should the ultimate solution not work out to the satisfaction of British shareholders. They feared that shareholders would blame them if they gave the companies advice which did not lead to satisfactory negotiations with the Argentines. British government representatives followed a hands-off policy. However, the Foreign Office advocated the transfer of the management of the railways to Buenos Aires and urged the gradual nationalization of the lines. They, like the company managers, rejected the idea of outright sale of the railways, since that would incur substantial losses to British shareholders due to the low market value of the railways. They saw no way of either raising enough capital on the Argentine market to make the purchase or turning the capital into sterling within a reasonable time. In the end, the British government chose to play the role of an interested spectator. It would assist the companies if asked. It would help the companies reach a satisfactory settlement of their grievances. It would lend its offices in any transfer scheme. But the government would not intervene on the railways' behalf. The government only wanted to act as a stabilizing agent, not a participant. As one member of the Foreign Office observed, the railways had not worked out their own policies. "I frankly confess," he wrote to his colleagues, "that I feel very hesitant about offering advice to these big independent organizations as to how to run their business, though I admit that the railway companies are in such a state of fright these days that I do not think they would in principle resent our offering them advice."[28]

When Justo proposed the gradual nationalization of the foreign-owned railways, he proposed a resolution of the railway issue. Companies could then develop transfer schemes; British government officials could feel relieved. Not only had the Anglo-Argentine trade agreement been successfully renegotiated, much to Britain's favor, but also the troublesome railway problem appeared settled, at least temporarily. The Argentine government, contented by maintaining the British meat market, also relaxed.

[28] Troutbeck to Foreign Office, June 9, 1936, PRO, FO 371/19760.

But the railway dilemma remained. Nationalistic Argentines, who concerned themselves neither with saving the British from financial difficulties nor with continuing the economic and political domination of the nation by the beef interests, still manipulated the railway issue to their own liking. Justo, cognizant of the emotional reaction to the two recently passed transportation bills, did not implement either law. During 1937, an election year, he made no move to antagonize the public. *Colectivos* still roamed Buenos Aires at large, unrestricted by central administrations.

11. The Transition

A fraudulent presidential election on September 5, 1937, brought Roberto M. Ortiz to office. The government, not the populace, selected the new president-elect and his running mate, Ramón S. Castillo. Neither represented a popular political faction. Indeed, the ticket reflected the growing split in the Concordancia. Ortiz and Castillo had little in common, weakening the Concordancia's leadership considerably. During their short-lived administration the two men worked against each other. Ortiz, a noted Anglophile, had served as legal adviser to some of the large British-owned railways. As a Radical politician he had accorded benevolent treatment to the railways while serving as Alvear's minister of public works and again as minister of finance under Justo. Like Justo, he became an antipersonalist Radical when he joined Alvear in splitting from Yrigoyen during the 1920's. Shortly after his inauguration as president of Argentina on February 29, 1938, Ortiz broke with Justo and the conservative wing of the Concordancia. On his own initiative Ortiz indicated that he would put an end to minority government and restore honest suffrage.[1] When a serious illness incapacitated him in July, 1940, the nominal control of the state passed to Vice-President Castillo. Castillo, upon assuming office, announced that as acting president he intended to carry out his own policies rather than continue those of Ortiz. He also reorganized the cabinet with men he could trust to carry out his orders. A staunch Conservative and pro-Axis in outlook, the shrewd Castillo acted as a representative of the pro-German military nationalists until shortly before his downfall on June 4, 1943.[2]

The economic planning of the Ortiz administration differed very little from that of Justo's, except that Ortiz advocated the principle of free trade and paid little attention to industrialization. He did not seem to comprehend a state-directed economic policy. He felt that Argentina could compete successfully in the world market because it produced large quantities of cheap, high-quality foodstuffs and raw materials. Since he could not practice free trade in the nationalistic world of the late 1930's, Ortiz had to modify his view. He did concede that Argentines should buy from their own industries what they could not obtain conveniently through foreign trade. Rather than promise blanket protection to domestic industries, Ortiz supported a policy that did not, in his words, "lose sight of the interests of the countries with which we maintain an active and balanced interchange."[3]

In spite of the fact that the Concordancia represented the cattle baron, Argentine domestic industries grew during the depression years. Industrialization posed new political, social, and economic challenges for the national government. For obvious reasons, the landholding members of the Concordancia wanted to

---

[1] *South American Journal* of September 16, 1939, pp. 261-262, ran an editorial that stated that Ortiz was a true democrat. It was convinced of Ortiz's good faith in undertaking electoral reforms. See John W. White, *Argentina*, pp. 165-166, for a contemporary observation by a foreign correspondent.

[2] For a good survey of the Ortiz-Castillo years see Robert A. Potash, *The Army and Politics in Argentina, 1928-1945*, pp. 104-181. Also see José Luis Romero, *A History of Argentine Political Thought*, trans. Thomas F. McGann, pp. 240-242.

[3] Roberto M. Ortiz, *Mensaje del presidente de la nación, 1939*, pp. 39-40.

keep the economic and political authority concentrated in their hands and feared that too much industrialization would lead to the loss of their power.[4] At the same time, the depression and the ensuing wartime situation gave impetus to steady growth of Argentine substitute industries, and an irreversible process began. Mechanization of the large farms made it possible for fewer persons to cultivate far larger areas. As a result, between 1930 and 1939 a surplus of displaced agrarian laborers swarmed into the cities in search of new jobs, providing an increasing urban labor force.[5] This situation, with the fact that the Argentines had to buy at home because the depression reduced their foreign purchasing power, explains in large part the increase of industrial production during the 1930's and the corresponding rise in living standards.[6]

Argentina had not become an industrial nation by 1940, although so-called substitute industries sprang up during the depression years. Argentine products replaced otherwise unobtainable foreign-made consumer goods. Only a small industrial base developed during the period. Argentina lacked the large steel, coal, and petroleum complexes needed to establish a viable industrial economy. The nation remained dependent upon foreign sources for heavy industrial equipment and many raw materials. Its economy was still predominantly agrarian, even though new industries freed Argentines from having to import most of their consumer goods. Despite the production of grains, cereals, and meats which continued to provide the mainstay of Argentina's economy, the demands made by the rising industrial sector brought increasing pressure upon the national government.[7] Native industrialists wanted to substitute their products for foreign imports wherever possible. Throughout the 1930's the Unión Industrial Argentina,

---

[4] Felix J. Weil, *The Argentine Riddle*, p. 97.

[5] Alejandro Bunge, *Una nueva Argentina*, p. 165.

[6] See Adolfo Dorfman, *Evolución industrial argentina*, pp. 73-169, 244-271.

[7] A number of articles in the *Anales de la Unión Industrial Argentina* during the 1930's were devoted to this problem; see especially "Amplificación de la nómina de materiales que los ferrocarriles pueden introducir libre de derechos," 49, no. 808 (April 1936): 9-24. The problem is briefly summarized in Lucio M. Moreno Quintana, "Características general de la economía argentina," *Revista de Ciencias Económicas* 27, no. 214 (May 1939): 411-446.

headed by Luis Colombo and aided technically by Alejandro E. Bunge before his death, campaigned for a general increase of tariff rates on foreign goods that competed with domestic manufactured goods. Though largely unsuccessful before the outbreak of World War II, their demands eventually influenced part of the New Deal-like programs espoused by the Castillo regime.

The growing industrial interests were at loggerheads with the foreign-owned railways regarding protection. The latter imported goods duty free under provisions of the Mitre Law. Technically the companies could import materials without paying duty if they needed the materials for the operation or maintenance of the lines. With some justification, the Argentine industrialists accused the British railways of abusing this privilege. The British imported everything possible, including the pens, paper, and inkwells used by the rural station masters.[8] To the Argentine industrialists this policy meant that the British-owned railways used their large purchasing power to support British rather than Argentine manufacturers. In the eyes of the Argentines this inequity appeared to subject Argentina to London.[9]

The industrial bloc attempted to introduce bills to Congress during 1936 and 1937 which would have established controls over the prices of commodities purchased by the railways. They wanted laws that would have forced the British-owned companies to buy any Argentine product available at a price equal to or lower than comparable imported goods.[10] Such a measure would have profoundly influenced Argentine economy because the railways provided a major market for British manufactured goods. But pro-British Conservatives in Congress thwarted efforts to close this large market to foreign goods. The British held tenaciously to this trade. As it turned out, many of the British-owned railway companies endured the difficult depression years because they made large

---

[8] See Diputados, *Diario*, June 9, 1937, p. 459. The list of goods imported free of duty by the railways included common glass, vases, wallets, uniforms of various types, towels, sheets, blankets, ropes, tickets, locks and keys, chairs, account books, and numerous other goods which were produced in Argentina.

[9] Ricardo M. Ortiz, *El ferrocarril en la economía argentina*, p. 29.

[10] For an example see Diputados, *Diario*, June 9, 1937, p. 459.

profits through interlocking construction and equipment companies which they owned.[11] The companies made profits by selling to a virtually closed railway market which they controlled. The combination of British manufacturer and Argentine Conservative kept alive the last vestige of the laissez faire economic philosophy in Argentina.

Ortiz accepted the concept of gradually nationalizing the railways. Shortly after he took office a spokesman for his administration announced that the government would continue Justo's plan to acquire the private railways slowly.[12] At the time, Argentine and British officials viewed the gradual transfer of the companies from British to Argentine hands as the best solution to the problem. Ortiz expressed satisfaction with the progress made by the newly acquired Central Córdoba Railway. He felt that its marked improvement under government supervision demonstrated the ability of Argentine personnel to meet the problems related to acquiring and operating the British-owned railways.[13] The immediate outlook for future purchases, however, seemed bleak. It had taken the Argentine Congress nearly two years to approve the purchase of the Central Córdoba. As of 1938 the government lacked the financial resources to buy more railways.

Under the circumstances the directors of the British-owned railways had little cause for optimism. They favored the eventual sale of the companies' holdings but knew that the transfer could

[11] Julius S. Duncan, "British Railways in Argentina," *Political Science Quarterly* 52, no. 4 (December 1937): 574; and *South American Journal*, May 10, 1941, p. 318.

[12] *South American Journal*, October 29, 1939, p. 424. Shortly after Ortiz's election, a prominent member of the Buenos Aires business community reported a conversation that he had had with the president-elect: ". . . he [Ortiz] thought it was necessary to take the preliminary steps towards nationalization of the railways over a period of years, with Government participation and assistance both in the capital structure and in administration. He thought the Railways would have constant trouble with the men unless a situation was created whereby a strike would be regarded as an infringement of the country's patrimony. As far as the public are concerned, they must be given the idea that they had an interest in the railways and be induced to cherish them, as it were, as part of a necessity vital to the country's existence" (Ovey to Eden, October 23, 1937, PRO, FO 371/20596).

[13] Ortiz, *Mensaje del presidente de la nación, 1939*, p. xxii. According to Ernesto Tornquist, *Business Conditions in Argentina*, no. 223 (July 1939), p. 67, the receipts and profits of the Central Córdoba increased noticeably under state ownership.

not take place immediately. The railways' future seemed uncertain. Carrying trade dropped off radically in 1937 and 1938. Droughts had reduced farm production. It appeared remote that the railways would ever recover the full value of their original investment and earning power.[14] The railways desired a few temporary concessions from the government. Greater coordination of the existing lines offered a possible solution. Closer cooperation with the Argentine authorities offered another. Ultimately, they wanted the government to repatriate their holdings. As summed up by the *South American Journal*, it seemed unlikely that the Argentine government could become a "full-fledged business partner" in the immediate future. "Taking over the British-owned railways is by no means an easy task for the Argentine Government, as apart from the very heavy sacrifices of a financial nature, . . . it must be remembered that once the property is acquired, there is the training of the necessary management personnel and the heavy expenditure involved in linking together all of the systems."[15]

The Ortiz administration treated the British-owned railways sympathetically. Like the British, the Argentine authorities wanted to make sure that negotiations concerning the purchase of the railways would be conducted in a spirit of mutual understanding once they began. Accordingly, the government revoked Article 67 of the General Railway Act of 1891 in October, 1938. That article had prohibited railways which served the same area from pooling their services and from reaching price agreements. Its revocation allowed the companies to merge services, a goal they had sought for over a decade. As the annual reports for the year 1939 reveal, the companies not only took advantage of the opportunity but also realized some improvements.[16] The Argentine government

---

[14] *South American Journal*, July 30, 1938, p. 105.

[15] Ibid.

[16] On September 23, 1935, President Justo submitted a proposal to modify the existing railway law by replacing Article 67. Although there was little outspoken criticism, there was little support. The bill was forgotten and finally resurrected by the Ortiz administration. See Trimble to SecState, September 27, 1935, DS, NA, RG 59, 835.77/267; and *South American Journal*, March 18, 1939, p. 296.

also introduced bills calling for the purchase of two small British-owned railways, the Entre Ríos and the North East Argentine railways.[17]

Ortiz got no further in his attempt to continue Justo's gradual acquisition scheme. He never met with British officials to work out details of a transfer. Despite repeated indications of willingness to purchase the British-owned railways, including the discussions during the renegotiation of the Anglo-Argentine trade pact in 1939, he made no concrete proposals. In renegotiating the Anglo-Argentine trade agreement, the Argentines encouraged future repatriation by agreeing to sell foodstuffs to Britain on credit. They intended to use part of their credit reserves to repatriate the railways.

British and Argentine authorities had already judged repatriation feasible. More recently a study prepared under the direction of Teodoro Sánchez de Bustamente for Instituto de Economía de los Transportes of the University of Buenos Aires worked out a method of purchasing the railways. Sánchez Bustamente thought the idea was wise. According to his study the foreign-owned railways were valued at approximately 2,502,906,267 pesos. The Argentine government could pay this sum over a period of fifty-six years with little strain on the economy, the study suggested. Ample precedents for such a step existed, especially the example of France, which had nationalized its entire railway network. Furthermore, in keeping with the growing economic nationalism of the late depression years, the report concluded, ". . . we ought to look after our own economic independence for it is as precious as our political independence."[18]

---

[17] American Embassy Report, January 18, 1939, DS, NA, RG 59, 835.77/318. According to this report the Argentine government was "definitely committed to state ownership and operation of railways."

[18] Universidad de Buenos Aires, Facultad de Ciencias Económicas, Instituto de Economía de los Transportes, *Los ferrocarriles argentinos de capital privado en los últimos once años, 1928-1939*, ed. Teodoro Sánchez de Bustamente, especially pp. 31-33. The suggested price is surprisingly close to the 2,665,296,000 pesos paid by Perón for the French and British railways in 1946 and 1947. There is ample evidence that the 1939 Anglo-Argentine trade agreement, by which the Argentine government agreed to let Britain pay for its purchases of meat and grains in blocked sterling, was arranged at the urging of the Argentine government so that it could begin the acquisition of the railways by building up credits in Britain. The British Public Record Office papers for the Foreign Office were closed for 1939 when

The almost simultaneous outbreak of World War II in Europe and the crippling illness of President Ortiz, which forced him to turn the effective control of the government over to Vice-President Castillo in July, 1940, dramatically affected the question of nationalizing the foreign-owned railways. The Indian summer of the Ortiz years gave way to the coolness of the Castillo era. A certain sense of urgency settled over the matter, but both British and Argentine observers doubted that they could reach a satisfactory arrangement. All agreed that the companies should become Argentine. Lack of political unity in Argentina frustrated attempts by the Castillo administration to take positive steps. Argentine solutions bogged down in partisan politics. The British-owned companies, which represented the largest foreign railway interest, could not present a workable proposal either.[19]

Searching for an answer, Castillo turned to Federico Pinedo, who served briefly as minister of finance under Justo (and again in the Illía government of 1963-1964). Castillo appointed Pinedo minister of finance and authorized him to consider the railway question within the broader context of Argentina's wartime economic development. As in the past, Pinedo represented the cattle barons. He did not hesitate to sacrifice Argentine interests in his effort to hit upon a scheme that suited the needs of his class. Of major importance, he had to bolster the agrarian segment of the economy, which now had to find new cash markets for commodities that had previously been shipped to Europe. Of course,

---

research for this chapter was undertaken in London, but documents in the National Archives in Washington, D.C. (especially those concerning commercial relations between the United States and Argentina), indicate that the Argentines insisted upon such an agreement with the idea of purchasing the railways. See especially Wilson to SecState, December 19, 1940, DS, NA, RG 59, 833.51/944. I am indebted to Mr. Dana Sweet for supplying me with much useful information concerning this point.

[19] On January 13, 1939, Conservative deputies from Entre Ríos, Juan F. Morrogh Bernard, Pedro Radio, Justo G. Medina, and Juan Labayen, introduced a bill to purchase the British-owned Entre Ríos and North Eastern railways for 4,522,496 pesos, or approximately 61 percent of the companies' capital value as computed by the director general of railways. See Diputados, *Diario*, January 13, 1939, p. 523, and *South American Journal*, October 29, 1938, p. 424, and January 28, 1939, p. 106. The sale was later postponed because the government was not in a position to finance such an undertaking.

foodstuffs continued to provide the nation with credit as European nations, particularly Britain, worked out wartime economic measures, but the producers could not survive indefinitely on credit. The government had to find a means of getting cash into the agrarian sector.

Castillo did emphasize industrialization and considered it politically expedient to do so. This emphasis also suited the Hispanic-*criollo* nationalism of the late 1930's concerned with the political autonomy and economic independence of Argentina, along the lines of certain fascist regimes in Europe. In this light, Pinedo drew up a comprehensive plan for solving Argentina's many economic problems. Known as the "Pinedo Plan," its concepts have been likened to Roosevelt's New Deal.[20] In many ways it offered Argentina a new deal, although its terms favored big agriculture, not big business.

The plan had three parts. First, Pinedo suggested that the government liquidate surplus agricultural products that had built up because of reductions in available markets.[21] To do this Pinedo urged the government to purchase such commodities directly from the producers for redistribution, thus assuring the agricultural interests a steady market for their goods. The Anglo-Argentine trade agreement of 1939 allowed the government to build up considerable trade credits in England. This part of the Pinedo Plan also encouraged local manufacturing and called for government-financed, low-cost housing projects, which served the dual purpose of supplying housing to low-income groups and employment to construction workers. The second part of the plan dealt with mobilizing the nation's financial resources for carrying out the above program. Here Pinedo recommended that the state help private enterprise and stimulate industrial activity. Among other

[20] Weil, *Argentine Riddle*, p. 158. For a complete discussion of the Pinedo Plan see *Review of the River Plate*, November 15, 1940, pp. 11-20.

[21] This paragraph is based on the Pinedo Plan found in Senadores, *Diario*, November 1, 1940, II, 314-332. Also *Review of the River Plate*, November 15, 1940, pp. 11-20, and *South American Journal*, January 31, 1941, p. 67. Pinedo called the plan a plan to "reactivate" the economy.

things, he included plans for the long-range financing of industry by strengthening the monetary controls of the Central Bank.

The third phase of the plan concerned the nation's foreign trade and its exchange rates. In this section Pinedo disclosed the true nature of the bill. Article 10, in particular, indicated the narrower goals of Pinedo's plan to aid the agrarian oligarchy. That article and the debates it evoked show that Argentine exporters would receive either foreign or national currency from the national government for their products. This benefited the cattle and cereal producers at a time when Argentina lacked foreign currency. The Argentine government would receive blocked credit from foreign powers in return for Argentine products. As the debates show, Pinedo believed that the government could benefit in this program by taking shares of foreign-owned companies in lieu of credits in blocked payments if it chose. At the same time, the elitist agrarian interests would be paid for their products by the national government. Ostensibly a reasonable plan, it appeared to critics of Castillo and Pinedo that the government planned to create internal banking and government agencies which would continue to serve the agrarian segment of the economy at the expense of the industrial segment.[22]

Article 10 of the Pinedo Plan also included a proposal for acquiring the British-owned railways. The scheme fit into the plan to stabilize Argentina's wartime economy. It suggested that Argentina turn to industrialization as a panacea. In defending this part of the plan, Pinedo and other spokesmen for the conservative cattle-wheat complex used the rhetoric of Argentine economic nationalism in their speeches. Some defended ties with England. According to ultraconservative Senator Matías G. Sánchez Sorondo, repatriation of the railways amounted to a patriotic undertaking and a sacrifice that Argentines had to make to support the Allied war effort.[23] Pinedo, however, spoke along narrower and more nationalistic lines. He now claimed that Argentina had to take measures to curtail the influence of foreign capital, which "used to

---

[22] See, for example, Paulino González Alberdi, *La situación económica del país.*
[23] Senadores, *Diario*, December 17-18, 1940, II, 420.

be efficient and beneficial for the national economy."[24] He stressed that there was a lack of such capital available for national enterprises. Furthermore, he added: ". . . this capital does not favor Argentine initiative and our growing aptitude for industrial techniques. This capital naturally tends to flow toward the groups of foreign interests with which it is connected." For that reason Argentine industries remained in inferior positions. Something had to be done to change the situation, Pinedo concluded.

The Concordancia's economic nationalism had a hollow ring. It did not appeal to the masses. Pinedo and his kind did not attack the British but held them up as "civilized." The "nationalistic" legislation they introduced had as its primary aim the defense of Argentine agrarian interests. The Pinedo Plan blatantly proposed to continue favoring the big beef and cereal industries. It showed an appalling lack of concern for the political aspirations of the Argentine public. As the record indicates, Pinedo and the Conservative oligarchs still gave preferential treatment to British interests, whether intentionally or inadvertently. They still looked guilty of *vendepatria* to large segments of the population. The Concordancia may have supported industrialization in word, but in deeds it protected the agrarian institutions.

The Pinedo Plan points out the duplicity of the Concordancia under Castillo's rule. In Article 10 the administration stated its intention to acquire shares of the British-owned railways as partial payment for foodstuffs sent to Britain during the war. The author of that clause, Pinedo, also wrote a similar proposal for the British-owned railways. That fact might not have been realized had Senator Sánchez Sorondo not introduced a bill in June, 1940, which called for the Argentine government to purchase all private utility companies operating in Argentina.[25] Sánchez Sorondo's bill resulted from his own initiative. At the time, he advocated the gradual acquisition of the foreign companies. He saw the need to protect the sovereignty of the nation: "Today it is more imperative than ever to nationalize the foreign-owned public utilities which

[24] Ibid., p. 419.
[25] Ibid., June 16, 1940, I, 243-244.

are operating under concessions granted by the national government. Two years ago, upon raising the question of acquiring the Central Córdoba Railway, I stated in this body that 'it is necessary, in face of reality, to find a formula which . . . will prepare for the future nationalization of the railways.' . . . Now the hour has arrived, and the only desirable formula is that which I am proposing today. . . . The economic and social aspects of the transportation companies are not the only things that come into action. There are, also, the interests of sovereignty. We are obligated by raison d'état to protect the integrity of the patrimony. . . . We ought to redeem these sources of wealth by making an indispensable sacrifice to the purpose of being, economically, the owners of our own production and of our transportation throughout the nation, and to initiate with this act the policy of practical independence, without which, we will remain, for the most part, under foreign domination and jurisdiction."[26]

The bill introduced by Sánchez Sorondo decided the fate of the Pinedo Plan. As with all bills, the proposal went to a Senate committee. In attempting to gain fuller understanding of the situation the committee asked the British-owned railway companies to submit proposals.[27] The companies responded readily and provided the committee with their own scheme, which their Argentine attorney Federico Pinedo had prepared. This occurred in June, before Pinedo's appointment as minister of finance. At the time, the matter drew little attention. It took on new meaning in December when Pinedo introduced legislation calling for repatriation of the foreign-owned railways along lines similar to those he had suggested to the British firms. An obvious conflict of interest existed. On the one hand, Pinedo introduced an economic program recommending the purchase of the railways. On the other hand, he authored the purchase scheme suggested by the railways to the Argentine government. Even members of the Conservative faction of the Senate believed that Pinedo and the companies had worked together to effect the sale of the railways. Opponents of the Con-

[26] Ibid.
[27] *South American Journal*, November 30, 1940, p. 343.

cordancia found another example of the corruption and *ven-depatria* that they abhorred.[28]

When pressed to explain his behavior, Pinedo admitted that he had helped the British-owned railways draw up a plan for selling their properties to the Argentine government. The newspapers had gotten the story essentially straight, he told the Senate. The British railways had consulted him for legal advice during a recent trip to London and later in Buenos Aires. He went on to add that "the work was very important, and it paid me, as it should have, a very *impressive* fee: £10,000."[29] This had occurred before he became minister. Pinedo claimed he had not used his present position to aid the companies, but few of his opponents believed him. The fee paid to him looked more like a fat kickback than a retainer for services. The Radicals jumped to the obvious conclusion that Pinedo had tried to serve two masters at one time. They accused him of working for the avaricious British and their greedy Argentine cohorts. Their chief spokesman, Atanasio Eguiguren, used the opportunity to embarrass the government. In a brief interchange with Pinedo he stated in disgust that "one of the serious evils and hindrances of our political system is that the lawyers of the great companies generally are deputies or senators (Pinedo: 'I was neither!') . . . ex-ministers, ministers, or even presidents, because disgracefully there have been cases of presidents with open offices."[30] Eguiguren continued his indictment in more nationalistic tones, "I have been against the Transportation Corporation of the Capital; I have been against the General Coordination of Transportation; I have been against the Central Córdoba Railway, and I have been against the purchase of the Pacific, because I believe that foreign capitalism has converted us into a colony . . ."[31] Eguiguren conceded that he supported Britain's war

---

[28] Senadores, *Diario*, November 17-18, 1940, II, 394-487, especially pp. 417-418. Also González Alberdi, *Situación económica del país*, pp. 19-21.

[29] Senadores, *Diario*, November 17-18, 1940, II, 417-418.

[30] Ibid., p. 418.

[31] Ibid. Eguiguren feared that Pinedo wanted to establish an economic dictatorship, which would have placed the rural provinces firmly under the control of urban-industrial interests (ibid., p. 436).

effort. But even though he supported Britain in the name of humanity, he would not "accept the form with which English capital treats us."

Despite Pinedo's predicament, the Pinedo Plan won the support of the Senate in mid-December, 1940, largely as a result of a Conservative majority. But the Chamber of Deputies buried the plan. Two factors explain the ultimate defeat of Pinedo's proposal. First, obvious partisan politics worked against it. Like most Argentine ministers of finance since 1930, Pinedo did not enjoy wide popularity. Many considered him an economic dictator because he advocated increased state control of the economy. Others considered him *siempre un maldito coimero*. Even members of the Conservative faction mistrusted Pinedo, many because they feared his development as a presidential aspirant.[32] Partisan politics also worked against the plan as Conservatives refused to work with Radicals and Radicals refused to make a truce with the Conservatives. The Radicals' leader, former President Alvear, would not support any Conservative legislation. He objected to backing the Pinedo Plan because he knew his party could not gain any political benefits by such action. Furthermore, Alvear had never advocated industrialization as a panacea to the nation's economic ills. Finally, most Radicals did not want the Castillo regime to get credit for the plan should it prove successful. They hated Pinedo, especially because of his long association with the Conservative oligarchs.[33] In this regard, the expressions of the more nationalistic members of the Radical party reflect another reason for the defeat of the Pinedo Plan. They branded the scheme as another of many efforts by which the pro-British elite worked to appease the British imperialists who continued to dominate Argentine economics. Anti-British Radicals believed that the plan frustrated the nation's development as an independent entity.

Actually, Pinedo's scheme offered nothing new or startling. His plan grew out of Justo's long-range purchase program. It also

---

[32] Bonsul to Welles, January 15, 1941, DS, NA, RG 59, 835.00/964. Also Rodolfo Lestrade, *Donde se prueba como se vende la patria.*

[33] Weil, *Argentine Riddle*, p. 168; and *South American Journal*, January 31, 1941, p. 66.

followed proposals made in 1940 by the Instituto de Economía de los Transportes of the University of Buenos Aires. Pinedo advised forming a mixed holding company in which the state and private interests worked as partners. The holding company would take over the debentures, guaranteed stock, and preferences of the railways for a 4 percent debenture, with a sinking fund of .5 percent guaranteed by the government. The British would retain 70 percent of the shares and the remaining 30 percent would go to the Argentine government. Under this arrangement the British elected seven of every ten members of the board of directors. Over a period of sixty years Argentines would replace the British representatives by gradually purchasing the British shares of the mixed company.[34]

Nationalistic opponents did not consider the scheme definite enough. They objected to the length of time it would take to make the railways Argentine. The plan did not strike them as a means by which Argentina would purchase the railways. Rather, they charged that it represented another attempt to save the British-owned railways from economic collapse, at the expense of the Argentine public. The railways, one opponent said, "would be British in *criollo* disguise."[35]

The defeat of the Pinedo Plan again set back efforts to nationalize the British-owned railways. Although its defeat did not alter the general economic policies of the Castillo government, it frustrated attempts to reach a solution satisfactory to Argentine and British interests alike concerning the fate of the railways. Pinedo resigned in disgust and defeat. His successor, Carlos Alberto Acevedo, followed a similar program. Soon after Acevedo's appointment, Castillo made it clear that he planned to continue the program, through the use of ministerial orders if necessary. Industrialization, key to the 1940's, became a major objective of the regime. According to Castillo, the goals of his administration included the initiation of large-scale working of the mines, develop-

---

[34] *South American Journal,* March 22, 1941, p. 207; and González Alberdi, *Situación económica del país,* pp. 19-21.

[35] Gonzalez Alberdi, *Situación económica del país,* p. 20.

ment of an Argentine merchant marine, and expansion of other extractive industries. As Castillo put it: "In the modern world these industries are the base of economic liberation and national autonomy. The exclusively agrarian and cattle raising nations are destined to servitude; this is the case of our past. We need coal, iron, copper, and diverse metals. We have them in abundance in the country, but disgracefully . . . we lack the machinery and the technicians necessary to realize our designs."[36]

Acevedo made industrialization a central point in his annual message on the national budget, which he delivered on May 29, 1942. Argentine industry had made significant strides during the war, he argued. These advances would continue with the restoration of normal international trade after the war ended. He believed that "in the postwar period our imports and exports will be different than before the war. Changes will be made in the fundamental structure of international commerce, and this country should be prepared for the situation so that she will not have to remain passive during the readjustment. We will not import products that our industries produce."[37]

Despite the fears of many rural spokesmen that the urban-industrial sector was establishing a dictatorial state-directed economy favorable to industrialization at the expense of agriculture, Argentina's wartime economy continued to depend largely upon exporting foodstuffs. As in the past, the railways played an important role in economics. They conveyed Argentine foodstuffs toward British ships, which then transported the products to British markets. The British still effectively directed the economic development of Argentina. Argentine industrialization took place, but always in a secondary role behind the agricultural industries.

The British-owned railways suffered several setbacks during the war years. Fuel shortages eventually forced the companies to burn maize in place of imported coal and increased the railways' operating expenses. Railway operation became increasingly

---

[36] As quoted by Carlos Ibarguren, *La historia que he vivido*, p. 495.
[37] Argentine Republic, Ministerio de Hacienda, *Proyectos financieros y económicos, 1941-1942*, p. 22.

difficult as a lack of new equipment made the replacement of outmoded equipment impossible. Losses due to breakdown became commonplace. The Castillo administration did little to alleviate the railways' problems. The government regularly turned down requests for rate increases between 1940 and 1942. Rate increases finally went into effect during April, 1942, at which time the government allowed an advance in freight rates of 10 percent and a 5 percent hike for passenger fares.[38] Even so, the companies gained nothing. They had to refund salary deductions to railway laborers in accordance with a presidential order of 1934, more than offsetting the increase in rates.[39] A presidential decree of October 17, 1941, set rigid restrictions on the use of fuels. The companies could not exceed 60 percent of their coal consumption nor 85 percent of their petroleum consumption for 1940. This restriction forced them to buy maize at inflated prices from the government, which hoped to sell surplus maize it had purchased from farmers.

As a result, the railways curtailed their services as an economy measure and incurred substantial losses of revenue. The only compensating factor, as far as the railways were concerned, was that the shortage of petroleum products, spare parts, and tires restricted highway competition.[40] British railway officials predicted financial disaster for the near future. Matters reached a new low. Because of wartime shortages of fuel and equipment the already antiquated railways became further run-down. Nearly reduced to scrap iron, they doggedly continued to run as an essential element of Argentina's economic life.

In a separate act President Castillo supported the long-neglected Buenos Aires Transportation Corporation in its efforts to force all *colectiveros* to join its ranks in late 1942. This proved an

[38] Tornquist, *Business Conditions in Argentina*, no. 232 (October 1941), p. 41.

[39] In 1934 President Justo intervened in a wage dispute between the British-owned railways and labor. The basic principle of his settlement was that there would be no distribution of profits to common shareholders until the wage cuts were restored, nor a restoration of wage cuts until receipts covered the whole of the industrial charges requested by the interest on debentures or mortgages.

[40] *South American Journal*, January 3, 1942, p. 5; and Tornquist, *Business Conditions in Argentina*, no. 235 (July 1942), p. 75.

unpopular decision. The *porteño* masses, who associated the
monopoly with the worst aspects of British economic imperialism,
immediately took to the streets in protest. The public generally
believed that the Buenos Aires Transportation Corporation had
been created solely to save the British-owned tramways from ruin.
Never popular in the minds of the average *porteños*, by 1942 the
tramways had fallen into disrepair. One citizen of Buenos Aires had
recently described the trams as being "large wooden boxes of loose
metal, slack screws and rattling windows which traverse the city
roaring and screaming like lions in a cage, . . . Their progress over
intersections of a line where streets cross is like the terrible battery
of artillery and the rattling of machine gun fire, every two or three
minutes, day and night. And when a curve has to be negotiated, the
antagonizingly high pitched shriek, such as a rat might emit on its
tail being squeezed, jars excruciatingly on the most tempered
nerves."[41]

Porteños felt that they deserved better transportation facilities
than those provided by these antiquated trams, many of which
were running until as late as 1962. Independent *colectivo* chauffeurs
still met much of the city's transportation needs. These men refused to give up their vehicles to the Transportation Corporation.
Until Castillo's decree the drivers had enjoyed a prolonged period
of benevolent treatment by national and local authorities. Neither
Justo nor Ortiz had given the British-dominated monopoly serious
support. Municipal leaders had been even less inclined to force the
colectivo drivers to adhere to the 1936 Municipal Transportation
Act. When Castillo issued his order in late 1942 that all the drivers
turn their vehicles over to the Transportation Corporation in
compliance with the law, the drivers began a popular wildcat
strike. Widespread rioting and the burning of several trams and
buses belonging to the British monopoly accompanied the strike.
Once again the *porteños* expressed familiar antipathy toward the
British.[42] They also showed hatred of the Castillo government.

[41] *Review of the River Plate*, January 10, 1941, p. 7.
[42] Ysabel F. Rennie, *The Argentine Republic*, pp. 301-302. Also see *Railway Gazette*, January 12, 1940, p. 47; January 19, 1940, pp. 79-80; May 8, 1942, p. 547; July 24, 1942, p. 78;
November 27, 1942, p. 513; and April 30, 1943, p. 432.

How long the hard-pressed British could maintain these enterprises became a matter of conjecture. Possible loss of the British-owned railways to a third power concerned many Argentine and British observers. They shared the fear that the British would possibly lose their Argentine railway holdings, either to the United States to pay for lend-lease loans or, in case of defeat, to Germany. In the latter case it seemed likely that the United States would have to intervene on the ground that German possession of the railways would have violated the Monroe Doctrine.[43] Once again fear of U.S. economic penetration entered into negotiations between the Argentine government and the British-owned railways.

British railway managers waited under a cloud of uncertainty. The statement by J. A. Goudge, taken from his annual report to the shareholders of the Buenos Ayres and Pacific Railway, sums up their position. After mentioning the possible acquisition of the British-owned railways by the Argentine government, he added:

We have heard nothing from that committee nor is there any indication yet of Government views, but we have since seen that in the Chamber of Deputies a member has also indicated the advisability that some steps should be taken to secure that the control of such vital services as those rendered by us should not pass into foreign hands, which might exert pressures and influences antagonistic to the national interests. It seems clear that public opinion in Argentina is awake to the position that might arise if the proprietorship of our securities should pass from their present owners either by reason of warlike action or financial pressure.[44]

The uncertain future of the British-owned railways looked better, at least from a psychological point of view, during the last months of the Castillo administration. The formerly pro-German president softened his official attitude toward the British. His motives for changing remain uncertain. Clearly he altered his stand. The recent realization that the Axis powers might not win played a large part in his decision. Rather than advocate the selection of a nationalist, pro-Axis Conservative, such as Carlos Ibarguren, for

---

[43] See *South American Journal*, November 31, 1940; Kennedy to Hull, August 12, 1942, DS, NA, RG 59, 835.77/369; and José Luis Torres, *Una batalla por la soberanía*, p. 129.

[44] *South American Journal*, November 30, 1940, p. 348. Article 16 of the Mitre Law set the expropriation price of the railways at their recognized capital value plus 20 percent.

his successor, he chose the less well known Robustiano Patrón Costas. The latter, while known as a German sympathizer, had long worked with British enterprises. He showed no indication after Castillo chose him in 1943 that he would change his position.[45]

President Castillo's seeming metamorphosis from Anglophobe to Anglophile occurred during the last year of his administration. He did not make as dramatic a change as some have professed, however. Castillo had always considered himself a friend of Great Britain, although he believed that Germany would win the war. Like all Argentine leaders, including Perón during his first year in office, he accepted Britain as a natural ally of Argentina. He waited longer than some other anti-British nationalists to express this feeling. Several politicians who had opposed British economic imperialism changed their attitudes toward Britain during the war. Many joined former President Marcelo T. Alvear, a leader of the Radicals, and former Minister of Finance Federico Pinedo in founding a pro-British patriotic organization called Acción Argentina.[46] The Socialists Nicolás Repetto and Alfredo L. Palacios became members of Acción Argentina. Previously they had led bitter fights against the British. But under wartime conditions both declared a moratorium on their anti-British campaigns. They feared German totalitarianism more than British capitalism. Repetto even went so far as to say that he considered British imperialism far more noble and progressive than the totalitarian imperialism of the Germans.[47] In ten years Repetto had changed his position radically. He had criticized the concessions made to the British under the Roca-Runciman Pact in 1933. By contrast, he wrote in 1943, "We are in a position to appreciate the significance of the introduction and diffusion of the railways, almost all of them English, that have served not only as a means of transportation, but also have contributed to the creation of the political unity of the nation and to the use of one national language, the acceptance of one code of

[45] Potash, *Army and Politics in Argentina*, pp. 178-181; and Romero, *History of Argentine Political Thought*, pp. 241-242.

[46] For a brief discussion of Acción Argentina see Arthur P. Whitaker, *The United States and Argentina*, pp. 64-65, and Rennie, *Argentine Republic*, pp. 270-281.

[47] "Argentina y Gran Bretaña," *Hechos e Ideas* 10, no. 37 (October 1940), pp. 84-85.

laws, and the awareness of a similar emotion toward the flag and anthem of the fatherland."[48]

Argentine nationalists split into two major camps by 1943. The majority of the liberals, including Socialists, Progressive Democrats, and Radicals, favored an Allied victory. A second powerful faction supported the Axis. Repetto's words spelled out the values of a new generation of Argentine liberals. Juan B. Alberdi, Domingo F. Sarmiento, or Julio A. Roca would have used similar language in their day. The same arguments had appeared at the dawn of the Argentine railway age. Because of his support of the Allied war effort and his fear of European and Argentine fascism, Repetto set aside his anti-British nationalism. Temporarily, at least, he referred to the British-owned railways as instruments of progress.

As the traditional political leaders of Argentina soon discovered, they did not speak for the broad base of the Argentine population. Rising militarists, mostly junior commissioned officers, led by such men as Colonel Juan D. Perón, held different views. They, along with the large urban labor population, remained staunchly anti-British and relatively unimpressed by England's war effort. In fact, many anticipated a German victory in Europe. Disillusioned by a political system that had ignored them, both groups sought a simpler solution to their mutual grievances. In June, 1943, they found an opportunity to begin accomplishing their objectives.

[48] Nicolás Repetto, *Política internacional*, p. 30.

12. Perón and the Anglo-Argentine Trade Negotiations

Few men have had a greater impact upon the political, economic, and social development of Argentina than Juan D. Perón. A complex individual whose politics defy definition, he controlled the nation between 1945 and 1955 by combining popularistic nationalism with aspects of Argentine corporativism and touches of traditional Argentine caudillism. His administration reflected the authoritarianism of Rosas, the liberalism of Sarmiento, the popularism of Yrigoyen, and the centralism of the Concordancia. Perón led an authoritarian government of the people, neither totalitarian nor democratic in the usual sense of the terms, but highly egocentric and dependent upon him at all times for all things. If Roca presented a new Argentina to the autocratic oligarchs of the late nineteenth century, and Yrigoyen signalled the emergence of the middle class as a political partner in the administration of the nation's traditional political system during the early 1900's, then Perón heralded the arrival of the common man, especially the lower-class workers from town and country, as an influential political factor.[1]

Perón succeeded because of his ability to act as a pragmatic, political opportunist. Free of any fixed ideology, he wanted to establish his own power over as wide a base as possible. Whether or not he had presidential aspirations as early as June 4, 1943, is academic.[2] He soon became concerned with power in its own right and obviously hoped to go as far as his abilities as a manipulator of men and emotions permitted. Though not an innovator of either issue or ideology, he had studied political history. He learned much from the examples of Hitler and Mussolini in Europe, Vargas in Brazil, Cárdenas in Mexico, and such Argentine leaders as Rosas, Sarmiento, Roca, and Yrigoyen. Like the latter, Perón was a farsighted politician. Whereas Yrigoyen led the middle class and personalized their struggle to obtain the rights they demanded, Perón did the same for the *descamisados*. Astute and knowledgeable of his nation's history, he played the game of Platine politics by ear.

Perón owed much of his success to his ability as a demagogue. He fulfilled many emotional needs of the Argentine public. Most demagogues understand the psychological demands of their

[1] Since his downfall in 1955, a number of polemical accounts of Perón have appeared, written by detractors and apologists of his regime. A most useful collection of readings in English is found in Joseph R. Barager (ed.), *Why Perón Came to Power*. Two dated works, Robert J. Alexander, *The Perón Era*, and George I. Blanksten, *Perón's Argentina*; offer worthwhile surveys of the regime before its downfall. Other more recent studies include Samuel L. Baily, *Labor, Nationalism, and Politics in Argentina*; Robert A. Potash, *The Army and Politics in Argentina, 1928-1945*; Aldo Ferrer, *The Argentine Economy*; José Luis Romero, *A History of Argentine Political Thought*, trans. Thomas F. McGann; Peter G. Snow, *Argentine Radicalism*; Peter H. Smith, *Politics and Beef in Argentina*; and Arthur P. Whitaker, *Argentina*. Also see Kalman H. Silvert, "Peronism in Argentina: A Rightist Reaction to the Social Problem of Latin America," in *Latin American History: Select Problems*, ed. Fredrick B. Pike, pp. 340-390; Peter H. Smith, "Social Mobilization, Political Participation, and the Rise of Juan Perón," *Political Science Quarterly* 84, no. 1 (March 1969): 30-49, and "The Social Base of Peronism," *Hispanic American Historical Review* 52, no. 1 (February 1972): 55-73. Among the many works in Spanish, the most pertinent to this study are Torcuato S. Di Tella, *El sistema político argentino y la clase obrera*; Carlos S. Fayt (ed.), *La naturaleza del peronismo*; Leopoldo Portnoy, *Análisis crítico de la economía argentina*; and Félix Luna, *El 45*.

[2] Potash, *Army and Politics in Argentina*, pp. 184-186; Luna, *El 45*.

followers for an authoritarian government; the usual causes are fear and the need for security or reassurance. Argentina of the post-1943 period presented a public in search of order. By that time the existing "democratic" political parties had been much discredited. The failure of the nation's constitutional government to operate in an orderly fashion thoroughly disillusioned the Argentine public. The middle class lay broken politically and expectant lower-class politicians yearned for power. Argentines needed reassurance that they could solve their own affairs. During the late war years and the early cold-war years, Argentines feared that their political system lacked the vitality to resist domination by one of the world powers.

The rise of Perón to power had its messianic aspects. Argentines awaited a leader who would forcefully initiate internal solutions to internal problems. They wanted protection from foreign powers. From a socioeconomic point of view, the nation needed leadership which would eliminate the insecurity that confronted the average citizen in his daily work. Though outwardly committed to industrialization, previous governments had not taken major steps toward achieving that goal. None had supported the nation's labor movement. None had identified the needs of a growing urban proletariat, swollen by unskilled rural laborers who left the land in search of a new life in Argentina's major cities. Uncertainty led to stagnation and in turn to economic chaos. In this setting Perón provided an example of courage and stability. His strong political image became a focus for many dissident groups. In his late forties, handsome and impressive in his military uniform, he epitomized optimism and strength. His choice of a dynamic wife completed his image of security and *macho*. His economic solutions proved daring, even if ill-conceived and misunderstood by those who tried to implement them. More than anything, he offered hope to a nation in despair.

Nationalism gave an important but intangible aura to the Perón mystique. He used symbols and ritual to gain the support of *criollo* migrants who had recently arrived at the cities of the nation. Through him the masses of uneducated and unskilled laborers came to believe that they had achieved a significant voice in the nation's affairs.[3] Perón appeared to many Argentines as the incarnation of the nation. As such he used a nationalism involving loyalty to the nation above all else to cajole and control labor. Those who objected to his reforms or opposed his authoritarian rule Perón branded as traitors and publicly decried. Perón's nationalism changed between 1943 and 1948. His dealings with the British-owned railways chronicle that change. During this period he frequently used the railways as a popular target. He also used the issue to gain support from labor, especially from the important railway unions, La Fraternidad and Unión Ferroviaria.

From the moment he took over as chief of the Department of Labor and Social Security on October 27, 1943, Perón made a concerted effort to win the backing of the two railway unions. They represented the best organized labor groups in the country. Unión Ferroviaria had the largest membership, since it included all railway workers not involved in driving locomotives. La Fraternidad, union of the locomotive drivers and firemen, began its activities at the turn of the century and considered its members among the elite of Argentine labor. For nearly half a century these unions had advocated the nationalization of the railway industry. By the 1940's they ardently opposed foreign capitalists, whom they felt exploited Argentine workers.

The workers' distrust and dislike of foreign employers made it easy for Perón to use antiforeign nationalism as a means of establishing rapport with the railway unions. By combining antiimperialism with basic "pork-chops" politics, he successfully bid for the support of the railway workers of the nation. The appeal of such nationalism stemmed from the workers' belief that income distribution would follow any action taken against foreign capitalists. On numerous occasions Perón encouraged such anticipation by forcing the railway companies to contribute to the workers' living standards through pay increases and improved fringe benefits. As a result, the railway workers equated social justice with improved working conditions and better pay. They blamed their miserable economic condition on profit-seeking

[3] Baily, *Labor, Nationalism. and Politics in Argentina*, pp. 116-117.

foreigners, who, to their way of thinking, "extended Downing Street to Argentina."[4] By forcing the British-owned railways and other foreign enterprises to assume an ever-increasing share of the financial burden of basic labor reforms and social programs that he implemented, Perón achieved the objective of gaining the support of labor while being strict with foreign capitalists. He became thought of as a friend of labor and an enemy of the oligarchy and foreign economic imperialists. To the average laborer, he personified their desire for social justice.

Essentially, Perón's programs responded to labor's demands for distribution of property and ownership of the nation's wealth. In so doing he won important support from Argentina's forgotten people. Workers had criticized previous governments for permitting foreign capitalists to make "excessive" profits while laborers starved. They believed that the Concordancia had acted only for the benefit of a handful of Argentines and foreigners at the expense of the majority. A suitable trilogy for such a government *El Obrero Ferroviario* once observed was *Dinero, Patria y Orden* ("Money, Patriotism, and Order").[5] Reformers had often attacked the system that held the mass of workers down, but they had done little to rectify the situation. Perón picked up the rhetoric of his predecessors. During 1944 government pressure led to wage increases of nearly 20 percent for railway workers. An annual Christmas bonus, an *aguinaldo*, often equal to a month's pay, also came from the coffers of the unhappy British companies. Thanks to Perón the workers' salaries increased noticeably. The workers also benefited from a number of government projects, such as improved social security insurance programs and the construction of clinics and hospitals for railway workers and their families.[6] Perón now proved that he not only advocated the doctrine of social justice but also practiced it and would back his works with tangible results. Workers in Argentina had reason to believe that their revolution had begun.

[4] *El Obrero Ferroviario*, October 16, 1942, p. 8.

[5] Ibid., April 1, 1943, p. 3.

[6] Based on information found in *South American Journal*, January 15, 1944, p. 32, and April 22, 1944, p. 223; and *El Obrero Ferroviario* (January 1944), pp. 1-2; (February 1944), p. 4; (May 1944), p. 1; and (June 1944), p. 16.

From a political view, Perón's revolution represented a brilliant manipulation of the laboring class. He and the magnetic Eva Duarte de Perón used revolutionary rhetoric even though they often held traditional goals. They did not alter the woof and warp of the Argentine social fabric, they only dyed it another shade. Basically, the social structure remained the same. The military continued to prevail as it had since 1930. The elite continued to exploit the masses. But to the vast majority of the workers Perón appeared to be a government official they could trust and respect. Conscious of their needs and responsive to their requests, he put himself above politics whenever he addressed them. When he asked the railway workers for cooperation, he joined them in a common cause. He told them of his dedication to their well-being and to the defense of the nation. "You must have confidence in me, my friends [*señores*], for I am a man who responds only to one political party and one ideology: the Fatherland."[7]

With considerable plausibility Perón told a May Day rally in 1944 that as secretary of labor and social security he had begun the struggle for social justice in Argentina. Stressing the social aspects of the June fourth revolution, he reminded his audience that unlike former governments the present administration had not forgotten its debt to the laboring class.[8] Now a powerful politician and a successful military man, Perón nonetheless identified his aspirations for creating a strong Argentina with the aims of the poor laborers. He understood their *criollo* goals: food to feed hungry families, a right to acquire property, and the privilege to educate their children. In a tribute to these poor he proclaimed himself a worker in May, 1944, when he became vice-president under the administration of his friend General Edelmiro J. Farrell. He credited the workers of Argentina for his promotion.[9]

British-owned railways took the burden of Perón's generous social legislation. In July the new military government rejected an appeal for higher freight and passenger rates sent to the Castillo

---

[7] *El Obrero Ferroviario* (January 1944), p. 6.
[8] Ibid. (May 1944), pp. 1-2.
[9] Ibid. (July 1944), p. 2.

regime in February, 1943.[10] Out of desperation, the British-owned railways sent a three-man mission to Argentina in September, 1943, headed by Sir J. Montegue Eddy, a man with years of experience in dealing with the Argentine government. The mission's members hoped to find a means by which the railways could operate until transferred to Argentine hands. In November, after some purposeful delay, the Argentine military government appointed a committee of three to meet with the Eddy mission. Hopes rose in Britain that the two commissions could reach "an integral solution."[11]

Such hopes proved premature. Two years of secret negotiations failed to produce a satisfactory agreement. By the end of the first year, the British had gained only a few concessions, all inadequate. In spite of new freight rates which permitted increases of up to 20 percent in some cases and a more favorable exchange rate of fourteen rather than fifteen pesos to the pound sterling for remittances, the railways ended 1944 with a deficit of nearly forty million pesos.[12]

Throughout most of 1945 the railway situation remained unchanged. The glorious railway age faced an ignoble end. Railway service deteriorated rapidly. Accidents became an everyday occurrence, mostly due to mechanical failures. Crews ditched their locomotives rather than plow into stalled trains ahead. Brakes failed and signals malfunctioned. Overcrowded passenger trains, broken equipment, ill-repaired rails, and neglected facilities caused numerous complaints from the Argentine public.[13] Wartime shortages of steel and other necessary commodities made renovation of the systems impossible.[14] Everyone knew that nothing would be

[10] *South American Journal*, July 31, 1943, p. 50.

[11] Ibid., August 21, 1943, p. 86; September 4, 1943, p. 109; and November 20, 1943, p. 231. The German-subsidized *El Pampero*, a popular newspaper aimed at lower-class readers, argued in its July 5, 1943, edition that the large remittances built up in Britain be used to repatriate the railways so that Argentina could construct the base for its economic liberation. This was a popular concept among working-class nationalists.

[12] Ernesto Tornquist, *Business Conditions in Argentina*, no. 244 (October 1944), p. 197, and no. 245 (January 1945), p. 25.

[13] Based on accounts in the daily newspapers for the period 1943-1946.

[14] Tornquist, *Business Conditions in Argentina*, no. 247 (July and August 1945), p. 83.

done to improve the situation as long as the railways remained in private hands. Under these deplorable conditions the Argentine public had legitimate complaint. They received miserable service from a dying industry. The British understandably anticipated an early settlement which would relieve them of both the financial and the psychological strain of operating railways in Argentina.

Rumors circulated in Buenos Aires in August, 1945, that the government planned to purchase the British-owned railways. Eddy squelched these rumors when categorically denying them and adding, "... there have been no such *pourparlers* of any kind ... neither have we, as to the present, been approached with any such object in view."[15] Two months later the morning newspaper *El Clarín* revealed details of the secret negotiations between the Eddy mission and the Argentine government. According to *El Clarín*, the British railway mission had submitted two proposals to the Argentines, neither of which the government had accepted. The first proposal provided for the nationalization of the railways through creation of a mixed company with a share capital of 1.896 billion pesos. The Argentine government would receive 20 percent of the shares, while the balance would be retained by the British. The second proposal reduced the share capital to 1.6 billion pesos, of which the government would hold 30 percent. This also proved unsatisfactory to the Argentines, who countered with a proposal of their own calling for a mixed company with a share capital of 1.4 billion pesos, of which the British would hold 800 million and the Argentine government 600 million. This did not suit the railway companies. Regarding outright purchase of the railways with the blocked sterling balance in London, *El Clarín* reported that "at all times the Government cast off the idea of 100 percent nationalization of the British-owned railways."[16]

In the meantime, the leaders of the railway unions continued to demand higher wages and an increased voice in the control of the private railways. They wanted a renovated and modernized

---

[15] *South American Journal*, September 1, 1945, p. 99.
[16] *El Clarín* was quoted by the *South American Journal*, December 8, 1945, p. 267. At a

railway network which would assure them future employment and improved working conditions.[17] Under the prevailing conditions they feared that the British-owned companies might collapse completely. They expected a revolution and anticipated radical changes in the operation of the railways through nationalization. As one writer stated in *El Obrero Ferroviario* of July 1, 1945: "We are in an epoch of reevaluation of all values, social, moral, economic, and financial. The railways also must endure this inevitable process of transformation that will make them into the instruments of progress and prosperity for the country, and for the thousands of men that they employ. . . . It is no longer possible for them to be instruments of exploitation of the working men."[18]

Telmo B. Luna, president of the Unión Ferroviaria, explained that railway workers wanted a better standard of living, which they believed they could achieve through nationalizing the railways. Like other labor leaders, Luna attacked the capitalists and their oligarch associates for not allowing the workers liberty. As he explained, "We want democracy, we want liberty, we want institutional normality, but we also want, above all things, a minimum of social justice to assure the laboring class the deserving and humane level of living to which they have the legitimate right to aspire."[19] Like the oppressed throughout Latin America, Argentine workers thought of freedom and liberty in terms of freedom from want and hunger. The workers' tautology held that democracy equalled the better life. To them, social justice meant freedom from want.

Perón's drive for political power and the *criollo* workers' push for a better life merged on the evening of October 17, 1945. During that day thousands of *descamisados* poured into Buenos Aires to protest the arrest of Perón on October 9. Perón's arrest had resulted from an attempted coup within the military government, but his friend Farrell remained president. Due to the efforts of

---

later date Sir Montegue Eddy admitted that *El Clarín*'s press release on the negotiations was "substantially correct" (see *South American Journal*, May 4, 1946, p. 239).

[17] *El Obrero Ferroviario*, July 1, 1945, p. 7.

[18] Ibid.

[19] Ibid., August 1, 1945, p. 3.

Evita Duarte; Cipriano Reyes, leader of the meat-packers union; and other loyal union leaders, Perón's labor friends repaid their debt to him for supporting unionization programs. Unruly workers roamed the city of Buenos Aires the week before October 17. The thousands who pushed toward the Casa Rosada that October evening represented the rank-and-file members of new urban and agricultural unions that Perón had helped found. The mob overflowed the Plaza del Mayo. They came to convince Farrell that they stood with Perón. They demanded his release from Martín García Island. Farrell could either fight the mob or free Perón. He chose the latter, and Perón returned a hero to the cheering crowd. From the balcony of the Casa Rosada he spoke briefly and emotionally to his followers. He promised to dedicate his life to becoming their president.

Perón understood the logic of the laboring masses. He knew they could be led. He also knew the economic plight of the British-owned railways. Upon his election as president in February, 1946, he made it clear that he would nationalize the railways. He did so partly to reward the workers, including the railway workers, who had supported his candidacy. During his campaign he had promised the railway unions increased participation in the management of the railways. He had another reason for nationalizing the railways: he wanted to fulfill the role as economic liberator of the country. In his inaugural address on June 4, 1946, Perón promised to lead Argentina's struggle for economic independence.[20] Although he did not specifically define that goal, he did announce to a joint session of Congress that within a matter of weeks the state would recover the public utility companies as part of his program to begin "the national aspiration of being economically and politically sovereign." He claimed that one day Argentina would "not owe as much as one centavo to the foreigner." He stated with assurance that, at the time, "Argentina will no longer be a colony in an economic sense."[21]

Sensitive to the urgent need to repatriate the railways, Perón

[20] Senadores, *Diario*, June 4, 1946, I, 44-45.
[21] Ibid., p. 64.

nonetheless followed a cautious policy in dealing with the British. Like his predecessors he did not purposefully bait the British. He controlled his anti-British nationalism behind the façade of a gentleman. Uncertain as to the best course of action, he let Britain take the initiative in reaching an agreement. He kept his nationalism at a low key throughout 1946 and did not personally admonish the British for their past record in Argentina. In contrast to his chief political opponents, the Radicals, Perón did not employ anti-British nationalism. When negotiations for transferring the railways began, Perón found the British stubborn bargainers, not easily moved by outbursts of xenophobia, which they had lived with since 1930.

A British trade mission to Argentina, led by Sir Wilfred Eady, superceded the Eddy mission in June, 1946.[22] Perón put his negotiations in the hands of his "economic czar" and friend, Miguel Miranda, president of the newly nationalized Central Bank. The negotiators discussed not only the railways, but also Argentina's blocked sterling balance in London and the renewal of the Anglo-Argentine trade contract. In many ways the situation paralleled that of 1933, before the signing of the Roca-Runciman Pact. This time Argentines appeared to have the upper hand. They represented the creditor nation, with a balance of blocked sterling amounting to some 130 million pounds. Furthermore, Britain continued to depend upon Argentina for 25 to 35 percent of its meat, but Britain had some advantages. The British market provided for over 80 percent of Argentina's surplus meat, and British ships carried nearly 90 percent of Argentina's meat exports. Postwar inflation meant that the blocked sterling balance lost its purchasing power each day it remained unused in Britain.[23]

Enough similarities existed between the negotiations of 1946

---

[22] *Review of the River Plate*, July 5, 1946, p. 6. Sir Wilfred Eady should not be confused with the chairman of the railway mission, Sir Montegue Eddy. Because of the similarity of their last names, their full names will be used whenever there is a chance of confusion. See also Harriman to SecState, June 14, 1946, DS, NA, RG 59, 635.4131/6-1446.

[23] *The Economist*, August 31, 1946, pp. 344-345; *Review of the River Plate*, July 5, 1946, p. 6. See also Tewksbury to SecState, August 14, 1946, and Messersmith to SecState, August 14, 1946, DS, NA, RG 59, 635.4131/8-1446.

and 1933 to give the Radicals cause for alarm. At least they attempted to exploit the situation to embarrass the Perón administration by calling attention to a possible reinstatement of the Roca-Runciman Pact.[24] While the Anglo-Argentine negotiations progressed in secret July through September, 1946, the Radical deputies in the Chamber of Deputies kept up a steady anti-Perón campaign. They combined attacks on Perón with anti-British attacks. The Radicals protested the secrecy of the negotiations and demanded that the Argentine press discuss the settlement of the meat and British-owned railway issues. The Argentine government refused to comply. Argentine papers carried no accounts of the talks. If an Argentine wanted to know recent developments he had to read the English newspapers. This situation angered the Radicals, but the Peronist majority defeated a Radical motion to have the discussions publicized on the ground that the nation should have faith in a president who had won the most honest election in Argentine history. In spite of their setback, the Radicals continued to insist upon open negotiations. They made an issue of this point because "the arrival of the British trade mission has an enormous transcendency for the future and the economic independence of the country." Argentines deserved to know the actions of the government, the Radicals asserted. Even though Argentines remained on friendly terms with the British people, the government carried on current negotiations with British imperialists, led by capitalists. The Radicals would not stand for this. Their party now opposed imperialism of any type.[25]

One of the chief spokesmen for the party, Arturo Frondizi, said that his generation embraced antiimperialism as an integral part of their political ideology. For that reason his party opposed

[24] Diputados, *Diario*, July 5, 1946, I, 470-471. As Félix Luna has recently demonstrated in *El 45*, the Radical party split during Perón's presidential campaign in 1945-1946. Many supported Perón; others followed an independent policy. The Radical minority in Congress represented a small but vociferous opposition faction led by Arturo Frondizi, Ricardo Balbín, and Solano Peña Guzmán. In 1946 the Radical faction also included Oscar López Serrot, Gabriel del Mazo, Emilio Donato del Carril, Luis Dellepiane, Ernesto Sammartino, Edmundo Leopoldo Zara, and J. Salvador Córdova.

[25] Diputados, *Diario*, July 5, 1946, I, 470-475; Messersmith to SecState, July 5, 1946, DS, NA, RG 59, 635.4131/7-546.

establishing mixed companies between government agencies and private foreign capitalists. Only complete nationalization of the railways would satisfy the Radicals. Frondizi criticized such organizations as the Directorate of Military Manufacturers in which the government joined with private capital to exploit the resources of the nation. He did not believe that Argentina could achieve economic recovery by drawing monopolistic capital into partnership with the state. The Radicals, he stated, "are of the opinion that nationalization should not be synonymous with statism, nor with the creation of large bureaucratic organisms in order to embark upon the unitary type of centralization that will unavoidably and necessarily lead to a totalitarian form of state."[26] In one of many speeches on the subject, Frondizi expounded his conviction: ". . . the state, in my opinion, should not enter into mixed companies with monopolists. The mixed company is not a means of working towards the nationalization of the public services: rather it is the legal procedure that the monopolists have adopted in the Argentine Republic in order to avoid the nationalization of their services. The Argentines should not assist them in this fraud."[27]

The Radicals' position reflected the extreme xenophobia of a party out of office in 1946 as it attempted to challenge the supremacy of the party in power. At the time, the Radicals could not accept gradual nationalization, largely because Perón proposed such a system. The Radicals continued a trend begun in the mid-1930's when young Radicals broke with Alvear and the traditional leaders of the Radical party. A faction of the Radical party had fought against the mixed-company idea under Justo. They sincerely believed it would continue British domination of the Argentine economy. Their position seemed extreme to most. As late as July, 1946, experienced observers felt complete nationalization of the British lines unlikely, primarily because they believed that Perón could not increase wages, modernize the railways, and still afford the purchase price of the companies. Others believed that,

[26] Diputados, *Diario*, August 1, 1946, I, 250.
[27] Ibid., August 7-8, 1946, I, 683.

despite public announcements, the Argentine government did not desire to take over the entire operation of the railways.[28] Previous administrations had turned down similar proposals in 1940 and 1945. When Sir Wilfred Eady suggested outright purchase of the railways at the outset of his negotiations with Miranda in July, Perón reputedly exclaimed, "We do not propose to use our blocked funds in order to buy out-of-date equipment."[29] Perón accepted a mixed Anglo-Argentine company as a natural alternative. Since this plan countered the Radicals' position, the Radicals escalated their demands. They couched their arguments in the same nationalistic rhetoric that popularistic politicians had used since 1930. In so doing they appeared more xenophobic than Perón, who remained nominally friendly with the British capitalists. Throughout 1946 he continued to deal with the British-owned railway companies through normal diplomatic channels without personally attacking them as imperialists.

Obviously Perón did not reject outright purchase of the British-owned railways; labor had not yet demanded such drastic action. In July the Unión Ferroviaria approved a resolution at its twenty-first general assembly which called for nationalization of the railways by the most economical method. This did not preclude outright purchase, but certainly did not demand it. The resolution supported Perón's pragmatic and flexible approach. The resolution simply reiterated the railway workers' demand for a voice in future railway activities. The workers regarded nationalization as the best method of achieving their goal. Union leaders did not trust the British-owned companies. They charged that the companies had produced enormous profits for the shareholders' benefit but had served Argentina only in a secondary

[28] *South American Journal*, April 20, 1946, p. 213; *Review of the River Plate*, July 5, 1946, p. 6; *Railway Gazette*, July 12, 1946, p. 33. See also Harriman to SecState, June 14, 1946; telegram, Harriman to SecState, July 26, 1946; Messersmith to SecState, July 26, 1946, DS, NA, RG 59, 635.4131/6-1446, /7-2646, /7-2646.

[29] *The Economist*, July 27, 1946, p. 154; and *South American Journal*, July 20, 1946, p. 27. See also telegram, Harriman to SecState, July 26, 1946, DS, NA, RG 59, 635.4131/7-2646. *The Buenos Aires Standard*, August 10, 1946, reprinted in translation an article that appeared in a new magazine called *Que* in which Miguel Miranda stated that "the railways do not interest me" and went on to explain why their purchase was not advantageous to Argentina.

sense. In recent years, the union argued, the British had allowed their rolling stock to fall into ill-repair, proof that they intended to support nationalization of the railways in order to "throw upon Argentina a public charge which she had mortgaged for half a century."[30] For that reason the resolution took a lukewarm attitude toward the creation of a mixed company.

In late August the Anglo-Argentine trade discussions reached an impasse over the blocked sterling balance. For obvious reasons, the British wanted to treat jointly the questions of the railways, meat, and blocked sterling; whereas, the Argentines made the separate settlement of the blocked sterling balance a prerequisite to other agreements. The Argentines felt that, if they could not receive cash, the British should pay them a 2.5 percent interest rate on their "investment." British officials, in contrast, would pay only .5 percent interest, the current rate paid on the London call market.[31] It was clearly to Britain's advantage to have the settlement of the meat contract and the railway question joined with the discussion of the disposal of the blocked sterling. Thus, they could use the railways as a means to pay off a substantial portion of the wartime debt. Perón's reluctance to sacrifice Argentine credit in return for the railways stalemated the British. They had to seek a compromise.

In early September the British trade mission announced its decision to break off negotiations and return to London.[32] That threat, whether intended as such or not, brought results. Within a few days the Argentines came to terms and signed an Anglo-Argentine agreement on September 17, 1946. That agreement, known as the Miranda-Eady Agreement, included terms for settling the three major issues. The agreement proposed the signing of a new Anglo-Argentine trade treaty, the details of which the two governments would work out at later meetings.[33]

[30] *El Obrero Ferroviario*, August 1, 1946, p. 2.

[31] *The Economist*, August 31, 1946, p. 344. See also Messersmith to SecState, July 26, 1946, DS, NA, RG 59, 635.4131/7-2646; Tewksbury to SecState, August 14, 1946, DS, NA, RG 59, 635.4131/8-1446.

[32] *The Economist*, September 14, 1946, p. 425.

[33] The English version of the Miranda-Eady Agreement is found in the *Review of the River Plate*, September 21, 1946, pp. 14-15, and *The Times*, September 18, 1946. It is also sum-

The Miranda-Eady Agreement established a mixed company to acquire the operating assets and liabilities of the British-owned railways. The agreement also provided several advantages for the new company, including exemption from all taxes, extension of the duty exemptions provided by the Mitre Law, a guaranteed operating revenue, and a contribution of 500 million pesos from the Argentine government for modernizing the lines over a five-year period. The Argentine government could purchase, upon reasonable notice, shares of the company at par value from any shareholder over an undisclosed number of years until it gained full control of the railways.

Argentine government officials considered the agreement a success. Miranda was happy, though not exuberant, and stated his belief that Britain and Argentina would always be close friends.[34] Even Perón, who had remained relatively quiet on the subject throughout the negotiations, expressed his opinion that the agreement reaffirmed "the traditional friendship between Britain and Argentina." He added: "We should be ungrateful if we did not recognize what other nations have done in this sphere [economic development], and particularly Great Britain, whose spirit of enterprise has conferred so many benefits of civilization. Consequently on this occasion we extend to her the expression of our gratitude, as in risking her capital in the construction of the great network of railways in Argentina she contributed to an extraordinary degree in making our country what she is today."[35]

Perón's words demonstrate the ambivalent nature of his nationalism. He did not begin as a frenetic xenophobe. Rather, he sought a rational solution to the dilemma. At times he assumed the

---

marized by *The Economist*, September 21, 1946, pp. 460-461. U.S. Ambassador George Messersmith claimed that in informal conversations with Juan A. Bramuglia and Juan Perón he convinced Perón to reach an agreement with the British trade mission. He credited Perón and Foreign Minister Bramuglia, not Miranda, with the terms of the new agreement (see Messersmith to Clayton, September 19 and 25, 1946, DS, NA, RG 59, 635.4131/-9-1946, /9-2546).

[34] *The Times*, September 17, 1946.

[35] *South American Journal*, September 21, 1946, p. 133; and excerpt from Perón's speech of September 17, 1946, republished in *Review of the River Plate*, March 5, 1948, p. 4. Also

role of a xenophobe. Certainly he encouraged his lieutenants to play that role on numerous occasions. But Perón had a pragmatic approach to politics. In September, 1946, the mixed-company idea appeared the best solution to a vexing problem. The Miranda-Eady Agreement provided a means of freeing Argentina's blocked sterling while permitting the repatriation of the railways. From an economic point of view the agreement seemed the wisest. Since he had not committed himself to the outright purchase of the railways, he did not suffer a political defeat in accepting the agreement's terms. Perhaps he exposed himself to criticism at home, but he still had the support of labor and the military, both of which approved the settlement.

The terms of the agreement also pleased the British railway and government officials. To them it "introduced the concept of partnership between the two parties which had been so lacking in the past."[36] British shareholders continued to control the majority of shares in the new company. They could expect higher revenues because of the assistance of a friendly Argentine government, which had a stake in the companies' equitable operation. At last management could undertake long-postponed modernization projects. The benefits impressed all Britons. Purchases of new equipment would be made almost exclusively from British manufacturers. By obtaining materials of all kinds from Britain the railways would "prolong considerably the present full employment of industrial plants."[37]

If the agreement led Perón to make laudatory comments about Britain's contributions to Argentina's economic development, it brought about an opposite reaction from his political opponents. A broad spectrum of the Argentine public criticized the Miranda-Eady pact, especially the establishment of a mixed company. Many believed that history had repeated itself; Perón had become another Roca. Even the two large conservative newspa-

---

see the *Buenos Aires Herald*, September 16, 1946, and September 17, 1946, and enclosure in Tewksbury to SecState, September 19, 1946, DS, NA, RG 59, 635.4131/9-1946.

[36] *The Economist*, September 21, 1946, p. 460. See also Messersmith to Clayton, September 25, 1946, DS, NA, RG 59, 635.4131/9-2546.

[37] *Railway Gazette*, September 27, 1946.

pers, *La Nación* and *La Prensa*, complained that economically Britain had got the better part of the arrangement.[38] *La Vanguardia,* the Socialists' newspaper, bluntly considered the mixed company a tragedy.[39] In the Chamber of Deputies, the Radicals accused Perón of having returned to the nineteenth century when the state guaranteed profits and security for the foreign-owned railways.[40]

The Miranda-Eady Agreement drew attacks from both the right and the left. In anger and disgust, Raúl Scalabrini Ortiz, a popular revisionist historian best known for his studies of the British-owned railways, wrote a scathing attack of the mixed-company idea. In *Los ferrocarriles deben ser del pueblo argentino,* published in 1946, he bitterly opposed British imperialism in the form of mixed companies. He believed that the Argentine economy suffered from such agreements.[41] A similar attack upon the agreement appeared in a sixteen-page pamphlet by Marcial González entitled *El convenio Miranda-Eady y sus repercusiones en la economía nacional,* also printed in 1946. González treated the agreement as a betrayal of the Argentine nation and claimed that Perón and Miranda had reverted to the techniques of Roca.

The most vitriolic criticism of the agreement came from the Radical members of Congress. They assumed a position of extreme antiforeign economic nationalism which contrasted markedly with Perón's flatulent acceptance of the mixed-company scheme. The Radicals had not participated in the negotiations. They had read British newspapers to keep abreast of recent developments. Upon completion of the pact they discovered that Perón had borrowed a scheme that they had shunned in 1940. As voiced by one of their members, Solano Peña Guzmán, the mixed-company scheme suggested by Miranda was less acceptable than Pinedo's plan to nationalize the railways had been in 1940. At least Pinedo's plan had assured the Argentines ownership of the railways at the end of fifty-six years, but the Miranda-Eady Agreement set no time limit. It might take forever to acquire the companies. Furthermore, Peña

[38] *La Nación,* September 21, 1946; and *La Prensa,* September 19, 1946.
[39] *La Vanguardia,* September 24, 1946.
[40] Diputados, *Diario,* September 25, 1946, V, 356.
[41] Falcoff, "Raúl Scalabrini Ortiz: The Making of an Argentine Nationalist," p. 94.

noted, the idea of a mixed company originated in Britain, not Argentina. "The origin of the mixed company was the proposition of the British railway directors in order to guarantee the protection of their capital investment. . . . Giving such privileges to foreign capital is a rare concept of *Argentinidad*."[42]

The mixed reaction to the Miranda-Eady Agreement must have bothered Perón. Although he had not assumed the role of the second San Martín as yet, he had advocated Argentine economic independence. The creation of a mixed company with the British did not achieve that goal. In fact, many Argentines considered it an act of *vendepatria*. To many Perón looked no better than his conservative predecessors in dealing with the pernicious British capitalists.

[42] Diputados, *Diario*, September 25, 1946, V, 352-356.

13. The Closed Door: Outright Purchase

The ink had barely dried on the signatures to the Miranda-Eady Agreement when a sudden and unexpected announcement that the Argentine government intended to purchase outright the foreign-owned railways, both British and French, aborted it. In mid-December the Argentine government bought three small French-owned railways for 182,796,174 pesos. In January of the following year the government began negotiations with the British for the outright purchase of their railway companies. On February 11, 1947, Britain and Argentina reached an agreement whereby the Argentines agreed to pay 2,482,500,000 gold pesos for the railways and their subsidiary properties. Argentina's blocked sterling balance in London provided the bulk of the purchase price. The rest would result from future shipments of foodstuffs to Britain under terms of a new Anglo-Argentine trade pact. The latter, known as the Treaty of the Andes, took a year to settle. The two nations did not sign the pact until February, 1948, thus delaying the final transfer of the British-owned railways until March 1, 1948.

A number of related factors explain Perón's decision to switch from a mixed company to the outright purchase. Postwar inflation and internal politics played an important part, but pressure from the United States proved to be the decisive factor. High-ranking State Department officials disapproved of provisions in the Miranda-Eady Agreement for disposing of the blocked sterling. In a letter from Secretary of the Treasury John Snyder to Chancellor of the Exchequer Hugh Dalton, written on October 31, 1946, Snyder informed the British official that his government considered the clause that tied Argentina's ability to dispose of the blocked sterling with her balance of trade with Britain in violation with the spirit of the U.S. loan to Britain in 1945. Obviously the State Department wanted to safeguard itself against attacks from domestic critics of the British loan. Acting through Secretary Snyder, the department warned the British against the inclusion of the objectionable clause in the Argentine agreement and against the use of similar provisions in future agreements with India and Egypt.[1] Under these circumstances, Britain had no other recourse than to reconsider the Miranda-Eady Agreement. The British government let the existing Anglo-Argentine trade agreement expire on December 31, 1946. In so doing the British considered the outright sale of the railways as the best way to wipe out the sterling balance, a solution they had preferred for years. Outright sale would eliminate Argentina's credit and put an end to Snyder's complaint. With luck, Britain might gain credit toward current trade deficits with Argentina.

[1] Secretary of the Treasury John Snyder's correspondence with Dalton was made public in February, 1947, and is discussed in *The Economist*, February 8, 1947, pp. 235-236. The Snyder-Dalton feud is also discussed by Alberto A. Conil Paz and Gustavo Ferrari, *Argentina's Foreign Policy, 1930-1962*, trans. John J. Kennedy, pp. 158-159; *Buenos Aires Herald*, February 13, 1947; and *South American Journal*, November 9, 1946, p. 214. See Snyder to Dalton, October 31, 1946, and Dalton to Snyder, December 17, 1946, General Records of the Department of the Treasury, NA, RG, Box 63. For background to Snyder's letter see the following documents in the Department of State Records: Office Memoranda prepared by E. A. Gilmore, September 24, 1946; October 1, 1946; and October 3, 1946; and Tewksbury to SecState, November 22, 1946, SD, NA, RG 59, 635.4131/9-2446, /10-146, /10-346, /11-2246, and enclosure 1, /11-2246.

Once again the specter of U.S. ownership appeared. In marked contrast with past Yankee threats, the British welcomed this one. It gave them new leverage in dealing with Argentina, to whom they wanted to sell their entire Argentine railway holdings. The British economic empire had begun its decline. The ruling party had little desire to hold on to the Argentine "colony." The Labor party had returned to power in 1945. Its leaders had long supported state ownership of land transportation systems in Britain. Now they prepared to nationalize the entire railway network of the British Isles. The Labor government also began negotiating the sale of British-owned railways throughout Latin America. On June 1, 1946, the British-owned Ferrocarril Mexicano sold its properties to the Mexican government.[2] Nearly two years later, on March 1, 1948, the British-owned railways of Argentina were officially transferred to the Argentines. On the same day the Uruguayan government announced that it had agreed to pay 7.5 million pounds for the remaining British-owned railways of Uruguay.[3] In all these cases the British government intervened on behalf of its citizens to bring about the successful sale of the railways.

Uneasy Argentines willingly cooperated with the British during January, 1947. Most feared that, unless Britain and Argentina complied with the United States' request, the United States might use the British-owned railways as collateral for the British loan. For that reason, Argentines felt that they had a choice to make between Argentine or North American ownership of the railways.[4] Moreover, Perón could not afford a delay. If the British refused to follow the provisions of the Miranda-Eady Agreement an alternative had to be found. Further delay would have had ruinous effects upon the Argentines' blocked sterling. Perón wanted to save the balance from being wiped out by postwar inflation. No advantage resulted from keeping the balance tied up in London in

---

[2] *Bulletin of the Pan American Union*, September, 1946, p. 530.

[3] *New York Times*, March 2, 1948; and *South American Journal*, March 6, 1948, p. 129.

[4] See José Luis Torres, *Una batalla por la soberanía*, p. 11, published in 1946, and Julio Irazusta, *Perón y la crisis argentina*, pp. 49-50, published ten years later.

long-term bonds at a low interest rate. As Perón later explained to a group of visiting United States congressmen: "We had large money deposits in the United States and Great Britain which we could not collect nor could we withdraw the equivalent in gold. Besides, we were getting no interest on our money. Meanwhile, world prices soared and our deposits were losing their original value. In this manner the time would arrive when we would not be able to buy anything with that money if the inflationary trend continued in the world. In that way we lost almost half our money."[5] Perón also wanted to implement his important Five Year Plan which he had announced in October.[6] Without assurance that he could repatriate the railways, his economic reforms meant nothing.

Discussions that led up to the final purchase of the British-owned railways were not helpful.[7] Once the two governments had agreed upon outright purchase as a mutually satisfactory solution to the long-standing railway problem, they only had to agree upon the price of the transaction. That decision took nearly a month. Sir Montegue Eddy, who represented the British-owned railways, claimed that under the expropriation provisions of the Mitre Law the railways were worth at least three billion gold pesos. Miguel Miranda, however, refused to accept the British price. He claimed that the Argentine government did not intend to expropriate the railways. Rather, Argentina would acquire them on the open market. Britain had offered to sell them on a voluntary basis. Miranda also scoffed at the British price. He considered the railways "scrap iron," and set their value at one billion gold pesos. In a statement he would later regret, he announced that Argentines considered Britain an old and warm ally. As a result his government would pay two billion gold pesos "for reasons of sentiment."[8]

---

[5] *President Perón Speaks to Members of the Banking and Monetary Committee of the House of Representatives of the United States*, p. 12.

[6] *The Voice of Perón*, p. 23; and *South American Journal*, October 26, 1946, p. 195.

[7] This paragraph is based on information found in the daily newspapers of Britain and Argentina. The latter contained little of note, however, and usually cited the British press, which was better informed, as its source of news. *The Times, Review of the River Plate*, and *South American Journal* were most useful.

[8] *La Nación*, January 22, 1947.

As a final rejoinder he remarked: "The British should not have forgotten, before they refused our proposal, that the railways are not a good business anywhere in the world. The railways will have high expenses and my impression is that within twenty years aviation will have liquidated much of their importance."[9]

Of course Miranda exaggerated the situation, but his intransigence stalemated the talks. In an effort to effect a rapid settlement, the British government intervened on behalf of the railway companies. In late January the British ambassador to Argentina, Sir Reginald Leeper, began negotiations with Miranda and Minister of Foreign Affairs Juan A. Bramuglia.[10] In short order the three men concluded their business. On February 11, 1947, they announced the results of their talks. The Argentine government acquired some sixteen thousand miles of track, amounting to approximately 66 percent of the nation's railway network. The government also acquired associated properties including real estate, grain elevators, station buildings, and one oil refinery.[11] In return, the British cancelled their wartime debt to Argentina.

The purchase plan met with a mixed reaction in Britain. A few dissenters opposed the liquidation of the British overseas investments. They lamented the demise of the British sphere of influence in Argentina. Others were displeased with the manner in which Argentina bought the British-owned railways. They resented the bluntness of a deal that swapped railways for meat. They could not accept Britain's dependence upon outside sources for foodstuffs. An editorial in *The Economist* of February 14, 1948, succinctly expressed the bitter feelings of many Britons. Entitled

---

[9] *Buenos Aires Herald*, January 21, 1947. Throughout the Miranda-Eady negotiations, between July and September, 1946, Miranda had earned the reputation of a hard bargainer. This reputation he carried into the 1947 talks. See translation of an article that appeared in *Que*, enclosed in Tewksbury to SecState, August 14, 1946, DS, NA, RG 59, 835.4131/8-1446.

[10] Bramuglia had long served as legal adviser to the Unión Ferroviaria. Previously he had served as Perón's chief assistant in the Ministry of Labor and Social Security, with the title of "Director General of Social Security." His appointment to both positions greatly pleased union members and helped win labor support for Perón.

[11] *The Times*, February 13, 1947; *La Prensa*, February 13, 1947; *Review of the River Plate*, February 14, 1947, p. 15.

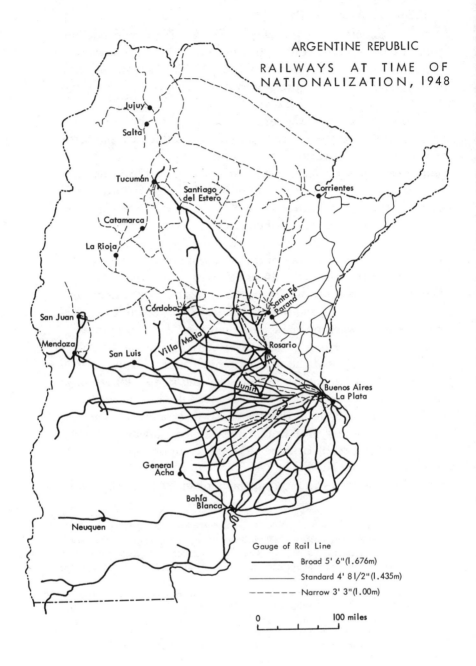

ARGENTINE REPUBLIC

RAILWAYS AT TIME OF
NATIONALIZATION, 1948

Jujuy

Salta

Tucumán

Santiago
del Estero

Corrientes

Catamarca

La Rioja

San Juan

Córdoba

Santa Fé
Paraná

Mendoza

Villa María

Rosario

San Luis

Junín

Buenos Aires
La Plata

General
Acha

Bahía
Blanca

Neuquen

Gauge of Rail Line

———— Broad 5' 6"(1.676m)

———— Standard 4' 8 1/2"(1.435m)

– – – – – Narrow 3' 3"(1.00m)

0   100 miles

"British Argentine Railways Bartered for Meat," the article discussed the terms of the Treaty of the Andes. In the course of analyzing the treaty the author stated: "To translate the tables and figures of the White Paper into more homely terms, Britain has been living like an improvident family which, failing to make both ends meet, first spends the accumulated capital of the past, then borrows from friends—from American friends, from Canadian friends, from South African friends—and when the loans are exhausted, begins to pawn the furniture. How else can one describe the latest deal with Argentina in which the whole capital asset represented by the British-owned railways is bartered away for eighteen months' supply of meat?"[12]

In general the British financial press reacted favorably to the outright sale of the railways. Shortly after the announcement of the Miranda-Eady Agreement in September, 1946, *The Economist* stated that the idea of a mixed company stood little chance of success, especially in light of the rising cost structure.[13] Although 1945 and 1946 had been record years, the cost of providing service had increased at a greater rate than the volume of trade. Perón's wage increases had cost the railways more than 25 million pesos during 1944, the railways' operating budgets had risen by 100 million

---

[12] *The Economist*, Fébruary 14, 1948, p. 249. The *Railway Gazette* of May 5, 1948, p. 272, quoted the following parliamentary question by Mr. J. S. C. Reid, M.P.: "If it be the fact that this year we are eating the Argentine railways, what are we going to eat next year?" In answer, the editor penned the following stanzas:

It should be very easy
in this be-rationed age,
to swallow up a railway
of any sort of gauge,
to whet our denture deeper
on engine, rail, and sleeper
Our hunger to assuage.

It should be very easy
to rid us of our fears,
And solve the little problem
of food for coming years.
When all the trains are swallowed
And rolling-stock has followed,
There's still the passengers.

E. C.

[13] *The Economist*, September 28, 1946, p. 515.

pesos between 1945 and 1946, and estimates called for an increase of another 140 million pesos in 1947. Wage increases formulated in September, 1946, placed a heavy financial burden on the undertaking at the outset.[14] Outright sale of the railways offered an attractive alternative. The *Buenos Aires Herald* concurred. Once the sale was assured, the *London Times* noted that "the outright sale is generally considered more satisfactory to the British than the mixed company . . . because a mixed company would have almost surely involved a conflict of interests and friction." To the point, the *Financial Times* of London said, "The outright purchase of the railways . . . might prove the best solution, since a bird in the hand is worth ten in the grass of the Pampas."[15]

Such observations proved correct. Britons had cause for a certain amount of joy. Shortly after the railways became Argentine in 1948, Perón embarked upon a renovation program and made considerable purchases of railway equipment in Britain, as well as in Canada and the United States. The Argentine government bought thirty Baldwin steam locomotives from the United States in June and ordered seventy-five more steam engines from the Cooper Bessemer Corporation. Orders for new rolling stock were placed in Canada, Great Britain, and the United States, including one for one hundred narrow-gauge flatcars from the United States. In August, the Argentine government accepted designs from the General Electric Company for the construction of sixty-five electric locomotives at an estimated cost of eighteen million dollars. Expenditures in Britain included the purchase of 250,000 tons of steel rails and fishplates, which pleased the British steel industry because it provided one of the largest steel contracts of the postwar years.[16]

In Argentina the announcement of the outright purchase received a far different reception than had the Miranda-Eady Agree-

---

[14] Ernesto Tornquist, *Business Conditions in Argentina*, no. 250 (April-May 1946), p. 54; *The Economist*, November 30, 1946, p. 884.

[15] *Buenos Aires Herald*, January 15, 1947; *The Times*, February 13, 1947; *Financial Times*, January 15, 1947.

[16] Robert J. Alexander, *The Perón Era*, p. 158; *El Obrero Ferroviario*, May 24, 1948, p. 5; *South American Journal*, August 14, 1948, p. 76, and September 25, 1948, p. 147.

ment. Both *La Nación* and *La Prensa*, formerly critical of the Miranda-Eady Agreement, approved the purchase. *La Nación* treated the development as a natural step in the evolution of the nation and hoped that the warm relationship between Argentina and Britain would continue. The editors of *La Prensa* assumed a "wait-and-see" attitude on the ground that it could not appraise the merits of the purchase until the state proved that it could operate and administer the railways efficiently. Although neither paper acclaimed the purchase in emotional terms, both supported Perón's actions.[17]

More important, the purchase greatly enhanced Perón's popularity among the nation's working class. Organized labor had openly supported the outright acquisition of the British-owned railways for decades. On September 12, 1945, the Confederación General del Trabajo (CGT) issued a proclamation favoring nationalization of the railways. During 1946 the two railway-workers unions passed similar resolutions. When the government announced the outright purchase in February, 1947, these unions staged public demonstrations to express their jubilation and to thank Perón. They believed that at last they would realize their aspirations. Wage increases, given shortly after the announcement of the purchase, further strengthened the workers' conviction that Perón would assure them a higher standard of living. Perón, a sagacious politician, allowed the workers to believe that he had acted unselfishly. He accepted their tributes but wisely presented the purchase as an act of the people, of the common man, and especially of the *descamisados*.[18]

The purchase had quieted Perón's critics, especially the Radicals. The Radicals had roundly attacked his handling of the railway issue in September. At the time they had considered him a continuation of the previous elitist-conservative military regimes, in spite of his professed nationalism and his association with Argentine labor. For months the Radicals campaigned for the complete

---

[17] *La Nación*, January 22, 1947, and *La Prensa*, February 13, 1947.
[18] *El Obrero Ferroviario*, November 1, 1945, p. 5; August 1, 1946, p. 2; March 1, 1947, p. 10; and March 16, 1947, p. 9; and *South American Journal*, June 22, 1946, p. 20.

nationalization of the railways. They made it clear that no other arrangement would satisfy them.[19] By choice the Radicals made antiforeign nationalism an important part of their ideology, but their scheme backfired. They assumed that Perón would not turn to outright purchase of the railways and planned to stamp his administration as guilty of *vendepatria*, a charge that stuck in Argentina of the mid-1940's with the adhesiveness that such names as "Red," "Commie," or "Pinko" did in the United States of the 1950's and 1960's. The Radicals also misjudged the British. They believed that the British did not want to give up the foothold in Argentina that the railways provided. This miscalculation caught the Radicals off guard. When the British pressed for the sale in early 1947 they had little to say except to criticize Perón for paying too much for what Miranda had unwittingly referred to as "scrap iron." They also chastised Perón for paying an inflated price out of "reasons of sentiment." Such criticism went unnoticed. The Radicals' attempt to out-nationalize Perón failed. The party suffered a major setback through a turn of events which led to the switch from the unpopular Miranda-Eady Agreement to the popular purchase plan of February, 1947.[20]

The purchase gave Perón an important victory over his critics. The victory proved all the more easy because the purchase suited Perón's own nationalistic scheme for the economic recovery of postwar Argentina. He had made repatriation of foreign-owned industries an integral part of his attempt to reactivate the nation's economy. State control of the railway system fit into the first Five Year Plan, announced in October, 1946. Obviously a certain portion of this much-acclaimed plan smacked of antiimperialism which Perón intended as partisan propaganda. He also framed the plan around an industrialization process to end Argentina's semicolonial economy. As Miguel Miranda emphasized at the signing of the railway agreement in February, "Argentine hearts are beating

[19] For examples of the Radicals' campaign in the Cámara de Diputados, see Diputados, *Diario*, August 1, 1946, II, 250; August 7-8, 1946, II, 683; September 12-13, 1946, IV, 466-471; September 25, 1946, V, 353-356; January 23, 1947, IX, 762-763.

[20] Ibid., July 4, 1947, II, 366.

proudly today because there is not a single foreign-owned railway line in Argentina, which fact enables Argentina to harness the entire railway system to the five year plan."[21] Expressing similar sentiments, the Peronista president of the Unión Ferroviaria, Telmo B. Luna, heralded the purchase as "an act of transcendental significance that will exercise a preponderant influence in the future economic development of the country . . . and the creation of conditions that are indispensable for making Argentina a great nation."[22]

The Five Year Plan had more to it than the redemption of the *patria*. It also provided a means for Perón to extend his personal control over the nation. Through the plan he would govern every aspect of Argentine economic life. All power would emanate from Perón as his economic reforms centralized state control. The purchase of the British-owned railways suited his purposes. It was a dramatic act in its own right and a step toward the economic independence of the nation. Moreover, it strengthened Perón's economic stranglehold on the Argentine people.

Shortly after the purchase, critics pointed out that the money would have been better spent if the government had undertaken the improvement of the railways rather than the acquisition of their useless equipment. The British-owned railways had few locomotives that had seen less than thirty years of service. The average locomotive had worked nearly fifty years; some had lasted over seventy. The rolling stock included decrepit vehicles. Under the circumstances, many felt that the Argentine government could have used the blocked sterling to purchase agricultural equipment, industrial machinery, automobiles, new locomotives and rolling stock, and innumerable items needed to implement the Five Year Plan. The single use of the blocked sterling contributed to Argentina's declining purchasing power and made the nation all the more dependent upon its agricultural industries. It seemed that the purchase best suited Britain's economy rather than Argentina's. As one Argentine exile suggested, "the best evidence that Argen-

[21] *The Times*, February 13, 1947.
[22] *El Obrero Ferroviario*, March 1, 1947, p. 1.

tina did not make such a good deal is that the British seem quite happy about it."[23]

If not economically sound, the purchase did prove a politically wise move. From the outset the mixed-company proposal had met with disapproval throughout Argentina. Because of the strength of antiforeign economic nationalism among Argentines, Perón found it inexpedient to support the mixed company, even though he had referred to it as an example of the "partnership" between Argentina and Britain. Perón realized that he had nothing to gain by supporting the Miranda-Eady Agreement. When given the opportunity to purchase the British-owned railways outright in January, 1947, he seized it. He did not repeat his actions of the previous July. Rather he accepted the British offer, thereby enhancing his own political career and redeeming his image as the economic liberator of Argentina. No one would accuse him of *vendepatria* again.

Because of its magnitude, the purchase of the British-owned railways marked a turning point in the growth of Argentine economic nationalism. From February, 1947, the symbolic meaning of the transaction far outweighed other aspects. The Perón administration committed millions of pesos to free the nation of British investors. Argentines celebrated the repatriation of the railways as signalling a new order. Perón had reversed the trends of the past, during which foreigners controlled the nation's economy. Ownership of their own railways led most Argentines to believe they could finally achieve the destiny their leaders had promised for over a century. The purchase also proved the political potency of economic nationalism. It provided a simple tool by which demagogues like Juan and Evita Perón could control the masses. A wartime atmosphere existed in which foreign imperialists became the common enemy of all Argentines. In that context the purchase of the British-owned railways represented a major victory in the struggle to obtain economic independence. Spokesmen for the Perón regime likened organized laborers to soldiers, the twentieth-century counterparts of General José de San Martín's vic-

---

[23] *New York Times*, February 13, 1947.

torious grenadiers. As expressed by one Peronista organ: "The recovery of the railways by the state cannot be considered as a business transaction. . . . It was no more a business transaction . . . than was the battle of Ayacucho, or the campaign for our national independence. . . . Liberty has no price."[24]

An anticolonial attitude prevailed in Argentina during 1947. Perón proclaimed the "Declaration of Economic Independence" of the Argentine Republic on July 9, 1947, in a ceremony held in the same Casa de Junín at Tucumán where an earlier generation of Argentines had announced their political independence exactly 131 years before.[25] Triumphantly, Perón stated that he had liberated Argentina from foreign imperialists who had controlled Argentina's economy since the mid-nineteenth century. What San Martín started, Perón finished. The former assured the nation's political independence; the latter gave the nation its economic independence. Argentines could now determine their own future. Bolstered by the purchase of the British-owned railways, an integral part of the events that led to the July proclamation, Perón boasted that Argentina had an important role as an independent world power.

Argentines reached a high point in the expression of their nationalism on the evening of March 1, 1948. On that memorable evening Argentines massed into the Plaza Britania to celebrate the transfer of the railways to Argentine control.[26] Although essentially a mass labor rally, the ceremony's theme depicted the whole nation's struggle for complete independence, economic as well as political. The setting combined nationalistic and militant symbolism. After due homage was paid to the statue of José de San Martín, political liberator of the Argentine Republic, railway whistles and churchbells signalled the beginning of the quasimilitary celebration. Seven military planes, recently acquired from Britain,

---

[24] From "Los ferrocarriles son argentinos," *Hechos e Ideas* 17, no. 47 (February 1948): 385.

[25] Argentine Republic, Senado de la Nación, *Documentos básicos de nuestra independencia, 1816 hasta 1947.*

[26] The official ceremony of March 1, 1948, is described in considerable detail by *La Prensa*, March 2, 1948; *Buenos Aires Herald*, March 2, 1948; *El Obrero Ferroviario*, March 16, 1948; and *New York Times*, March 2, 1948.

flew overhead and dropped harmless bombs that burst high over the heads of the expectant throng to release thousands of tiny flag-bearing parachutes as souvenirs of the occasion. Behind the rostrum on which the main speakers were located was an enlarged map of the Argentine railway system, appropriately labeled in gigantic print, "Now They Are Argentine." To one side, but in prominent view, was the original Argentine locomotive, the ancient and venerable "La Porteña," which had been imported from England in 1857 to run on the first six miles of Argentine railway constructed by the Ferrocarril del Oeste in Buenos Aires.

Significantly, the hundreds of thousands of workers who jammed the plaza in front of the large Retiro station came as much to pay tribute to Perón as they did to celebrate a major achievement in the nation's history. They wanted to cheer Perón, economic liberator of the republic. The crowd showed obvious disappointment when it learned that Perón would not attend the festivities because he had suffered an attack of appendicitis in the morning. Shouts of "We want Perón" drowned out the public address system. Compact groups of *descamisados* abandoned the plaza when they realized that he would not speak. The speakers could not be heard above the din and the police had to hold back the unruly mob on several occasions.

Despite Perón's absence, the celebration proceeded as planned. The first speaker, José G. Espejo, secretary general of the CGT, set the pattern for the adulation of Perón. He praised the latter for ending the rape of Argentina by the British-owned railways. That action, he added, restored the rights of the workers. Now they had to prove that Argentines could run the railways on their own. Alfredo Sivoli, vice-president of La Fraternidad, followed Espejo. He compared San Martín and Perón in glowing terms: "Both had the common objective of gaining the independence and liberty of the sons of America. The former [San Martín] . . . unsheathed his sword in order to liberate half a continent, and for this reason we venerate San Martín as the Saint of the Sword. To the other [Perón] we owe the economic liberation of the *patria*."[27] In a similar manner, Juan Rodríguez of the Unión

[27] *La Prensa*, March 2, 1948.

Ferroviaria linked Perón's campaign for economic independence directly with the labor movement. He called Perón the best of all Argentines, a friend of labor. "Perón, Perón, Perón! He is the heart of us. . . . Do not forget that this day of glory for the country and the people is also a day of glory for Perón. Do not forget that in these moments, economic independence represents geographic and political independence. And if San Martín was the Saint of the Sword, I proclaim Perón Saint of the Worker."[28]

After the labor leaders spoke, the official activities ended with the reading of Perón's prepared speech by General Juan Pistarini, minister of public works. In that capstone speech Perón no longer spoke of the British with affection as he had in September, 1946. Rather, he reiterated what he had put forth in the Declaration of Economic Independence. He bitterly charged that foreign imperialists had used the railways as instruments of economic domination. The purchase of the railways helped achieve economic independence. This important conquest over the foreign imperialists fulfilled Perón's promise to liberate the worker. In words made all the more dramatic because of the operation he underwent that morning, Perón's speech stated: "I consider the act that we are celebrating today so important that I firmly believe that if my political career, or even my physical life were to end today I would die with the intimate satisfaction that I had paid off my debt to Argentina. . . . Men perish. The *patria* remains, and its well-being is what matters."[29]

[28] Ibid.
[29] Ibid.

Conclusion

Perón's purchase of the British-owned railways proved a popular act in 1948 because of its symbolic value. It represented the touchstone of his campaign to make Argentina socially just, politically sovereign, and economically independent. Significantly, Perón heralded the purchase as a "conquest that never would have been accomplished if a government of the workers had not come to office."[1] He often referred to the purchase as a victory over foreign imperialists. In Peronista rhetoric the comparison of the purchase to a military victory seemed appropriate because of Perón's attempts to regiment the Argentine workers. Although he never used the word *regiment* in this connection, since 1945 he had more than once called organized laborers an "army" that he would lead to battle in the struggle for social justice and economic independence. Previously, the quest for economic independence and social justice had been led by political parties which challenged the ruling elite. Under Perón economic nationalism became an integral part of the ruling party's platform.

[1] *La Prensa*, March 2, 1948.

The acquisition of the British-owned railways highlights the fact that two currents of Argentine political and economic development met in the mainstream of Peronist politics. There, antiforeign economic nationalism, which had increased steadily during the present century, merged with the popular massification of the nation's simplistic political system. Popular nationalism provided Perón with a convenient way to broaden his base of support. On numerous occasions he encouraged the mass of urban workers to back his political movement by using popular antiforeign nationalism. Workers, who had received little political attention before 1940, readily pledged themselves to Perón during the mid-1940's. Understandably, they joined Perón's legions to win the battle for economic independence. Victory, they believed, would assure them social justice and improved living standards.

Perón rode the wave of economic nationalism to increase popular support for his regime. He did not have to create an issue in the British-owned railways. Rather, he had only to keep alive the masses' antipathy toward the British. He did not invent economic independence and social justice as campaign slogans. These already existed as well-conceived goals of Argentine nationalists. Even members of the Conservative oligarchy had used similar phrases since 1930. Opposition to foreign economic influence had become an important plank in the platforms of every party that opposed the ruling oligarchy after 1890.[2] The Socialist leader Juan B. Justo sought to rid the nation of foreign imperialists in order to bestow the benefits of social justice upon the masses. The Radicals under Hipólito Yrigoyen professed similar beliefs. Popular politicians, such as Lisandro de la Torre and Alfredo L. Palacios, also spoke out against foreign-owned enterprises, such as the British-owned railways. In so doing they won widespread support from the Argentine public.

The history of the British-owned railways reflects the evolution of Argentine economic nationalism since the fall of Rosas in 1852. During the first stage, Argentina's prevailing economic

[2] José Luis Romero, *A History of Argentine Political Thought*, trans. Thomas F. McGann, pp. 183-193.

nationalism remained liberal and optimistic. Leaders of the traditionally antiforeign interior provinces joined *porteños* in seeking the assistance of foreign capitalists in building railways throughout the country. The honeymoon period ended by 1890. At that point economic nationalism entered its second stage. Disillusioned by the crash of 1890, opponents of the pro-European oligarchs became increasingly critical of the role played by foreign entrepreneurs. Their criticism often amounted to political attacks against the elite. As Argentines became less inclined to stand in awe of the British companies, the government officials found it harder to defend the companies from criticism. During the brief interlude of Radical rule between 1916 and 1930, potential xenophobes controlled the government. The Radicals failed to implement many antiforeign measures, but they did encourage the spread of xenophobia. After the effects of the 1929 Wall Street crash reached Argentina, Argentine economic nationalism entered a third stage. During the depression years the conservative Concordancia turned to nationalistic solutions for Argentina's economic dilemmas. They may have favored one particular economic sector, but their programs were nationalistic. Critics of the Concordancia, from both the right and the left, took even stronger positions against foreign economic imperialism of the type symbolized by the large British-owned railways. When proponents of antiliberal nationalism triumphed in 1943, Argentine economic nationalism entered its fourth stage. Xenophobia became an official government policy of the leaders of the new Argentina.

The popular reaction to the repatriation of the British-owned railways demonstrates the narrow definition of economic independence held by most Argentines. To the great majority in 1948, economic independence meant the withdrawal of all forms of foreign economic influence from the nation. When the nineteenth-century laissez faire policy failed to meet Argentina's economic needs, and as the nation turned toward diversification through industrialization after World War I, the repatriation of the railways became an important part of a popular political ideology that promised social justice on a broad scale when and if Argentina won its economic independence. Purchasing foreign-owned enterprises and accumulating credits against the most advanced nations of the world appeared to lead to a new and free Argentina. In such a climate of opinion, the British-owned railways served as fixed symbols of retrogressive foreign intervention and a target for anti-foreign demonstrations. Because of this attitude, Perón and his associates equated the purchase of the railways with attempts to improve the working conditions and living standards of all Argentines.

In the long run the purchase had devastating results. The nationalization of the British-owned railways and other foreign-owned utility companies contributed directly to the economic crisis that has plagued Argentina since 1950. The railway purchase hastened the withdrawal of European investment and exhausted the capital reserves that Argentina had built during the war years. Nationalization of the railways accounted for over 90 percent of the reduction of British investments in Argentina from 356,212,586 pounds sterling in 1946 to 69,428,083 pounds sterling by 1950.[3] Argentines had to replace British capital with their own. This they failed to do. Perón needed large amounts of capital to carry out his industrialization programs. The Argentine economy would have benefited more if the reserves had been used to develop local industries. New Jobs could have been created for unemployed workers. Consumer goods could have been produced in Argentina, rather than imported. Acquisition of the railways did little to stimulate the economic growth of the nation. The railways were not reproductive industries. They did not create new jobs, except through the expensive and wasteful system of featherbedding.[4]

Perón did not turn to outright purchase of the railways because of nationalism alone. In large part he reacted to pressures from the United States and Britain, but nationalism provided an

---

[3] *South American Journal,* January 28, 1950, p. 42. Of the 356,212,586 pounds invested in Argentina in 1946, 252,131,866 were invested in railways. British holdings in Argentine government bonds dropped from 29,940,570 pounds in 1946 to 5,666,450 in 1950. Also see United Nations, "The Problems of the Economic Development of Argentina," *Economic Bulletin for Latin America* 4 (1959): 15-16.

[4] United Nations, "The Problems of the Economic Development of Argentina," pp. 15-16.

excellent rationalization for the act. In buying the railways Perón fulfilled the nationalistic urge of thousands of Argentines and their leaders. He became the economic liberator of the nation. As such he encouraged Argentines to liken him to the great hero, General José de San Martín. The emotional aspects of economic nationalism outweighed the economic realities of a policy that contributed to Argentina's financial difficulties. Perón permitted mobs to destroy the records of the British-owned companies. In a nationalistic frenzy the Argentines destroyed years of invaluable information concerning the details of running the railways. Such an act emphasized the fact that no matter what the causes were, Argentines used emotional rather than economic standards to measure the success of the repatriation of the railways.

GLOSSARY

aguinaldo: Christmas present, frequently paid to employees in the form of a month's pay bonus.

Argentinidad: word coined in 1910 by the cultural nationalist Ricardo Rojas to describe an intense concept of national identity.

Casa Rosada: Argentine presidential palace in Buenos Aires.

caudillo: political boss or chief who bases power on a complex balance of force, wealth, kinship, and charisma.

chacra: small isolated farm, usually for the purpose of growing wheat or some other grain.

Concordancia: name given to the conservative coalition that governed Argentina between 1932 and June 4, 1943.

criollo: indigenous American, especially used in this study to identify indigenous movements that have reacted to foreign ideologies and innovations.

descamisado: term used by Juan and Evita Perón to identify their working-class followers; literally, the term suggests a ragamuffin, but the Peróns used it as one of endearment.

estancia: large farm or ranch estate, frequently comprising thousands of unused acres of land.

estanciero: owner of an *estancia*.

gaucho: mixed racial horseman of the Argentine pampa; the term also suggests strong Argentine sentiments.

litoral: coastal region of Argentina above the province of Buenos Aires.

pampa: extensive and fertile plains of Argentina.

porteño: resident of a port city; in Argentina the term refers to the native of the city of Buenos Aires.

vendepatria: in general, one who sells out his country to foreign imperialists.

BIBLIOGRAPHY

Unpublished Material

Buenos Ayres and Pacific Railway Company Limited. Minute Book of General Meetings. No. l: general meetings from February 13, 1883, to June 1, 1964. Nos. 32, 36, and 37: receipts and correspondence noted for September 13, 1945-March 25, 1948; also board meeting records, May 31, 1932-March 20, 1934; June 26, 1941-August 23, 1945; and September 13, 1945-March 25, 1948.

Jordan, David C. "Argentina's Nationalist Movements and the Political Parties: 1930-1963." Ph.D. Dissertation, University of Pennsylvania, 1964.

Merkx, Gilbert W. "Political and Economic Change in Argentina from 1870 to 1966." Ph.D. Dissertation, Yale University, 1968.

Platt, D. C. M. "Latin America: Business Archives in the United Kingdom." Mimeographed. Exeter, 1964.

Reports on the Value of Railway Undertakings of the Four Broad-Gauge Railways, May, 1945.

Sweet, Dana R. "A History of United States Argentine Commercial Relations, 1918-1933: A Study of Competitive Farm Economies." Ph.D. Dissertation, Syracuse University, 1971.

Government Documents

Agote, Pedro. *Report on the Public Debt: Banking Institutions, and Mint of the Argentine Republic and on the National and Provincial Estimates and Taxation Laws.* Translated by L. B. Trant. Buenos Aires: Stiller and Laas, 1887.

————. Argentine Republic. Junta de Administración del Crédito Público Nacional. *Informe del presidente del Crédito Público Nacional Pedro Agote sobre la deuda pública, bancos, acuñación de moneda y presupuestos y leyes de impuestos de la nación y de las provincias, 1881-1888.* 5 vols. Buenos Aires, 1881-1888.

Argentine Republic. Cámara de Diputados. *Diario de sesiones.* 1862-1955.

————. ————. *Diario de sesiones* (Daily Issue). Buenos Aires, 1936-1948.

————. ————. *Investigación parlamentaria de los ferrocarriles garantidos de la nación.* Buenos Aires: Imprenta del Congreso de la Nación, 1891.

————. ————. *El parlamento argentino, 1854-1947.* Buenos Aires: Imprenta del Congreso de la Nación, 1948.

————. Cámara de Senadores. *Diario de sesiones.* Buenos Aires, 1862-1955.

————. ————. *Diario de sesiones* (Daily Issue). Buenos Aires, 1934-1948.

————. *Comisión especial de representantes de empresas y obreros ferroviarios.* Buenos Aires: Gmo Kraft, 1930.

————. Dirección de Informaciones y Publicaciones Ferroviarias. *Origen y desarrollo de los ferrocarriles argentinos.* Buenos Aires: "El Ateneo," [1946].

————. Dirección Nacional de Vialidad. *La coordinación nacional de los transportes: Mas opiniones de la prensa del país.* Buenos Aires: Gerónimo J. Disce y Cía, 1936.

————. Junta honoraria para el estudio de la situación económica y financiera de los ferrocarriles. *Informes, y conclusiones, y recomendaciones de la junta honoraria nombrada para el estudio de la situación económica y financiera de los ferrocarriles por el P.E.N.* Buenos Aires: Gorral, Tusso y Vita Impresores, 1935.

————. Ministerio de Hacienda. *Proyectos financieros y económicos, 1941-1942.* Buenos Aires, 1942.

————. Ministerio de Obras Públicas. Dirección de Publicidad Ferroviaria. *Los ferrocarriles particulares en la Argentina.* Buenos Aires, 1938.

————. ————. Dirección General de Ferrocarriles. *Estadística de los ferrocarriles en explotación.* 50 vols. Buenos Aires, 1892-1943.

————. ————. ————. *Estadística gráfica de los ferrocarriles en explotación, 1857-1935.* Buenos Aires, 1937.

————. Obras Públicas e Industrias. *La crisis ferroviaria argentina.* Buenos Aires: Obras Públicas e Industrias, 1933.

————. *Poder ejecutivo nacional, 1932-1938.* Buenos Aires: Obras Públicas, 1938.

————. Presidente. *Mensajes de President Roca.* Vol. 1. Buenos Aires:

Editorial Aranjo, 1941.

———. *Registro oficial de la República Argentina, 1854-1863.* Buenos Aires, 1882-1895.

———. Senado de la Nación. *Documentos básicos de nuestra independencia, 1816 hasta 1947.* Buenos Aires, 1951.

———. *Tercero censo nacional: Leventada el 1 de junio de 1914.* Vols. 7 and 10. Buenos Aires: Talleres Gráficos de L. J. Rossi y Cía, 1917.

Castillo, Ramón S. *Mensaje del presidente de la nación, 1941.* Buenos Aires: Compañía Impresora Argentina, 1941.

Farrell, Edelmiro J. *Mensaje del presidente de la nación, 1944.* Buenos Aires: Compañía Impresora Argentina, 1944.

Great Britain. Board of Trade. Department of Overseas Trade. *Report on the Financial and Economic Conditions of the Argentine Republic.* London: His Majesty's Stationery Office, 1921-1945. [Title varies.]

———. ———. Overseas Economic Surveys. *Argentina: Economic and Commercial Conditions in the Argentine Republic.* Edited by J. G. Lomax. London: His Majesty's Stationery Office, 1948.

———. House of Commons. *Parliamentary Debates.* London: His Majesty's Stationery Office, 1930-1948.

———. Public Record Office, London. Foreign Office. Commercial. Series F.O. 368.

———. ———. General Correspondence 1900-1905. Series F.O. 6.

———. ———. General Correspondence: Political, 1906-1937. Series F.O. 371.

———. *Reports on the Value of Railway Undertakings of the Four Broad-Gauge Railways.* London, May, 1945.

———. Treaties. *Convention between the Government of the United Kingdom and the Argentine Republic relating to Trade and Commerce, with Protocol, May 1, 1933.* London: His Majesty's Stationery Office, 1933.

———. Treaties Series no. 27 (1948). *Exchange of Notes between the Government of the United Kingdom and the Argentine Government Accepting the Agreement of the Sale of the British-Owned Railways in Argentina.* Buenos Aires, February 13, 1947. London: His Majesty's Stationery Office, 1948.

Irigoyen, Hipólito, ed. *Hipólito Irigoyen: Pueblo y gobierno.* 12 vols. Buenos Aires: Editorial Raigal, 1956.

League of Nations. Economic and Financial Section. *International Statistical Yearbook of the League of Nations, 1926.* Geneva: League of Nations, 1927.

President Perón Speaks to Members of the Banking and Monetary Committee of the House of Representatives of the United States. Buenos Aires: November 31, 1951.

United Nations. "The Problems of the Economic Development of Argentina." *Economic Bulletin for Latin America* 4 (1959): 15-16.

United States. Chamber of Commerce of the United States of America in the Argentine Republic. *Comments on Argentine Trade* 12, no. 8 (March 1933): 15-44.

———. Department of Commerce. Bureau of Foreign and Domestic Commerce. Latin American Transportation Survey Section. "The Railways of Argentina." Prepared by Emerson R. Johnson. Mimeographed. Washington, D.C., 1943.

———. National Archives, Washington, D.C. Department of State. Correspondence of the American Legation in Buenos Aires, 1862-1944. Microcopy and decimal files. Record Group 59. [Used for commercial, general political, and economic information.]

Universidad de Buenos Aires. Facultad de Ciencias Económicas. Instituto de Economía de los Transportes. *Los ferrocarriles argentinos de capital privado en los últimos once años, 1928-1939: Posibilidad económica-financiera de su nacionalización.* Edited by Teodoro Sánchez de Bustamente. Buenos Aires: Imp. de la Universidad, 1940.

Books, Pamphlets, and Articles*

Acevedo, Edberto Oscar. "Situación actual de la historia argentina." *Estudios Americanos* 60, no. 43 (May 1955): 353-396.

Alberdi, Juan B. *Bases y puntos de partida para la organización política de la República Argentina.* Buenos Aires: Francisco Cruz, 1914.

———. *The Life and Industrial Labors of William Wheelwright in South America.* Boston: A. Williams and Co., 1879. In Spanish version, *La vida y los trabajos industriales de William Wheelwright en la América del Sur.* Paris: Libería de Garnier Hermanos, 1878.

Aldao de Díaz, Elvira, ed. *Cartas íntimas de Lisandro de la Torre.* Buenos Aires: Editorial Futuro, 1941.

Alexander, Robert J. *An Introduction to Argentina.* New York: Frederick A. Praeger, 1969.

———. *The Perón Era.* New York: Columbia University Press, 1951.

———. *Prophets of the Revolution.* New York: Macmillan, 1962.

Amadeo, Mario. *Ayer, hoy, mañana.* Buenos Aires: Ediciones Gure, 1956.

Amadeo, Santos Primo. *Argentine Constitutional Law.* New York: Columbia University Press, 1943.

*Studies of nationalism are indicated by asterisks.

Amaral, Edgardo L. *Anecdotario de Lisandro de la Torre, y debate sobre el comunismo.* Buenos Aires: Comisión Nacional de Homenaje de Lisandro de la Torre, 1957.

"Amplificación de la nómina de materiales que los ferrocarriles pueden introducir libre de derechos." *Anales de la Unión Industrial Argentina* 49, no. 808 (April 1936): 9-24.

Ara, Guillermo. *Leopoldo Lugones.* Buenos Aires: Editorial la Mandrágora, 1958.

Arena, Domingo. *Batlle y los problemas sociales en el Uruguay.* Montevideo: Claudio García y Cia, n.d.

Baily, Samuel L. "Argentina, Twentieth Century." In *Latin America: A Guide to the Historical Literature.* Edited by Charles C. Griffen and J. Benedict Warren, pp. 556-570. Austin: University of Texas Press, 1971.

————. *Labor, Nationalism, and Politics in Argentina.* New Brunswick: Rutgers University Press, 1967.

Balestra, Juan. *El noventa: Una evolución política argentina.* Buenos Aires: "La Facultad," 1935.

Barager, Joseph R. "The Historiography of the Río de la Plata Area." *Hispanic American Historical Review* 39, no. 4 (November 1959): 588-642.

————, ed. *Why Perón Came to Power: The Background to Peronism in Argentina.* New York: Knopf, 1968.

*Barker, Ernest. *National Character, and the Factors in Its Formation.* London: Methuen & Co., 1928.

Barres, Francisco. "Reseña de los ferrocarriles argentinos." *Boletín de la Asociación Internacional Permanente* 26 (1926), no. 71: 96-104; no. 72: 27-33; no. 73: 21-30; no. 74: 26-35; no. 75: 20-26.

*Barzun, Jaques. "Cultural Nationalism and the Meaning of Fame." *Nationalism and Internationalism.* Edited by Edward Mean Earle, pp. 3-17. New York: Columbia University Press, 1950.

Batlle, Jorge, ed. *Batlle, su obra y su vida.* Montevideo: Editorial "Acción," 1956.

Beltrame, José. *La crisis de los ferrocarriles argentinos de propriedad privada.* Buenos Aires: Lotito Hermanos y Cía, 1946.

Bishop, Nathaniel. *The Pampas and Andes: A Thousand Mile's Walk across South America.* Boston: Lea and Shepard, 1869.

Blanksten, George I. *Perón's Argentina.* Chicago: University of Chicago Press, 1953.

Borges, Jorge Luis. *Leopoldo Lugones.* Buenos Aires: Editorial Troquel, 1955.

*Breton, Albert. "The Economics of Nationalism." *Journal of Political Economy* 72 (1964): 376-386.

Bruce, James. *Those Perplexing Argentines.* New York: Longmans, Green and Co., 1953.

Brunstein, Jacabo. *Estudio técnico y general de los ferrocarriles argentinos.* Buenos Aires: Imprenta Lurati, 1928.

Bryce, James. *South America: Observations and Impressions.* New York: Macmillan and Co., 1912.

Bucich Escobar, Ismael. *Los presidentes argentinos, 1826-1918.* Buenos Aires: Juan A. Herrera, 1918.

Buenos Ayres Great Southern Railway Company, Limited. *Report of the Directors to the Proprietors and Statement of the Revenue and Capital Accounts, 1924-1934.* London, 1924-1934.

Buenos Ayres Western Railway Company, Limited. *Report of the Directors to the Proprietors and Statement of the Revenue and Capital Accounts, 1922-1937.* London: Waterlow and Sons, 1922-1937.

Bunge, Alejandro. *La economía argentina.* 4 vols. Buenos Aires: Agencia general de liberías y publicaciones, 1928-1930.

———. *Ferrocarriles argentinos: Contribución al estudio del patrimonio nacional.* Buenos Aires: Imprenta Mercatali, 1918.

———. *Una nueva Argentina.* Buenos Aires: Guillermo Kraft, 1940.

Bunkley, Allison W. *The Life of Sarmiento.* Princeton: Princeton University Press, 1952.

Burgin, Miron. *The Economic Aspects of Argentine Federalism, 1820-1852.* Cambridge: Harvard University Press, 1946.

Cané, Miguel. *Expulsión de extranjeros.* Buenos Aires: Impr. de Sarrailh, 1899.

Cárcano, Miguel Angel. *Realidad de una política.* Buenos Aires: M. Gleizer, 1938.

*Carr, E. H. *Nationalism and After.* London: Macmillan, 1945.

Carranza, Neptalí. *Oratoria argentina.* 5 vols. Buenos Aires: Administración Vociaro, 1922.

Carrera, Héctor I. *El engaño de las nacionalizaciones totalitarias.* Buenos Aires: Ediciones Gure, 1955.

Castro, Juan Francisco. *Sarmiento y los ferrocarriles argentinos.* Buenos Aires: Ministerio de Educación de la Nación, 1950.

Castro, Juan José. *Treatise on the South American Railways and the Great International Lines.* Montevideo: La Nación Steam Printing Office, 1893.

Chianelli, Pascual. *Situación económica y financiera de los ferrocarriles argentinos en el ejército 1934-1936*. Buenos Aires: L. J. Rossi, 1936.

Chitti, Juan B., and Francisco Agnelli. *La fraternidad*. Buenos Aires: Ravaschino Hnos., 1937.

Cochran, Thomas C., and R. E. Reina. *Entrepreneurship in Argentine Culture: Torcuato Di Tella and S.I.A.M.* Philadelphia: University of Pennsylvania Press, 1962.

Coelho, Augusto J. "El rescate de los ferrocarriles argentinos." *Revista de Economía Argentina* 1 (August 1918), 199-204.

Conil Paz, Alberto A., and Gustavo Ferrari. *Argentina's Foreign Policy, 1930-1962*. Translated by John J. Kennedy. Notre Dame: University of Notre Dame Press, 1966.

Courbel, Juan B. "El ferrocarril transandino de Salta a Antofagasta." *Revista de Ciencias Económicas* 11, nos. 18-19 (1923): 16-26.

Cruz Machado, Daniel. *Frondizi: Una conducta, un pensamiento*. Buenos Aires: Soluciones, 1957.

Cuccorese, Horacio Juan. *Historia de los ferrocarriles en la Argentina*. Buenos Aires: Editorial Macchi, 1969.

Cúneo, Dardo. *Juan B. Justo y las luchas sociales en la Argentina*. Buenos Aires: Editorial Alpe, 1956.

Dagino Pastore, Lorenzo. "El nuevo ferrocarril." *Revista de Ciencias Económicas* 22, no. 168 (July 1935): 633-658.

Damonte Taborda, Raúl. *¿A donde va Perón? De Berlin a Wall Street*. Montevideo: Ediciones de la Resistencia Revolucionaria Argentina, 1955.

Denis, Pierre. *The Argentine Republic*. Translated by Joseph McCabe. New York: Charles Scribner's Sons, 1922.

*Deutsch, Karl W. *Nationalism and Social Communication: An Inquiry into the Foundations of Nationality*. New York: Technology Press of M.I.T. and Wiley, 1953.

―――. "Social Mobilization and Political Development." *American Political Science Review* 60, no. 3 (September 1961): 493-514.

Díaz Alejandro, Carlos F. *Essays on the Economic History of the Argentine Republic*. New Haven: Yale University Press, 1970.

Díaz Arana, Juan José. "El rescate de los ferrocarriles argentinos." *Revista de Economía Argentina* 1 (September 1918): 275-279.

Dickmann, Adolfo. *Nacionalismo y socialismo*. Buenos Aires: Porter Hnos., 1933.

Dickmann, Emilio. *Nacionalización de los ferrocarriles: Un problema técnico-económico argentino*. Buenos Aires: La Vanguardia, 1938.

Díez, Manuel María. *Régimen jurídico de las comunicaciones*. 5 vols.

284   Bibliography

Buenos Aires: Jesús Menéndez, 1936-1938.

Discursos y documentos políticos de Dr. Ricardo Cabellero. Edited by Roberto A. Ortelli. Buenos Aires: Sociedad de Publicaciones el Inca, 1929.

Di Tella, Guido, and Manuel Zymelman. Las etapas del desarrollo económico argentino. Buenos Aires: EUDBA, 1967.

Di Tella, Torcuato S. El sistema político argentino y la clase obrera. Buenos Aires: EUDBA, 1964.

Dorfman, Adolfo. Historia de la industria argentina. Buenos Aires: Escuela de estudios argentinos, 1942.

————. Evolución industrial argentina. Buenos Aires: Editorial Losada, 1942.

Duncan, J. S. "British Railways in Argentina." Political Science Quarterly 52, no. 4 (December 1937): 559-582.

Dunsdorfs, Edgars. The Australian Wheat-Growing Industry, 1888-1948. Melbourne: The University Press, 1956.

Ellis, Hamilton. British Railway History. 2 vols. London: George Allen and Unwin, 1959.

*Emerson, Rupert. From Empire to Nation. Boston: Beacon Press, 1962.

Emiliani, Rafael. Reorganización económica, política y social. Buenos Aires: De Martino, 1920.

Etcheguía, Gregorio. Los ferrocarriles argentinos vistos por ojos argentinos. Buenos Aires: Sociedad Impresora Americana, 1938.

Falcoff, Mark. "Raúl Scalabrini Ortiz: The Making of an Argentina Nationalist." Hispanic American Historical Review 52, no. 1 (February 1972): 74-101.

Fawcett, Brian. Railways of the Andes. London: George Allen and Unwin, 1963.

Fayt, Carlos S., ed. La naturaleza del peronismo. Buenos Aires: Abelardo Perrot, 1967.

Ferns, Henry S. Argentina. New York: Frederick A. Praeger, 1969.

————. Britain and Argentina in the Nineteenth Century. Oxford: Clarendon Press, 1960.

————. "Britain's Informal Empire in Argentina, 1806-1914." Past and Present 4 (November 1953): 60-75.

Ferrer, Aldo. The Argentine Economy. Translated by Marjory M. Urquidi. Berkeley: University of California Press, 1967.

"Ferrocarriles." Diccionario histórico argentino. Edited by Ricardo Piccirilli, III, 648-651. Buenos Aires: Ediciones Históricas Argentinas, 1953.

"Ferrocarriles." Gran enciclopedia argentina. Edited by Diego A. de Santillán, II, 313-317. Buenos Aires: Ediar Sociedad Anónimo Editores, 1957.

Fillol, Tomás Robert. *Social Factors in Economic Development: The Argentine Case*. Cambridge: M.I.T. Press, 1961.

Flores, María. *Woman with a Whip*. New York: Doubleday, 1953.

Fournier, Leslie T. *Railway Nationalization in Canada*. Toronto: Macmillan Company of Canada, 1935.

Gálvez, Manuel. *El solar de la raza*. 2d ed. Buenos Aires: Editorial Tor, 1936.

————. *Vida de Hipólito Yrigoyen: El hombre de misterio*. 2d ed. Buenos Aires: Kraft, 1939.

————. *Vida de Sarmiento: El hombre de autoridad*. Buenos Aires: Emecé Editores, 1945.

García, Juan Agustín, *Sobre nuestra incultura*. Buenos Aires: Editorial Claridad, 1922.

García Mellid, Atilio. "Etapas de la revolución argentina." *Hechos e Ideas* 10, no. 70 (January 1950): 31-80.

Germani, Gino. *Estructura social de la Argentina*. Buenos Aires: Editorial Raigal, 1955.

————. *Política y sociedad en una época de transición*. Buenos Aires: Editorial Paidos, 1962.

Giménez, Ovido. "La conferencia Otawa y nuestra producción ganadera." *Revista de Ciencias Económicas* 20, no. 133 (August 1932): 542-547.

Glauert, Earl T. "Ricardo Rojas and the Emergence of Argentine Cultural Nationalism." *Hispanic American Historical Review* 43, no. 1 (February 1963): 1-13.

González, Joaquin V. *Mitre*. Buenos Aires: El Ateneo, 1931.

González, Marcial. *El convenio Miranda-Eady y sus repercusiones en la economía nacional*. Córdoba, 1946.

González Alberdi, Paulino. *La situación económica del país: El plan Pinedo, plan de la oligarquía*. Buenos Aires: Editorial Problemas, 1941.

González Clement, Aurelio. "La reforma de la constitución nacional y los medios de transportes." *Revista de la facultad de Ciencias Económicas* 2, no. 13 (May 1949): 413-440.

Graham, Richard. *Britain and the Onset of Modernization in Brazil, 1850-1910*. London and New York: Cambridge University Press, 1968.

Grahame, Leopoldo. *Argentine Railways: A Review of Their Position, Conditions, and Prospects*. New York: Penskarf, Lyon and Co., 1916.

Green, Otis H. "Gálvez's 'La sombra del convento' and Its Relation to 'El

Diario de Gabriel Quiroga.' " *Hispanic Review* 12 (1944): 196-210.

———. "Manuel Gálvez, 'Gabriel Quiroga,' and 'El mal metafísico.' " *Hispanic Review* 11 (1943): 314-327.

———. "Manuel Gálvez, 'Gabriel Quiroga,' and *la maestra normal.*" *Hispanic Review* 11 (1943): 221-252.

Guaresti, Juan José. "La coordinación de los transportes." *Revista de Ciencias Económicas* 23, no. 165 (May 1935): 525-538.

Grummon, Stuart Edgar, trans. *A Sarmiento Anthology.* Princeton: Princeton University Press, 1948.

Halsey, Frederic M. *Railway Expansion in Latin America.* New York: Moody Magazine and Book Co., 1916.

Hanson, Simon G. *Argentine Meat and the British Market.* Palo Alto: Stanford University Press, 1938.

———. "The Farquhar Syndicate in South America." *Hispanic American Historical Review* 17, no. 3 (August 1937): 314-326.

———. *Utopia in Uruguay: Chapter in the Economic History of Uruguay.* New York: Oxford University Press, 1938.

Harris, Seymour E., ed. *Economic Problems of Latin America.* New York: McGraw Hill, 1944.

*Hayes, Carlton J. H. *Essays on Nationalism.* New York: Macmillan, 1928.

———. *The Historical Evolution of Modern Nationalism.* New York: R. R. Smith, 1931.

———. *Nationalism: A Religion.* New York: Macmillan, 1960.

Hernández Arreguí, Juan José. *Imperialismo y cultura: La política en la inteligencia argentina.* Buenos Aires: Editorial Amerindia, 1957.

———. *La formación de la conciencia nacional: 1930-1960.* Buenos Aires: Ediciones Hachea, 1960.

Hierro Gambardella, Luis. "Batlle y los entes autónomos." In *Batlle, su obra y su vida,* edited by Jorge Batlle. Montevideo: Editorial "Acción," 1956.

Hirschman, Albert O. *Journeys toward Progress: Studies of Economic Policy-Making in Latin America.* New York: Twentieth Century Fund, 1963.

———, ed. *Latin American Issues: Essays and Comments.* New York: Twentieth Century Fund, 1961.

Hunter, Holland. *Soviet Transport Experience: Its Lessons for Other Countries.* Washington, D.C.: Brookings Institution, 1968.

Hutchinson, Thomas J. *The Paraná with Incidents of the Paraguayan War and South American Recollections from 1861 to 1868.* London: Edward Stamford, 1868.

Ibarguren, Carlos. *La historia que he vivido*. Buenos Aires: Ediciones Péuser, 1955.

Ingenieros, José. *Sociología Argentina*. Buenos Aires: Talleres Gráficos Argentinos, n.d.

Irazusta, Julio. *Perón y la crisis argentina*. Buenos Aires: La Voz de la Plata, 1956.

————, and Rodolfo Irazusta. *La Argentina y el imperialismo británico*. Buenos Aires: Editorial Tor, 1934.

Jefferson, Mark. *Peopling the Argentine Pampa*. New York: American Geographical Society, 1926.

Jeffrey, William Hart. *Mitre and Argentina*. New York: Library Publishers, 1952.

Jenks, Leland H. "Britain and American Railway Development." *Journal of Economic History* 11, no. 4 (1951): 375-388.

*Johnson, Harry G., ed. *Economic Nationalism in Old and New States*. Chicago: University of Chicago Press, 1967.

Johnson, J. *The Economics of Indian Rail Transport*. New York: Allied Publishers, 1963.

*Johnson, John J. "The New Latin American Nationalism." *The Yale Review* 54, no. 2 (December 1964): 187-204.

————. *Political Change in Latin America: The Emergence of the Middle Sectors*. 2d ed. Stanford: Stanford University Press, 1962.

————. "Whither the Latin American Middle Sectors." *Virginia Quarterly Review* 37, no. 4 (Autumn 1961): 508-521.

Justo, Juan B. *La realización del socialismo*. Buenos Aires: La Vanguardia, 1947.

Kautsky, John H., ed. *Political Change in Underdeveloped Countries: Nationalism and Communism*. New York: Wiley, 1962.

Kennedy, John J. *Catholicism, Nationalism, and Democracy in Argentina*. Notre Dame: University of Notre Dame Press, 1958.

Kirkpatrick, Frederick A. *A History of the Argentine Republic*. Cambridge: Cambridge University Press, 1931.

*Kohn, Hans. *The Idea of Nationalism: A Study of Its Origins and Background*. New York: Macmillan, 1951.

————. *Nationalism: Its Meaning and History*. Princeton: D. Van Nostrand, 1955.

Korn, Alejandro. *Influencias filosóficas en el evolución nacional*. Buenos Aires: Editorial Claridad, 1936.

Lafiandra, Félix, ed. *Los panfletos: Su aporte a la revolución libertadora: Recopilación, comentario, y notas*. Buenos Aires: Itinerarium, 1955.

288   *Bibliography*

Lafond, Georges. *Les chemins de fer argentins.* Paris: Société d'études et d'informations économiques, 1926.

Lazarte, Juan. *Lisandro de la Torre: Reformador social americano.* Buenos Aires: Editorial Americale, 1941.

Lestard, Gaston H. *Historia de la evolución económica argentina.* Buenos Aires: Bernabé y Cía, 1937.

Lestrade, Rodolfo. *Donde se prueba como se vende la patria: El juicio político al Dr. Federico Pinedo.* Buenos Aires: Edito Patria, 1940.

Lewis, Colin. "Problems of Railway Development in Argentina, 1857-1890." *Inter-American Economic Affairs* 22, no. 2 (Autumn 1968): 55-75.

"Ley Mitre." *Gran enciclopedia argentina.* Edited by Diego A. de Santillán, V, 314-315. Buenos Aires: Ediar Sociedad Anónimo Editores, 1957.

López Basanta, J. *Cultura ciudana: La economía argentina.* Buenos Aires: Editorial Fides Librería, 1954.

Lugones, Leopoldo. *Historia de Sarmiento.* Buenos Aires: Babel, 1931.

Luna, Félix, *Alvear.* Buenos Aires: Libros Argentinos, 1958.

————. *El 45: Crónica de un año decisivo.* Buenos Aires: Editorial Jorge Alvarez, 1969.

Mabragaña, Heraclio, ed. *Los mensajes: Historia del desenvolvimiento de la nación argentina redactada cronologicamente por sus gobernantes.* 6 vols. Buenos Aires: Compañía Oral de Fósforos, [1910?].

Mcdougall, John Lorne. *Canadian Pacific: A Brief History.* Montreal: McGill University Press, 1968.

McGann, Thomas F. *Argentina, the United States and the Inter-American System, 1880-1914.* Cambridge: Harvard University Press, 1957.

Magnet, Alejandro. *Nuestros vecinos argentinos.* Santiago de Chile: Editorial del Pacífico, 1956.

Mansilla, Lucio V., ed. *Retratos y recuerdos.* Buenos Aires: El Ateneo, 1927.

Martel, Julián (José María Miro). *La bolsa.* Buenos Aires: Ediciones Estrada, 1946.

Martínez Estrada, Ezequiel. *Radiografía de la pampa.* 5th ed. 2 vols. Buenos Aires: Editorial Losada, 1961.

Matienzo, José Nicolás. *El gobierno representativo federal en la República Argentina.* Buenos Aires: Impr. de Coni Hermanos, 1910.

————. *La revolución de 1890 en la historia constitucional argentina.* Buenos Aires: Editorial Argentina de Ciencias Políticas, 1926.

Mazo, Gabriel del, ed. *El pensamiento escrito de Yrigoyen.* Buenos Aires:

Luis Casartelli, 1945.

———. *El radicalismo.* 2 vols. Buenos Aires: Ediciones Gure, 1957.

Meinvielle, Julio. *Política argentina: 1949-1956.* Buenos Aires: Editorial Trafac, 1956.

Meira, Gregorio A. *Reflexiones que sugiera la actual industrialización del país: Bases para un plan industrial.* Rosario: Universidad Nacional del Litoral-Santa Fe, 1945.

Moreno Quintana, Lucio M. "Características general de la economía argentina." *Revista de Ciencias Económicas* 27, no. 214 (May 1939): 411-446.

———. "La recuperación de la economía nacional." *Revista de Ciencias Económicas* 25, no. 189 (April 1937): 259-268.

Nazar Anchorena, Benito A. *Los ferrocarriles en el código civil: Naturaleza jurídica de la propriedad ferroviaria.* Tucumán: Bonetto y Cué, 1928.

Nichols, Madeline W. *Sarmiento: A Chronicle of Inter American Friendship.* Washington, D.C., 1940.

Olariaga, Luis. "El porvenir de la economía argentina." *Revista de Ciencias Económicas* 15, no. 72 (July 1927): 811-820.

Ortiz, Ricardo M. *El ferrocarril en la economía argentina.* 2 ed., rev. Buenos Aires: Editorial Problemas, 1958.

———. *Historia económica de la Argentina, 1850-1930.* 2 vols. Buenos Aires: Editorial Raigal, 1955.

Ortiz, Roberto M. *Mensaje del presidente de la nación, 1939.* Buenos Aires: Compañía Impresora Argentina, 1939.

Palacio, Ernest. *Historia de la Argentina, 1515-1938.* Buenos Aires: Edicione Alpe, 1954.

Palacios, Alfredo L. *En defensa de las instituciones libres.* Santiago de Chile: Ediciones Ercilla, 1936.

Palcos, Alberto. *Sarmiento: La vida, la obra, las ideas, el genio.* 3d ed. Buenos Aires: El Ateneo, 1938.

*Pearson, Lester B. "Beyond the Nation-State." *Saturday Review*, February 15, 1969, pp. 24-27, 54.

Pellegrini, Carlos. *Discursos y escritos del Dr. Carlos Pellegrini.* Edited by Domingo de Muro. Buenos Aires: Martín García, 1910.

Pendle, George. *Argentina.* London: Oxford University Press, 1963.

———. "Railways in Argentina." *History Today* 8, no. 2 (February 1958): 119-125.

Pennington, A. Stuart. *The Argentine Republic: Its Physical Features, History, Fauna, Flora, Geology, Literature and Commerce.* London: Stanley Paul and Co., 1910.

Perón, Juan D. *La fuerza es el derecho de las bestias.* Havana, Cuba: Santiago Touriño, 1956.

———. *La política internacional argentina.* Buenos Aires, 1948.

———. *The Voice of Perón.* Buenos Aires, 1950.

Phelps, Vernon L. *The International Economic Position of Argentina.* Philadelphia: University of Pennsylvania Press, 1938.

Pinedo, Federico. *En tiempos de la república.* 5 vols. Buenos Aires: Editorial Mundo Forense, 1946.

Pinto, Estevão. *Historia de una estrada-de-ferro de nordeste.* São Paulo: Livraría José Olympio Editora, 1949.

Platt, D. C. M. "British Bondholders in Nineteenth Century Latin America—Inquiry and Remedy." *Inter-American Economic Affairs* 14, no. 3 (Winter 1960): 3-43.

Portnoy, Leopoldo. *Análisis crítico de la economía argentina.* Mexico City: Fondo de Cultura Económica, 1961.

Potash, Robert A. *The Army and Politics in Argentina, 1928-1945: Yrigoyen to Perón.* Stanford: Stanford University Press, 1969.

Pugliese, Mario. "Nacionalismo económico, comercio internacional bilateral, e industrialización de los paises agrícolas, desde el punto de vista de la economía argentina." *Revista de Ciencias Económicas* 27, no. 219 (October 1939): 917-950.

Pulley, Raymond H. "The Railroad and Argentine National Development, 1852-1914." *The Americas* 23, no. 1 (July 1966): 63-75.

Rabinovitz, Bernardo. *Sucedió en la Argentina (1943-1956): Lo que no se dijo.* Buenos Aires: Ediciones Gure, 1956.

Ramallo, Carlos M. *Algunos consideraciones sobre coordinación de los transportes.* Buenos Aires: L. J. Rossi, 1936.

Ratti, Luis P. *El transporte por ferrocarril.* Buenos Aires: Jesús Menéndez, 1936.

Rebuelto, Emilio. "Ferrocarriles del continente sudamericano." *Talleres Gráficos del Ministro de Obras Públicas* 6, nos. 3 and 4 (March-April 1912): 81-112.

———. "Historia del desarrollo de los ferrocarriles argentinos." *Boletín de Obras Públicas de la República Argentina* 5, nos. 5 and 6 (November-December 1911): 113-172.

———. "Historia del desarrollo de los ferrocarriles argentinos." *Boletín de Obras Públicas de la República Argentina* 8, nos. 1 and 2 (January-February 1913): 1-32.

Rennie, Ysabel F. *The Argentine Republic.* New York: Macmillan Co., 1946.

Repetto, Nicolás. *Mi paso por la política: De Uriburu a Perón.* Buenos Aires: Santiago Rueda, 1957.

―――. *Política internacional.* Buenos Aires: La Vanguardia, 1943.

Rippy, J. F. "Argentina: Late Major Field of British Overseas Investment." *Inter-American Economic Affairs* 6, no. 3 (1952): 3-13.

―――. *Latin America and the Industrial Age.* 2d ed. New York: G. P. Putnam's Sons, 1947.

Robbins, Michael. "The Balaklava Railway." *Journal of Transport History* 1, no. 1 (May 1953): 41-42.

―――. *The Railway Age.* London: Routledge and Kegan Paul, 1962.

Rodríguez Yirgoyen, Luis. *Hipólito Yrigoyen, 1878-1933: Documentación historica de 55 años de actuación por la democracia y las instituciones.* Buenos Aires, 1934.

Rögind, William. *Historia del Ferrocarril Sud, 1861-1936.* Buenos Aires, 1936.

Rojas, Ricardo. *La argentinidad.* 2d ed. Buenos Aires: La Facultad, 1922.

―――. *Los arquetipos.* Buenos Aires: La Facultad, 1922.

―――. *Blasón de la plata.* Buenos Aires: J. Roldán, 1922.

―――. *Eurindia.* 2d ed. Buenos Aires: La Facultad, 1924.

―――. *El profeta de la pampa: Vida de Sarmiento.* Buenos Aires: Editorial Losada, 1945.

―――. *El radicalismo de mañana.* Buenos Aires: L. J. Rossi, 1932.

―――. *La restauración nacionalista.* 2d ed. Buenos Aires: La Facultad, 1922.

Romero, Francisco. *Alejandro Korn.* Buenos Aires: Editorial Losada, 1940.

Romero, José Luis. *El desarrollo de las ideas en la sociedad argentina del siglo XX.* Mexico City-Buenos Aires: Fondo de Cultura Económica, 1965.

―――. *A History of Argentine Political Thought.* Translated by Thomas F. McGann. Stanford: Stanford University Press, 1963.

Ronald, Juan. *El problema de los ferrocarriles argentinos.* Buenos Aires: The Standard, 1945.

Rosa, José María. *La caída de Rosas.* Madrid: Instituto de Estudios Políticos, 1958.

―――. *Defensa y perdida de nuestra independencia económica.* 2d ed. Buenos Aires: Editorial Haz, 1954.

Royal Institute of International Affairs. *Nationalism.* London: Oxford University Press, 1939.

Rutter, W. P. *Wheat-Growing in Canada, the United States and the*

Argentine. London: Adam and Charles Block, 1911.

Saldías, Adolfo. *La evolución republicana.* Buenos Aires: Editorial Raigal, 1919.

Salera, Virgil. *Exchange Control and the Argentine Market.* New York: Columbia University Press, 1941.

Sánchez, Luis Alberto. *Nueva historia de la literatura americana.* Santiago, Chile: Ediciones Ercilla, 1943.

Sánchez de Bustamente, Teodoro. "La coordinación de transportes de la ciudad de Buenos Aires." *Revista de Ciencias Económicas* 27, no. 218 (September 1939): 811-840.

————. "¿Estatización o industria privada en materia de servios públicos de transportes y comunicaciones?" *Revista de Ciencias Económicas,* 2d ser., 31, no. 267 (1943): 963-973.

————. "La vialidad en la República Argentina: Su evolución y estado actual." *Revista de Ciencias Económicas* 22, no. 150 (January 1934): 35-68.

Santander, Silvano. *Yo acuse a la dictadura.* Buenos Aires: Ediciones Gure, 1957.

Sarmiento, Domingo F. *Estados Unidos.* Buenos Aires: Emece-Editores, 1942.

————. *Life in the Argentine Republic in the Days of the Tyrants.* Preface and biography by Mrs. Horace Mann. New York: Collier, 1961.

Scalabrini Ortiz, Raúl. *Los ferrocarriles deben ser del pueblo argentino.* Buenos Aires: Editorial Unión Revolucionaria, 1946.

————. *Historia de los ferrocarriles argentinos.* Buenos Aires: Editorial Reconquista, 1940.

————. *Política británica en el Río de la Plata.* Buenos Aires: Editorial Reconquista, [1940].

Scobie, James R. *Argentina: A City and a Nation.* New York: Oxford University Press, 1964.

————. *La lucha por la consolidación de la nacionalidad argentina, 1852-62.* Buenos Aires: Librería Hachette, 1964.

————. *Revolution on the Pampas: A History of Argentine Wheat, 1860-1910.* Austin: University of Texas Press, 1964.

*Shafer, Boyd C. *Nationalism: Myth and Reality.* New York: Harcourt, Brace, 1955.

*————. *Nationalism: Interpreters and Interpretations.* Washington, D.C.: American Historical Association Service Center for Teachers Series, 1959.

Sherbinin, Betty de. *The River Plate Republics: Argentina, Uruguay, Paraguay.* New York: Coward-McCann, 1947.

Sherrington, Charles Ely Rose. *The Economics of Rail Transport in Great Britain.* 2 vols. New York: Longmans, Green and Co., 1928.

*Silvert, Kalman H., ed. *Expectant Peoples.* New York: Random House, 1963.

————. "Peronism in Argentina: A Rightist Reaction to the Social Problem of Latin America." In *Latin American History: Select Problems; Identity, Integration, and Nationhood,* edited by Fredrick B. Pike. New York: Harcourt, Brace and World, 1969.

Smith, Peter H. *Politics and Beef in Argentina: Pattern of Conflict and Change.* New York: Columbia University Press, 1969.

————. "Los radicales argentinos y la defensa de los intereses ganaderos 1916-1930." *Desarrollo Económico* 7, no. 25 (April-June 1967): 795-829.

————. "The Social Base of Peronism." *Hispanic American Historical Review* 52, no. 1 (February 1972): 55-73.

————. "Social Mobilization, Political Participation, and the Rise of Juan Perón." *Political Science Quarterly* 84, no. 1 (March 1969): 30-49.

Snow, Peter G. *Argentine Radicalism: The History and Doctrine of the Radical Civic Union.* Iowa City: University of Iowa Press, 1965.

*Snyder, Luis L. *The Meaning of Nationalism.* New Brunswick, N.J.: Rutgers University Press, 1954.

Soares, Ernesto E. *Ferrocarriles argentinos: Sus origenes, antecedentes legales, leyes que los rigen y reseñas estadísticas.* Buenos Aires: Compañía Impresora Argentina, 1938.

Solberg, Carl. *Immigration and Nationalism: Argentina and Chile, 1890-1914.* Austin: University of Texas Press, 1970.

————. "The Tariff and Politics in Argentina, 1916-1930." *Hispanic American Historical Review* 53, no. 2 (May 1973): 260-284.

Sommi, Luis V. *El monopolio inglés del transporte en Buenos Aires.* Buenos Aires: Editorial Problemas, 1940.

Stover, John F. *American Railroads.* Chicago: University of Chicago Press, 1961.

*Sulzbach, Walter. *National Consciousness.* Washington, D.C.: American Council on Public Affairs, 1943.

Talbot, Frederick A. *The Making of a Great Canadian Railway.* Philadelphia: J. B. Lippincott Co., 1912.

Taylor, Carl C. *Rural Life in Argentina.* Baton Rouge: Louisiana State University, 1948.

Thompson, Norman, and J. H. Edgar. *Canadian Railway Development: From the Earliest Times.* Toronto: Macmillan Co., 1933.

Tornquist, Ernesto. *Business Conditions in Argentina.* Buenos Aires: Ernesto Tornquist y Cía, 1910-1955.

Torre, Lisandro de la. *Las dos campañas presidenciales, 1916-1931.* Buenos Aires: Colegio Libre de Estudios Superiores, 1939.

Torres, José Luis. *Una batalla por la soberanía.* Buenos Aires: Domingo E. Taladriz, 1946.

Valle, Aristóbulo del. *Discursos políticos.* Buenos Aires: Administración Voccaso, 1922.

————. *La política económica argentina en la decada del 1880.* Edited by Luis V. Sommi. Buenos Aires: Editorial Raigal, 1955.

Vanger, Milton I. *Batlle y Ordóñez of Uruguay: The Creator of His Times, 1902-1907.* Cambridge: Harvard University Press, 1963.

Vedía y Mitre, Mariano de. *La revolución del 1890.* Buenos Aires: L. J. Rossi, 1929.

Vega, Juan Carlos de la. *Discursos contra la tiranía.* Rosario: Ruiz, 1956.

Velar de Irigoyen, Julio. *Bernardo de Irigoyen: Algo en torno a una vida argentina.* Buenos Aires: Talleres Gráficos, 1957.

La vida de los ferrocarriles y la competencia en los transportes: Memorial presentado el gobierno argentino por las compañias de ferrocarriles. Buenos Aires, 1931.

Vigil, A. [pseud.]. *Railway Propaganda and Publicity: A Study Prepared for the Institute of Transport—Argentine and the River Plate Centre.* Buenos Aires: Institute of Transport—Argentine and the River Plate Centre, 1939.

Villafañe, Benjamín. *La tragedia argentina.* Buenos Aires, 1943.

Weil, Felix J. *The Argentine Riddle.* New York: John Day Co., 1944.

Westwood, J. N. *A History of Russian Railways.* London: George Allen and Unwin, 1964.

Wheelwright, William. *Introductory Remarks on the Provinces of the La Plata and the Cultivation of Cotton: Paraná and Córdoba Railway, Report of Allan Campbell: Proposal for an Interoceanic Railway between the Rio de la Plata and the Pacific. Being a Paper Read at a Meeting of the Royal Geographic Society. January 23, 1860, p. 36.* London, 1861.

Whitaker, Arthur P. *Argentina.* Englewood Cliffs, N.J.: Prentice-Hall, 1964.

————. Nationalism in Latin America: Past and Present. Gainesville: University of Florida Press, 1962.

————. *The United States and Argentina.* Cambridge: Harvard University Press, 1954.

————, and David C. Jordan. Nationalism in Contemporary Latin America. New York: Free Press, 1966.

White, John W. *Argentina: The Life Story of a Nation.* New York: Viking, 1942.

Williams, John H. *Argentine International Trade under Inconvertible Paper Money, 1880-1900.* Cambridge: Harvard University Press, 1920.

*Wright, Quincy. "Symbols of Nationalism and Internationalism." In *Symbols and Values: An Initial Study,* edited by R. M. MacIver, pp. 383-403. New York: Conference on Science, Philosophy and Religion in Their Relation to the Democratic Way of Life, 1954.

Wythe, George. *Industry in Latin America.* New York: Columbia University Press, 1945.

Zamboni, Humberto. *Peronismo: Justicialismo, juicio crítico.* Córdoba: Editorial Assandro, 1956.

Zea, Leopoldo. *The Latin-American Mind.* Translated by James Abbott and Lowell Dunham. Norman: University of Oklahoma Press, 1963.

Periodicals and Newspapers

Anales de la Unión Industrial, 1925-1936. [Known as *Argentina Fabril* from January, 1937, to January, 1944.]
Bandera Argentina.
Board of Trade Journal.
Buenos Aires Herald.
Buenos Aires Standard.
Bulletin of the Pan American Union.
C.G.T. (Buenos Aires).
The Economist.
Financial Times (London).
The Financier (London).
Hechos e Ideas.
Herapath's.
Killick's Argentine Railway Manual.
La Nación (Buenos Aires).
New York Times.
El Obrero Ferroviario (Buenos Aires).
El Pampero (Buenos Aires).
La Prensa (Buenos Aires).
Railway Gazette (London).
Railway News.
Railway Times.
Review of the River Plate.
Revista de Ciencias Económicas.

Revista de Economía Argentina.
Revista de la Facultad de Ciencias Económicas.
South American Journal.
The Times (London).
Wall Street Journal (New York).

INDEX

302